Bones That Float

Enjoy

Kari Grady Grossman

Bones That Float

A Story of Adopting Cambodia

Kari Grady Grossman

Wild Heaven Press
wildheaven.com

First Edition

Cover, map and interior design by Anne Austin

Cover image © 1995 Deborah Koff-Chapin
The image on the cover of this book is reproduced from SoulCards by Deborah Koff-Chapin. For information on SoulCards and TouchDrawing, the technique through which the image was created, go to www.touchdrawing.com. Fine art giclee prints of this image (SoulCards #12) are available through the website.

Grady Grossman, Kari
    Bones That Float, A Story of Adopting Cambodia / Kari Grady Grossman.
    —1st ed.

ISBN-13: 978-0-9792493-0-3
ISBN-10: 0-9792493-0-9

Library of Congress Control Number: 2007921810

Wild Heaven Press, PO Box 707, Fort Collins, Colorado, 80522
wildheaven.com

25% of the proceeds from the sales of Bones That Float, A Story of Adopting Cambodia benefit Friends of the Grady Grossman School, a 501(c)(3) non-profit organization, supporting education in Cambodia. Please help us make a difference, visit www.GradyGrossmanSchool.org.

Printed in the United States of America

Dedicated to
Eric Ratanak Grady Grossman,
my teacher,

George Grady Grossman,
my love,

and Shanti Charu Grady Grossman,
my light.

And for
The students and teachers at the Grady Grossman School in
Chrauk Tiek village, Kampong Speu province, Cambodia

and
adoptive families everywhere.

Acknowledgements

The writing of this book has been a journey to comprehend, consciously, what adopting a child from Cambodia has made me a part of; or perhaps I was always a part of it and this event only served to lay awareness bare. Whichever the case, the journey would not have been possible without the friendship, support, advice, encouragement and expertise of a small army of people I am proud to know, and humbled to have been assisted by.

To my dear friend, Amanda Maly Prom, who patiently taught me how to cook Cambodian and adopted our family into hers with an open heart; to Amanda's husband, Andy Ben, and their children, Alisa and Odom, for giving me countless hours of Amanda's time; to Sokun Prom and Neang Om, Amanda's parents, for their strength and their memories; to Dani Prom for filling in all the blanks and his South Dakota hospitality; to the rest of the Prom family, especially Malis, David and Tom, for appearing in this book.

To my friend and partner, Sovann Ty, whose name remains changed even here, at his request, to protect his identity. You know who you are. I am deeply indebted for your service to our cause at the Grady Grossman School, for your travel companionship, for answering copious e-mails, for keeping me out of harm's way, for your honesty and for always trying to do the right thing.

To my readers, for their time, thoughtful feedback, constructive criticism and above all, their positive reinforcement at various stages of the manuscript: Araya Gunderson; Suzy Blanchet; Susan Gray Gose; Bruce Hampton, who kept me on the historical high road; Molly Hampton, our number one customer; Chavawn Kelly; Robert Kline; Tita Legras; John Long; Tean Ly, for her knowledge of Khmer; Jeanne Malmgren, for her attention to detail; Jill Marshal; Deryle Matland and Charolette Sheedy.

For all the people who have touched our adoption of Grady and his country: Lee Slater, for the matchmaking and hand-holding; Dr. Nancy Hendrie of The Sharing Foundation; Yiet Ly and the staff of Roteang Orphanage, who watched over our son until we were united; Bernie Krisher and his American Assistance for Cambodia staff, who gave us the opportunity to build a school in our son's honor and who continue to transform education in Cambodia; Sharon Blender, Susan Borst, Pam Sweetser and the rest of the Cambodian Heritage Camp family, for giving us a place to call home.

To the people who gave me the time I needed by providing love and attention to my children: Annalissa Purdum; Piper Champion; Marilyn Toms; Miss Jean; Kristy Kaiser and Joyce Groathouse.

I am thankful to Bob Gordman for solid writing-business advice and to Bill Boycott for keeping and running the sweat lodge.

I am grateful to my family and friends for their undying support: my mother, Sandy Rine Grady Keenan, a teacher who raised me to be compassionate; and my father, Bill Grady, who gave me the bug for adventure; my parents-in-law, Rick and Susan Grossman, for their financial support of this project; and to my cheerleaders: Jacki Blakeman, for the use of her lodge; Tim Brown and Anne Casey; Coralee Flug, who introduced me to network marketing; Lisa Lowham, the wonder neighbor; Jagoe Reid, the keeper of the list; Anne Reber, the energy infuser; and the Artist Way Circle, who kept the energy flowing.

Above all others, the person who made this journey possible is my husband, George. This book is as much his achievement as it is mine. With his love, anything is possible.

Contents

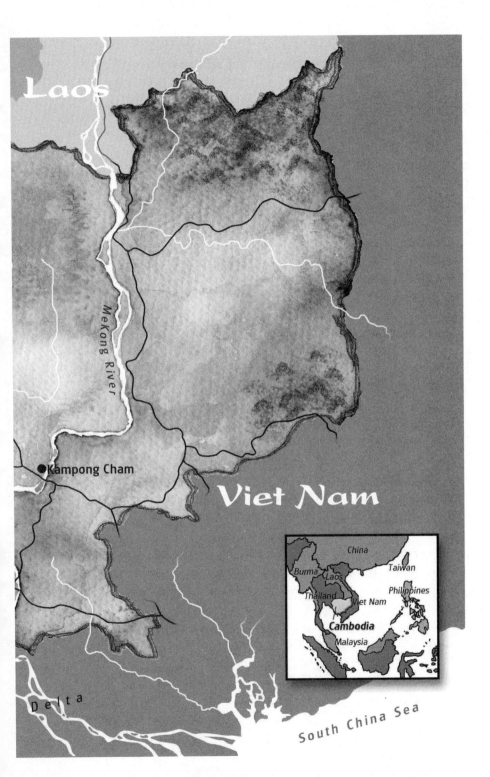

Chronology of Events

1954 Cambodia peacefully gains independence from France, ending colonial rule.

1960 Prom family business established in Battambang, Cambodia.

1965 America enters the war in Viet Nam under direction of President Lyndon Johnson. Sovann Ty is born.

1966 Ho Chi Minh Trail established. King Sihanouk claims neutrality for Cambodia.

1968 Richard Nixon is elected president of the United States. Kari Grady is born.

1969 U. S. starts bombing North Vietnamese sanctuaries inside Cambodia, along the Ho Chi Minh trail.

1970 March: Lon Nol overthrows King Norodom Sihanouk. Sihanouk aligns with his former adversary, the Khmer Rouge. April: Nixon announces U.S. troop withdrawal from South Viet Nam. Maly Amanda Prom is born. Sovann's father dies.

1971-73 Cambodian War. North Vietnamese/Khmer Rouge fighting Lon Nol/U.S.

1973 Paris Peace Accords end U.S. war in Viet Nam. North Vietnamese withdraw from Cambodia. Khmer Rouge takes over fighting against Lon Nol. U.S. carpet bombs Cambodia for 200 consecutive days. Maly's sister, Srey Pau, is born. Kari enters kindergarten.

1974 Cambodian War continues. Prom family business moves to Pailin. Maly's brother, Atuit, is born. Sovann's sister, Theary, last seen.

1975 April 17: Fall of Phnom Penh to Khmer Rouge. Prom family removed to Kampong Kohl. Sovann removed to Takeo province.
April 30: Fall of Saigon.

1976 Khmer Rouge establishes Democratic Kampuchea with Pol Pot as prime minister. Maly's sister, Srey Pau, dies. Maly's baby brother, Atuit, dies. U.S. celebrates bicentennial.

1977 Democratic Kampuchea starts a border war with Viet Nam. Maly is taken to Daikon Camp. Her baby sister, Eline, is born, lives 10 months and dies. Sovann runs away to another work collective.

1979 January: Viet Nam captures Phnom Penh and establishes a government called the People's Republic of Kampuchea (PRK). Prom family migrates back to Battambang. Khmer Rouge fight Vietnamese from camps in the Cardamon Mountains and on the Thai border. The Prom family escapes to Khau I Dang refugee camp, Thailand. Sovann survives in a ditch while the front line passes through Takeo, then returns to his mother's village.

1981 United Nations votes to retain the seat of Cambodia for the Khmer Rouge government of Democratic Kampuchea. Fighting between Khmer Rouge and Viet Nam continues.

1982 Coalition government of Democratic Kampuchea formed on the Thai border. Prom family is sponsored to emigrate to the U.S. Maly Prom enters school in the fifth grade in Denver, Colorado. Sovann enters Vietnamese primary school. Kari enters high school.

1984-86 Heavy fighting on the Thai border between Viet Nam/PRK and Democratic Kampuchea. Sovann enters secondary school. Kari graduates from high school.

1987 Hun Sen and Norodom Sihanouk begin peace process. Maly enters North Glenn High School in Denver and changes her name to Amanda.

1989 Vietnamese troops withdraw from Cambodia. Prom family business established in Mitchell, South Dakota. Sovann graduates from Phnom Penh Accounting School and takes a job with the Ministry of Economy and Finance in Koh Kong province.

1990 United Nations Transitional Authority in Cambodia (UNTAC) established. Amanda graduates from high school, marries Andy Ben, and moves to South Dakota to join the family business. Sovann battles malaria and tuberculosis. Kari graduates from college.

1991 Norodom Sihanouk returns to Cambodia for the first time since 1979. Amanda's first child is born. Sovann quits Ministry of Finance and finds a job at ASEAN hotel.

1992 UNTAC arrives in Cambodia with 20,000 peacekeepers. Sovann begins servicing the prostitution industry as a moto taxi driver.

1993 Prince Ranariddh Sihanouk elected prime minister. Norodom Sihanouk is re-crowned King, with two co-prime ministers: Prince Ranariddh Sihanouk and Hun Sen. Amanda opens China Garden in Lander, Wyoming.

1994 Kari marries George Grossman.

1996 Hun Sen overthrows Prince Ranariddh Sihanouk. Many Khmer Rouge soldiers defect to Hun Sen's government. Amanda's second child is born. Sovann marries Ngim; their first child dies in utero.

1997 Sovann's first child is born.

1998 Pol Pot dies in the jungle from unknown causes.

2000 Ratanak is born and relinquished to an orphanage at three months of age.

2001 March: Eric Ratanak Grady Grossman is adopted and brought to U.S. The Grady Grossman School is established. Sovann begins working with adoptive families.
December: U.S. suspends adoptions from Cambodia by American citizens, because of accusations of corruption.

2003 UNICEF report estimates 670,000 orphaned children in Cambodia.

2005 USAID/Holt International Children's Services releases Cambodia Orphan Survey documenting 7,697 orphaned children housed in child-care facilities.

2007 Adoption of Cambodian children by U.S. citizens remains closed.

13

Author's Note

The events in this story are real; yet of the three lives portrayed here, I lived only one. With the other lives, those of my two friends, I have done my best to convey them accurately. I've changed the names of people living in Cambodia who appear in this book, and often I have changed place names. That was done at their request and for their protection, because Cambodia is still a lawless place. I've chosen to spell Viet Nam as two words (the way Vietnamese refer to their country), and I've chosen to spell Khmer words in English phonetically because I could find no consistent written translation in the Roman alphabet. For the purpose of narrative flow, I have condensed the chronology of my personal journey, combining events that actually transpired over three separate trips to Cambodia and four years of e-mail communications. Beyond my personal journey, I hope that this story inspires a deeper sense of humanity, through the Cambodian connection to us all.

A River Like Me

"We can do no great things,
only small things with great love."

Mother Teresa

The river is flowing backwards, my first clue that Cambodia is going to show me a new perspective. In the middle of the rainy season, the Tonle Sap River helps the swollen Mekong drain slowly into the ocean by absorbing the overflow and reversing its course. This river is like me: taking in Cambodia from two different directions, two different outlooks – as an American and as a mother of Cambodia.

On the far side of the river, a fisherman casts his butterfly net into the water while his son poles their sampan under the bronze glow of thick, sun-drenched clouds. At the water's edge, two small children fight like beasts over a loaf of French bread. A man with an amputated leg holds out a blackened baseball cap for my donation. The left breast logo on his tattered polyester shirt says McDonald's – most likely a garment factory reject.

From across the wide, backward-flowing river, I hear loud banging.

"A new hotel?" I ask my driver.

"No, that is the new building for the U.N. authorities who come to convict the Khmer Rouge criminals," he says.

Cranes and hammers graft cement and steel to the bank of this ancient confluence, giving birth to a great hall and a new era, maybe the era of justice. In that hall elderly Khmer Rouge leaders will be held accountable for war crimes, 30 years after those crimes were committed.

Looking toward the skeletal building rising from the riverbank, I wonder if the "crimes against humanity" phase of the Khmer Rouge trials will produce an explanation capable of untying the knot in my stomach.

The knot has been there since my heartstrings found their way to Cambodia in March 2001, when my husband, George, and I adopted our son, Grady, at an orphanage outside Phnom Penh. My river was flowing downstream then, toward family and future. Yet the current changed its course that day, when an eight-month-old boy crawled into our arms and Cambodia's story crawled in with him. Our lives were unexpectedly rocked by the ripple effect of a war, a quarter-century past, that defined our new son's life. Today Cambodia is a country of 14 million people, with half its population under the age of 18. One out of every eight Cambodian children will either die before the age of five, or be orphaned before he turns 15.

Two lives twist and untwist with mine in this book, in the eddies that form along the barrier of cross-cultural communication. One of them escaped Cambodia and realized her dreams in America; the other didn't. Amanda Prom, my neighbor and friend, was once a little girl called Maly. She survived genocide and rebuilt her life in small-town Wyoming, where she runs a Chinese restaurant. Sovann Ty, my driver and now my business partner in an education project, never escaped Cambodia. He continues to navigate violence, poverty and corruption toward an uncertain future, clinging to the hope that one day he, too, will touch American soil.

The river in our story sometimes flows backward toward 1970, when the war in Viet Nam spilled into Cambodia and swallowed little Maly Prom, along with the rest of Cambodia's tenacious people and ancient culture. Other times the river flows forward from the place where I jumped into the twisting current, opening my heart to a child who needed me, and a taxi driver in contemporary Cambodia who could show me the reasons why. Until then, I never understood what "we all are one" meant. When my husband and I adopted a little boy, and in turn adopted his country, we unearthed a connection in our souls to a disregarded and long-suffering people. The mystery of our union gives me hope that in the end, love will win.

one

A Mystical Path to Motherhood

"Adoption feels like a genetic connection because it links you directly, not only to your own gene pool, but to the genes of all humanity, all the way to the roots from which we all originated… Adoption carries the added dimension of connection not only to your own tribe but beyond, widening the scope of what constitutes love, ties and family. It is a larger embrace."

Isabella Rossellini, adoptive parent

O n the longest day of the year, after the turn of the new millennium, a ceremonial fire crackled in the lodgepole pine forest below our cabin. We read the list one last time and, without looking at each other, tossed it into the fire. I stared at the paper edges curling up into golden streaks. As the words dissolved into brown patches of ash, a small trail of white smoke ascended into the air. We didn't speak. That smoke drew love, fear and intention from two hearts, my husband's and mine. A breeze whisked our wish to the treetops and the night wind whispered, "It's gone. It's out there." A small puff of smoke carried our dream – a child to call our own.

The summer solstice of 2000 was not the first time we had tried this avenue of prayer. The earth smelled of burning pine, and the timber creaked as the wind picked up speed. The forest felt like an ancient cathedral bigger than anything man-made, less contrived and a little more open to the possibility of a higher force. A sudden whisper from the pine boughs sent a chill up my spine. Someone had to be listening.

Our fire burned on the bank of Little Warm Springs Creek, part of the drainage system for melted winter snows of the Wind River Mountains. These headwaters feed life to much of the western half of the United States. Isolated within two mountain ranges and the Wind River Indian Reservation, we had found a spirituality that felt right for the landscape. Centuries of ash and rock blown from the Yellowstone caldera have been piled, eroded, and sculpted into the Absaroka Mountain Range to the north. To the south, ancient limestone mountains thrust skyward, baring a backbone of earth's volcanic crust and creating a powerful statement – the Wind River Range. We live between these two ranges, in Wyoming's Wind River Valley, where there's little rainfall to encourage anything to grow except sagebrush, lodgepole pine and the occasional cottonwood. Inspired by the land and its wildness, we'd worked hard to eke out a living since moving to Wyoming in 1993 as twentysomething ski bums, George becoming a photographer and I a freelance writer. We'd come to appreciate how shallow soil holds shallow roots, for plants as well as people. A careful cultivation of attachment to the earth is required to thrive here.

The Native American sweat lodge ceremony had become my lifeline, once the world of marriage and family that I had previously understood dissolved into the distance. It had been two years since the day a doctor's sterile voice stated dryly, "It's impossible for you two to conceive a child." *Infertile* had been stamped like a scarlet letter onto the envelope of our loving, harmonious, magical marriage. Case closed. I wondered what on earth we had done to deserve this. I crawled on my belly many times, under the willow arches of a blanketed dome, to enter a

Being a fertile woman unable to have babies felt like a cruel joke. Male medical issues may account for half of the infertility equation, but our society simply doesn't discuss it. The first few times George and I bravely shared this personal information with our closest confidants, we were questioned about our sex life, as if no one knows how the reproductive system works. We were ill-prepared for infertility to be confused with impotence, or sperm production to be mistaken for libido. How embarrassing to explain the mechanics to your mother. What could possibly strike a man more to his core? I wished my body were the obstacle. I wanted desperately to protect George from snide judgments of his masculinity. Eventually, we decided not to discuss it with anyone else. I felt betrayed – not by my body, but by love itself.

Like most young couples married more than a few years, we heard plenty of hints from our parents about their desire to become grandparents. The family tree is expected to continue growing. It seemed unfair that life kept moving forward. None of the people around me seemed stuck. Children laughed; toddlers cried; happy news and baby showers were announced. Yet those joys were off-limits to me. Emotional strength previously had served me well, yielding a competitive disposition with a stubborn aversion to failure. Now love was holding me hostage in my own life process. Though I didn't fit the label of "barren woman," I still felt its historical scorn, like a slightly defective and pathetic failure in the family arena. How many times I wanted to wipe the piteous, "Oh, you poor woman" look from someone else's face!

I had fancied myself the purest of earth mommas, envisioning a judicious pregnancy: prenatal yoga; organic nutrition; midwife-attended home birth; breastfeeding – the works. They were not helpful delusions while I wrestled with the options that lay before me. I was a champion of the "natural way. " Yet, in an attempt to thwart what felt like God's effort to deny me my birthright, I began to shoot up synthetic hormones every day. Infertility treat-

sweat lodge, the ceremonial womb of Mother Earth, in hopes o finding an explanation.

Each time it is the same: In the warm, earthy darkness, the disembodied voices of six or seven people who have gathered for the ceremony offer their prayers to the four directions – East, South, West, North – then Grandfather above, Earth Mother below, and the spirits of the place. The air slightly tinged with smoke, red rocks glowing in the central pit, the hot smell of damp earth, the drum beats and songs in an ancient tongue … the sweat lodge has an amazing power to make me prayerful. I was raised Catholic, married a Jew, and studied Buddhist chants, yet no previous experience came this close to creating in me a physical connection with God. Perhaps, when you're forced to let go of your own tribal and genetic identity, it's natural to embrace another.

I never spoke of my heartache to the other voices in the darkness. My prayers were pleading and silent: "Why, God, Grandfather, Divine Spirit – whoever You are – why are you doing this to me?" The ache was not so much for a child to cuddle, what psychoanalysts label "the empty lap syndrome." I simply felt as though the next stage of my life was waiting for me, but the door to it was locked. No matter how hard I pounded, that door wasn't going to open. The full weight of my soul pushed against it, even as I sank down, down, down into isolation. I felt intensely stuck.

It just didn't make sense; we were a strong, healthy, young couple. Together we had ridden bicycles 3,000 miles to Alaska, climbed mountains, paddled rivers, started a business and learned the names and habits of hundreds of wild things. We were one with Nature, we thought. But somehow God had forgotten to give my husband sperm, or at least enough to beat the odds. "There must be some mistake," I thought. "Surely God knows better. George is humble and generous, respectful and self-sacrificing. With more dads like him, the world would be a better place."

ments – the drugs, the procedures and the improbability – made me feel like I was being exploited by my own desperate heart-strings. Since I was the fertile one, we assumed our two-month, $20,000 in-vitro fertilization attempt would work. It didn't. Not one of the specialists from the medical office ever called to say they were sorry. We could only afford to do it once, and that one shot had failed. We cried in bed for three days.

I couldn't fathom the failure. I had prayed so hard in the sweat lodge. It had been a potent New Year's Eve, Earth Mother rotating slowly toward the dawn of a new millennium, and I had felt certain that God was listening. I felt a spirit guiding me. Was it a figment of my imagination? Where were my angels when I needed them? Months passed, my mind blanketed by a haze of unreality. Life itself poured from the holes in my heart. At odd times of the day, I would embrace George just to stop the flood from sweeping me into oblivion. I was no longer strong. The very *thought* of our children had died and, along with them, our dreams for a family. My will was defeated.

One day we actually visited a sperm bank website, and read the detailed descriptions of each donor. None described my husband: a man with a natural aptitude for intimacy and communication; secure in his masculinity; gentle; funny; adventurous and powerfully handsome. We scanned the catalog entries for key adjectives: dark-haired; blue-eyed; Jewish; educated and athletic. I felt like a cow and George felt useless. We turned off the computer and never discussed it again.

Everywhere I looked, my gaze fell upon books and television programs that glorified pregnancy and detailed the magical mysteries of childbirth – as if that were the only authentic way to become a parent. My impulse toward rage made breastfeeding look like a brazen badge of maternal vanity. I didn't like the cynical person I had become, but my mind clouded over with gloom each time someone else announced a pregnancy. It simply wasn't a joyful subject to me. Every reference to family jewels, genes and blood alienated my determination to find a resolution to our predicament.

Enter a little puff of smoke.

As the sun finally set on the summer solstice that year, we stood before the snapping pine in the fire pit, about to enter the sweat lodge again – only this time with no demands for a solution. An energetic healer had told us to make the list, burn it and have faith. On that paper was written our wishes for a child:

1.) a spiritually advanced soul
2.) a soul with something to teach us
3.) a soul we have something to teach
4.) a soul with enough flexibility to enjoy and benefit
    from our lifestyle and one last wish for all three of us:
5.) the financial needs for this family to be met

Letting go of the physical need to have biological children sent a swift pulse of liberation through my body so suddenly that my eyes twitched. Watching those wishes go up in smoke, everything at last made perfect sense. I'd always felt destined for a more mystical path to motherhood.

George looked at me and whispered, "Did you feel that?" I had: a slight pulling sensation from the smoke floating away.

"You know," I whispered back, "I've been thinking about adoption my entire life." George closed his eyes and inhaled a deeper breath than he'd taken in months. His sigh captured the unspoken truth that stood between us – his desperate guilt and my hidden disappointment – and released it into the fire. We were moving on.

Every test to gain permission from local, state and federal authorities to adopt a child was as anxiety-ridden as a prenatal exam. Yet there was no due date to plan the rest of our lives around. We were strapped to an emotional roller coaster: filling out forms; waiting; more forms; more waiting; being judged on paper as to whether we were fit to parent. The waiting required absolute submission to the divine, for adoption is a manifestation of the soul, a birth of the heart. You consciously will a child into your life, and there is magic in it.

Mysteriously, that little puff of smoke found its way from the Wind River Mountains of Wyoming all the way to Phnom Penh, Cambodia.

I had been meditating every day, asking the energy of my heart to radiate toward our child, wherever he or she was. Country and race, we decided, did not matter. Our conversation about domestic versus international adoption was short. Why wait for a child to be born in America and for us to be selected by a birth-mother, we reasoned, when we could give our love to a child in an orphanage who already was waiting for a family? We knew several couples who had adopted Chinese girls, and we joined their communication network. Our lives changed forever on the day one of those families sent us an e-mail about children waiting for parents in Cambodia.

When I read that simple message, a gentle, invisible hand took hold of my heart, and Cambodia has been a part of my soul ever since. Calls around the country ate up my days; the issues of abject poverty in a war-torn nation crowded my consciousness, merging with the bureaucratic details of Cambodia's adoption process. Overwhelmed, I did what any levelheaded woman does when confronting her fear of the unknown: I called my mother.

"Mom, I just learned about orphaned children in Cambodia," I said.

From her kitchen in Maine she answered, "Cambodia – you're kidding me! I just got back from the beauty parlor, where I met a lady who told me all about the adoption process in Cambodia."

Mom had written down the names and telephone numbers of the exact same people I had already called during my two-week, fact-finding mission. During the conversation, George arrived with the mail and plopped the new issue of *National Geographic* in front of me. The cover story was about Cambodia. I looked skyward and said, "Okay, I got it!"

Adoption is a *soul birth*. Our labor began on December 18, 2000, when we received word of a five-month-old boy who had been living at an orphanage near Phnom Penh for several months. His name, Ratanak, wrapped itself like a mellow love song around my heart. George and I both knew instantly that he was our son. Three days later we received a picture and one-page fax that told us his height and weight and described his health in one word: "good." His date was July 1, 2000 – ten days after our ceremonial fire when we had burned the list of our wishes. With little debate we faxed back our acceptance. We had no idea when we might hold him the first time. We'd just given birth and the child was held up before our eyes, but we couldn't touch him until someone far away said we could.

We waited three months. Our faith strained. I nurtured my boy from afar, watching over him with my soul. It was all I could do to keep from going crazy. When the phone call finally came, we were on a plane in only three days.

When we met our son at Roteang Orphanage outside Phnom Penh City, it was not love at first sight. How could it be? We were in a room with 50 gorgeous children all younger than two. The details of how each child came to the orphanage were unique, yet the causes repeated themselves: some parents had died; some babies were foundlings, others were relinquished by family members simply because they didn't have enough food to feed them. Thank God someone else does the matchmaking; otherwise, we would never have been able to choose.

Ratanak was quiet and introverted, though he enjoyed the doting attention of his nanny, Yiet Ly, who slept next to him on the tile floor. He was eight months old – clean, toothless and chubby. He did not babble, he did not eat solid foods, and he did not crawl. But he did persistently try to get to his feet, determined to forgo the use of his knees for propulsion. He seemed indifferent to the other children, solitary, with a knack for entertaining himself; secretly I wondered if there might be something wrong. The nannies asked us if we liked him, so eager to please that it seemed as though they would gladly exchange him for another child. George shot me a sideways glance, and a sudden protective urge in my gut burst into a hasty, "Yes, we like him! Absolutely!"

Yiet Ly mothered Ratanak as if he were her own. She was acutely aware of his habits and signals for food, sleep and attention. Holding him, I felt like a kidnapper. I was now officially his mother, but Yiet Ly knew him better than I did. Ratanak was curious about me, but looked to Yiet Ly for reassurance. I knew it was going to take time for us to bond, but I wanted the magical family I'd imagined to begin right away. We were afraid to remove him from the orphanage before the paperwork was complete, so he remained in the care of Yiet Ly while we waited five more weeks for the Cambodian court to decide our fate.

Between visits to the orphanage, George and I made a photographic assignment of the countryside, to give our son a pictorial history of his homeland. But which image of Cambodia would we document for him? Her ancient stone temples and luscious, tropical beauty? Or the miserable conditions that lead to thousands of orphaned and abandoned children? I liked to think that the invisible hand holding my heart was the spirit of my baby boy, but more often it felt like the collective consciousness of Cambodia, with a very specific agenda. The images we would take home with us seemed almost preselected, our guide to them provided by Providence, in the form of a charmingly ambitious moto taxi driver named Sovann Ty.

Motos, a ubiquitous form of transportation in Cambodia, are miniature motorcycles with long seats, easy to maneuver through crowded streets and inexpensive to operate. Moto taxi drivers are a-dime-a-dozen in Phnom Penh, lingering on every street corner and badgering passersby to take a ride. Beleaguered by the desperate need of Cambodians to earn U.S. dollars, George and I had become accustomed to incessant offers of rides, goods and favors. One day we were standing outside the Royal Palace of King Sihanouk, pondering a map of the city, when Sovann approached us. He was different. With two easily understood English phrases – "Where are you going? Can I help you?" – he hooked us. We dropped our guard and began asking a myriad of questions. Sovann's friendly conversation and genuine assistance was a welcome prospect, and for 3000 Cambodian riels (about 75 cents), he offered to take us anywhere we wanted to go in the city. As a bonus, he would act as our interpreter and guide.

We squished our backsides, Cambodian-style, onto the long banana seat of Sovann's red moto. As he eased into the incessant flow of vehicles, we joined the lifeblood of the city. Cars with steering wheels on either the right or left side merged with trucks of all sizes, motos, bicycles, pushcarts, any kind of wheeled vehicle that could possibly transport people, pigs, produce, bamboo, chickens, or children: They all fought for a place in the transit hierarchy. The occasional stop sign or traffic light was largely ignored; a honk and a flash of the headlights communicated the ever-changing rules of the road. The governing principle took its cue from the social structure of Cambodia itself: He who is bigger wins.

Even though most of the vehicles were open, hardly anyone wore a helmet. Whole families squeezed onto a single moto: one child between the handlebars; another on the gas tank; father driving with a toddler between his knees; mother riding sidesaddle with a baby on her hip. The most I counted was eight. Our adoption agency had warned us not to ride motos; rather to err on the side of safety and hire a car and driver befitting our situation. Yet George and I sought the edgy connection to humanity in the streets, to participate in Cambodian life. I reassured myself that my child had already lost one set of parents; surely, Lord Buddha would not subject him to the same fate twice.

"Are there a lot of accidents?" I asked Sovann.

"My mother die instantaneously in the street," he shouted over his shoulder to me.

A few years ago, he explained, she had been riding sidesaddle on a moto taxi, returning from her sister's funeral, when a truck hit them. At the scene, the truck driver paid off the policeman with a few thousand riels. Sovann couldn't afford to waste his hard-earned money to buy an audience with a judge, so he let the matter drop.

"No good law," he said. "Cambodia very corrupt."

We sped past a mixed marriage of ancient Khmer and French colonial architecture lining wide boulevards and rotundas, which created a Champs Elysées impression, on the way to gold-leafed Buddhist temples. Everything needed a paint job.

The grime-covered walls of Phnom Penh, chipped by bullet holes, hide a glorious and cruel history. The time when the international press referred to Cambodia as "the jewel of Asia" is long gone. Thousands of shanties are crammed between dirt alleyways; naked street children and limbless beggars signify how far the country has fallen. Sovann pointed with equal pride to the embassies of Thailand, France, and the United States, and to the office buildings that host a variety of non-governmental organizations. The capital city's main industry appeared to be humanitarian aid.

Sovann delivered us to a small palm thatch resort, run by a Frenchman on the outskirts of town, where he thought we might enjoy the small zoo and a dip in the pool. The $3 entrance fee included a foot massage. Sovann, who had no intention of waiting outside with his moto taxi, expected us to pay for his recreation and food as a fringe benefit of the profession.

"You want to race me?" he asked, as we stood ready to dive into the swimming pool. His childlike suggestion was such a surprising contrast to his usual nose-to-the-grindstone posture that I said "Sure." He counted, we jumped, and my body churned breathlessly through the splashing and bubbles, as I put forth my best effort at the American crawl. I easily beat him to the other end. Watching him approach my side, I was amazed that he made any progress at all. His perfectly straight arms thrashed up and down, in a chopping fashion, while his head swayed side to side. I couldn't tell if his legs were kicking. He hoisted himself onto the pool edge with a huge grin.

"Sovann, who taught you to swim?" I asked.

"Soldiers," he said, "During Pol Pot time. My job to collect, um ... the stuff from the cow ... you know." He made a motion toward his backside.

"Manure?" I guessed.

"Yeah, I follow cow across river for dat," he said. "The soldier on river side, dey yell at us, 'Swim!' If you not swim, dey shoot you."

He was ten years old and had never learned to swim until the day a Khmer Rouge soldier pushed him and several other young boys into the river with a bayonet to their backs. As Sovann sank under the peaceful water, he considered that it might be best to die. But instinct compelled his legs to kick and arms to crawl to the surface, where he splashed his way to the other side. He would spend the next 14 hours, until dusk, collecting manure in the hot sun.

"Can you spell dat, please?" Sovann asked, handing me the latest edition of *Cambodia Daily,* the folded edge of which bore several handwritten English words I had already spelled for him. In response to my inquisitive stare he answered, "The one that mean stuff from cow." I smiled and wrote "manure" on the paper. It was a little game we played.

Cambodia Daily is the English-language newspaper published in Phnom Penh. Sovann buys one every day from the young paperboys, who sell them on the sidewalk in bare feet and dirty T-shirts. News items from Southeast Asia and the world are printed in both English and Khmer on the first two pages. Page three features a vocabulary and grammar lesson printed in English. Sovann completes it religiously. What he can't learn from *Cambodia Daily*, he gleans from daily readings of the Khmer-English dictionary, page by page. His gift for language and steadfast determination has produced perhaps the most polished English spoken by a moto driver in Phnom Penh.

Sovann has learned almost everything he knows about the United States from reading *Cambodia Daily*. The presidential election of 2000 holds a particular fascination for him. Having voted in the first election held in Cambodia in more than forty years, with United Nations peacekeepers monitoring the polls, Sovann struggles to grasp how an American candidate who didn't get all the votes could have won the election. The Electoral College defies cross-cultural description. But Sovann insists that he needs to understand it if he's to realize his dream of going to America to become a migrant fruit picker.

"Life in Cambodia is a struggle," he often says, when he can't find the words to explain its social and political problems. He imagines a future founded on stories of Cambodian refugees who have made good on the promise of the American dream. Cambodia has no employable use for a man of his obvious intelligence, aptitude and entrepreneurial spirit. He doesn't believe my description of urban poverty, nor does he care that life in America is a struggle for migrant fruit pickers. He has given up on Cambodia.

One afternoon Sovann drove us to an old school on a nondescript block near the city center. At the end of a long, whitewashed cement wall is a sign: "Khmer Rouge Genocide Museum. Foreigners $2, Cambodian Nationals Free." The compound once held Tuol Svay Prey, a prestigious high school and primary school. Now it's a testament to Khmer Rouge crimes. After the Vietnamese government took control of Phnom Penh in 1979, they discovered S-21 at Tuol Sleng: the secret police's main torture and execution center. The new government simply left it as it was.

Along the outdoor walkway, the classroom doors are open. The inside has never been cleaned; blood still stains the checkered tile floors. A bare, rusted spring cot still has iron manacles chained to its steel leg posts. Other instruments of torture lie scattered about: a whip; a chain; an electric cattle prod. In the former lecture halls, cement slapped between uneven brick walls randomly divide the room into small isolation cells. At the rate of 100 per day, an estimated 16,000 people were tortured into "confessions" of plotting against the Khmer Rouge communist revolution. The executioners kept meticulous records, in order to prove their own loyalty to the party. Wallet-sized, black-and-white photographs of every prisoner, before and after their torture session, line the walls. Many portraits are of women and several are holding babies. Their hollow eyes are expressionless, as if their spirits have already left their bodies. Tightly drawn lips silently speak of the depth of human cruelty.

The deep-rooted smell of death in that place tied my stomach in a knot. Sovann's face gave no hint of emotion, his gaze remaining neutral as he moved slowly from room to room. There was a sign written in Khmer. Sovann read it for us: "Do not cry out in pain, this is annoying to the party."

Only seven people are known to have survived Tuol Sleng, most of them artists kept alive to make portraits of Pol Pot and other party leaders. In the last room, an artist's work details the many tortures he witnessed inside the prison. One image depicts a man's fingernails being pulled off, another shows a drowning. The last piece takes up the entire wall at the end of the room. It's a giant map of Cambodia, made entirely out of the bones and skulls of Cambodian people, her fertile waterways rivers of blood.

Unable to turn my back to the wall, I walked backwards to the exit, my eyes drinking in the enormity of an unknown horror. The words "Auschwitz," "Hitler" and "Holocaust" had held a deep and singular meaning since the first time I heard them as a child, and I felt a sharp distress that despite my college education, this was the first I'd ever heard of Tuol Sleng.

Roughly seven or eight miles outside the city, near the village of Cheung Ek, we walked around large pits that had served as mass graves for the many victims of Tuol Sleng. Cambodians call it *The Killing Fields*, after the Oscar-winning movie from 1986 – just one of hundreds of mass gravesites throughout the country. At the center stands a tall white tower, about ten feet square and 100 feet high, filled to the top with skulls. A small thatched roof shelters one pit from the rain. A hand-painted sign reads: 167 males, 57 females, 16 children. On a nearby tree, a red arrow points to a worn patch of bark where another sign says: "Place where executioners beat … children." My knees weakened and I sank to the ground. A grazing cow meandered into one of the pits; I mindlessly started picking grass and pitched it toward him.

"Sovann, where did you live when the Khmer Rouge took over Cambodia?" George asked.

"Precinct Three, Phnom Penh," he said. "Before the communists took over the nationwide country of Cambodia, my mother sold the lottery and my father worked for the Sokarlay Restaurant to scrape a living."

"What happened to your family?" I asked.

"My father die of disease. I had four sisters and one brother in 1975, but my oldest sister and cousin disappear in 1977."

The cow followed us back to the place where the moto was parked. A silence stiffened the hot, steamy air, making it difficult to breathe. The moto seat was scalding hot. Sovann was watching the cow as he started the engine and turned to me.

"Manure, it mean feces?" he asked. "So I can say, 'I collect cow manure.' That is polite?"

"Yeah," I answered. "That would be polite."

✳   ✳   ✳

Four weeks after George and I arrived in Cambodia we were issued an adoption decree for our son; finally it was time for Ratanak to leave the orphanage. He fell asleep in my arms before

saying goodbye to his nanny. Quietly backing away, Yiet Ly tried
not to cry, but I could see her pain. I kissed her for him.

Beads of sweat poured off mother and son as we clung to each
other in the back seat of our taxi. During that bumpy ride, I felt
my heart stretching as we gradually put distance between an
eight-month-old baby and everything he'd ever known. We were
becoming not just parents, but adoptive parents, and no one had
warned us about the sudden shift of consciousness that comes
with it. Ratanak's resting body lent peace to the floating sensation of my soul's abrupt expansion. From now on we'd occupy
the space between two worlds – together.

Laying the little cherub down, George and I eyed each other
across the expanse of our king-sized hotel bed. We were in a
foreign country, no one spoke English, and there was a baby on
the bed. What did we do now? When 24 hours passed without
a poop in the very first diaper our son had ever worn, George
paced the room in nervous anticipation.

Ratanak did all the teaching, and blossomed before our eyes.
Within forty-eight hours he was crawling across the floor at top
speed, pulling himself up on the walls, babbling for attention
and laughing when he got it. He deliberately positioned himself
in front of my face, looked me squarely in the eye, and laughed
and laughed – as if he knew it was finally okay to come out of his
shell. At Ratanak's mandatory physical examination to obtain an
immigration visa, the Cambodian doctor for the U.S. Embassy
was amazed at our bond. He asked how long we'd been together
and George answered, "Two days!" Imagine that, I thought, and
without breastfeeding.

At the embassy we had to take an oath that we would have
him vaccinated. Weighing the pros and cons was not an option.
What difference did it make, anyway? The child had already run
the gauntlet of deadly diseases during the most vulnerable days
of his life: tuberculosis; polio; typhoid; malaria; hepatitis A, B

and C; parasites; AIDS, all of them rampant in Cambodia. He must have had some protection, either from our hearts across the globe, or from his very own angels. We felt certain that God wanted him to live.

At long last we boarded a plane at Pochentong International Airport with our precious son, bound for Wyoming. After three years of trying to get pregnant, 10 months of jumping through adoption paperwork hoops, one month of visits to the orphanage, the courts, the ministries and the embassy — all to gain permission to love a child — the stress finally exploded from my stomach. Between bouts of projectile vomiting, I held a damp washcloth to my forehead. Tears streamed down my face as we waited on the runway for take-off. I was too sick to take care of Ratanak, so George took over while I gazed numbly out the window. In that exhausted, trance-like state, I perceived real angels for the first time. There were hundreds of them under the wings of the plane, and the spirit of my paternal grandmother nestled over my shoulder, her strong presence telling me not to worry anymore.

The wheels of the airplane left the ground and released the grip of despair from my soul. At the same moment, the umbilical cord of my son's Cambodian life was cut. We were flying through the air together, as a family, ungrounded but whole.

We flew stand-by through six airports and twelve time zones as if the wheels of international travel had been greased. Every connection was on time, and we were seated on every flight in business class, with a bassinet for the baby. We arrived home two hours earlier than expected. Inside a bathroom at the Los Angeles airport, I was hurrying to change a diaper and wash my hands, while juggling Ratanak on my hip. A woman entered the room and pinched his cheek, saying, "He's going to change the world." I gave her a cursory nod, having no desire to encourage conversation in my harried state. But as I scurried out the door, she added, "Old souls are being born right now."

My stomach has always been my emotional Achilles heel and it continued to protest for days after our arrival home, trying to digest the experience of Cambodia. Before we left, the goal had been about us, and our desire for a family – fairly selfish motivations. The adoption journey reflected a more selfless purpose. Or perhaps it was that my grief had found its home, in a place where heartache knew no bounds.

two

Family

"A mother is likened unto a mountain spring that nourishes the tree at its root, but one who mothers another's child is likened unto a water that rises into a cloud and goes a long distance to nourish a lone tree in the desert."

The Talmud

I smell Cambodia as soon as I walk in the door of Café Wyoming. The thick and tangy essence of coconut milk and curry accompany the scented waves of sweet lime and galangal root. The welcoming smell bridges the step back into our western American community. Amanda Prom and her mother have driven 70 miles from Lander to bring *Samla Kh'tih Satch Moin* (Chicken Yellow Curry), to our potluck baby shower in Dubois. During our adoption wait, I had found Amanda in the *Riverton Ranger*, in a newspaper article about her first trip back to Cambodia after escaping the war zone twenty years ago. I was thrilled to discover that my son would not be the only Cambodian in Fremont County, Wyoming, after all.

Amanda and I made our introductions over the telephone, and our friendship blossomed in long chats and Sunday afternoon lunches that often ate up the best hours of Amanda's only day off. Intrinsically, she seemed to recognize both the restless unease of waiting, and the point when reason defies purpose. "Do whatever it takes to get your son out of Cambodia," she often said to me.

At our baby shower Amanda gave Ratanak a golden necklace with an R on it, in keeping with Cambodian tradition, to bring the child good luck and prosperity. Amanda's own baby jewelry was cut up and sold in tiny increments before she turned ten; it helped her family survive. Her mom's face glows when she holds Ratanak; a miraculous, lighthearted giggle accompanies her tickles. From where does a woman who has watched four of her own children die summon such spontaneous joy?

We had brought Ratanak from the tropical jungles of Southeast Asia to the northern Rocky Mountains, and the climate change was a shock. Dry mountain air sucked all the moisture from his skin, nose and lips. My neighbors brought humidifiers and a space heater, so we could replicate a steamy jungle habitat in the bedroom. A spring snowstorm raged outside the window and the mountains protested their awakening from winter's slumber, while I swam through a haze of hot steam to find the crib.

When I kissed Ratanak's head, and whispered his new name – Grady – it sounded strange. My Irish surname didn't easily fit his Asian face but he responded to both with equal degrees of perception. In darkness tinged by the glow of a smiley-face nightlight, I contemplated the Talmud's wisdom. The distance to my little lone tree was very far indeed. Now that he had been uprooted, I wondered if I had absorbed enough of the nutrients of his lost past to bring cultural nourishment to our desert.

Among the secret imaginings in my heart, the circumstances under which Ratanak was likely born triggered potent visions of his birthmother, a shadow woman I considered my sister. Was she desperate and alone? Or did she have her mother, or a midwife, to attend the birth? Knowing there is a woman in the shadows who will miss all the great moments of our son's life – first teeth, first steps, first fall through the dog door – I was left to wonder what led her to release this magnificent child into the karmic current, and a fate that included me. We were told that she could not feed him.

Within the year, we moved our family 70 miles east from Dubois to Lander, Wyoming, where Amanda operated a restaurant. She had become a willing surrogate for the culture our son left behind, and for the kin he will never know. A part of me was hoping that her friendship, and Grady's happy childhood, would transform the malaise in my heart into an emotion more useful than guilt.

* * *

Everyone laughs except me, the joke passing in the sounds of a language I barely understand. Khmer has a rhythm like a sputtering engine, alternating between guttural and nasal diphthongs, and punctuated by a rich medley of inimitable consonants such as *bp, dt,* and *ch'ng.* I can pick out only a dozen or so words, but I enjoy listening to the clucks and dips and the high-pitched rise at the end of a sentence. I smile and giggle anyway. That's what you do when you're hanging out with the girls. Amanda explains the words that describe the creative and explicit ways their young sons communicate the need to go to the bathroom. Now that my two-year-old is potty training, I can relate.

"Yesterday he stood up in his chair," I announce, "And before I could get him down, he peed all over his breakfast." Laughter fills the cement block room and I instantly become a naturalized citizen of their sisterhood.

We are making Cambodian egg rolls – 400 of them – on a metal table in the storeroom of China Garden Restaurant, which is owned by Amanda and her husband, Andy Ben. My job is peeling back the thin sheets of dough, trying not to tear them, so they can be filled with a salad of shredded pork, cabbage and carrot, which has been flavored with exotic spices and mild soy sauce. The egg rolls are a special preparation for Amanda's youngest brother's wedding feast. The family would never serve their guests Chinese egg rolls, even though they run the only Chinese restaurant in town. They're Cambodian; they don't eat Chinese food.

Most of the customers who pass through Amanda's restaurant mistakenly assume she is Chinese, despite the fact that she has a circular face, full lips, round eyes and curls in her jet black hair – all characteristic of Southeast Asians. It's strange how an obvious difference such as skin color can snuff out the brain's reception of the more subtle details in another person's face. Most of the Cambodians I know say that all white folk look alike, too. To sharpen my perceptive skills, I play a game whenever boarding airplanes of trying to guess the ethnic origins in Asian faces. Korean, Japanese, Chinese and Vietnamese features are usually easier for me to decipher than the subtle difference between Cambodian, Thai and Lao, who present the genetic blend of India and China in varying proportions.

Despite its political turmoil of the past 60 years, Southeast Asia has always been, and continues to be, the melting pot between China and the Indian subcontinent. This cultural confluence follows the curves of the mighty Mekong River and flows into the borderlands of Laos, Cambodia, Thailand and Viet Nam. Hindu, Buddhist, Muslim and Christian religions all lay claim to some of their history. Through all the resulting skirmishes between such diverse cultures, the savvy inhabitants of the fertile valleys became powerful merchants on the trade routes of both land and sea. In this religiously volatile and economically strategic location, the Khmer race evolved, blending Polynesian ancestry with the ethos of East Indian explorers and molding a people independent in spirit, hierarchical in nature and hungry for power (a hunger that has never been fully satisfied), beneath an outwardly shy and gracious nature.

Each spring, the Mekong River carries snowmelt down from the Himalayan Mountains and spreads it throughout Southeast Asia as the river winds its way toward the South China Sea. Summer monsoons bring even more swell to the river as it passes through Cambodia, until the sheer volume of water surpasses the river system's capacity to discharge into the ocean and forces its largest tributary, the Tonle Sap River, to flow backwards. The reversing current causes the Tonle Sap Lake to double in size, flooding central Cambodia. This yearly saturation of surrounding mangrove forest creates a huge freshwater fishery. Consequently, Cambodian cuisine centers on fish. Blending the chop, shred and stir-fry techniques of China with the spicy heat of Indian cuisine, a distinctive style captures the flavor of the world's most fertile river system and distills it into a taste defined by two words: fish sauce.

Fish sauce – a clear, brown liquid gathered from fermented salty fish after it's pressed – is used like table salt in Cambodia. It's also one of the reasons that Amanda won't serve Cambodian food in her restaurant. You can't make Cambodian food without fish sauce, and fish sauce stinks. She's afraid it will scare away customers.

Around this metal table in the China Garden storeroom, I witness a kind of sisterhood I've never known. For a moment, even though I'm white on the outside, I feel brown on the inside, united with my friend and her family by the domestic chores of daily living. Amanda's sister, Malis, has driven seven hours from Denver and her sister-in-law, Savy, twelve from South Dakota. In Cambodia, extended families usually live in the same village. Now that this family is spread out over the vast mileage of the American West, the instinct toward togetherness puts lots of miles on the car.

I can't recall the last generation in my family that lived together in the same town. With family members scattered from Maine to Florida and Seattle, we couldn't get much farther apart and still live in the same country. Reflective of a nation of immigrants and rebels, Americans long ago cast off the security of family clans, in favor of staking a claim to a life independent of what came before us. Watching these happy sisters chatter away in a foreign language makes me wonder if the desire to live such a long distance from my family is a distinctly American impulse.

Lander, Wyoming is a sleepy town of about 8,000 people, nestled against alpine foothills at the southern end of the Wind River Range. Our town is an island of humanity amid the vast sea of arid sagelands that define the eastern slopes of the Rocky Mountains. It's a long way from nowhere, we like to say.

It's a long way from Cambodia, too. Transracial families are not exactly commonplace here. I've gotten used to inquisitive looks at the grocery store. Most of the brown faces around our town are Arapahoe and Shoshone people from the nearby Wind River Indian Reservation. Sometimes my son is mistaken for American Indian; his skin is just a slightly more olive shade. Between strong traditions of extended family among Native tribes, and a dark history of prejudice from the white man, the idea of white parents raising an Indian child is rather taboo in these parts. But lately I've noticed that when I look my American Indian neighbors in the eye, I see more details than I saw before. Something in my perception has changed that I can't identify, but it feels as though a filter has been lifted that I never knew was there.

Suddenly Grady runs into the room, clutching at my leg to reach the goodies on the table. He hates fish sauce, but loves egg rolls. I carefully break off a piece from the pile of fried rolls we're snacking on, and he crawls up on the stool beside me to munch his treat. I catch Amanda's soft gaze upon him. An indiscernible mixture of happiness and heaviness lingers behind her warm, round eyes.

"Lucky boy," she whispers deeply, the urge to slap his butt restrained by the belief that he must have done something noble in a past life to deserve this. Already he has surpassed all the sacrifice and struggle of her 34 years.

Large bowls of new ingredients are carried into the storeroom. Amanda's mother, Neang, whom I call *M'yiey* for grandma, gives me meticulous instructions for constructing the perfect spring roll – another hand-rolled appetizer, this one fresh instead of fried. Carefully I layer rice noodles, fried pork, mint leaf, bean sprouts and two small shrimps onto a piece of wet rice paper, then fold the edges around this clever pile of flavors and shape it into a tidy, small, see-through envelope. I immediately dip my first creation into the *tirk trei* sauce and shove it in my mouth. The smell of sweetened fish sauce, garlic and peanut arouse my tongue to savor the comings and goings of each exotic spice. I lick my fingers clean. We're like two shrimps in a spring roll, Amanda and I, wrapped together in a translucent little world, where the misery and mystery of Cambodia defines the borders of both our souls.

M'yiey picks up Grady and tries to persuade him to eat rice. He won't, protesting the same way he does when I offer it. He prefers Kraft macaroni and cheese. M'yiey shakes her head in disbelief. Nevertheless, I notice how easily Grady blends into this scene. Everyone in the room is Cambodian but me. His face slides right into place in a Cambodian family portrait, and I suddenly feel very different from my own child. This is the angst of the transracial adoptive mother – knowing I cannot give my child all the answers to his heritage, nor an ethnic self-image that's complete and authentic. He's Cambodian on the outside and Caucasian American on the inside. George and I made a choice for him, and that choice changes the core of his being forever. We chose family over culture. We hope that once he is old enough to know his own mind, he will agree with our decision.

"Nudder one, peas," he begs, pointing to a crisp egg roll.

"When my kids that age, I only hear Khmer come from their mouth," Amanda says. In her small sigh, I think I hear the sound of a reluctant peace. I have never heard her son or daughter speak a word of Khmer, even though it's the language she uses to converse with them. They always reply in English.

Love and guidance, health care and education are important things I can give my son, but the one thing I can't give him is the ability to speak his native tongue – and that makes me feel inadequate as his mother. Instead, I will depend on my friend to at least make the tones familiar to his ear. Sitting at this table munching egg rolls in his Oshkosh B'Gosh overalls – chubby, happy and healthy – he listens and eats, while thousands of children living in orphanages in Cambodia wait. They wait for their lives to begin, they wait for birthparents to return, they wait for someone to notice them, they wait for their country to provide health care and hope. It won't. The most common cause of an unfinished childhood in Cambodia today is death by diarrhea.

Hot egg rolls return from the fryer and the pile of fresh spring rolls grows, too. More family members arrive, greeting their mother and sisters in rapid-fire Khmer. It's the first time I've met Amanda's extended family, and they're an impressive bunch: articulate; polite and outgoing. Each sibling owns a Chinese restaurant in a rural western town, having forgone the impulse to remain enclosed in the subculture of a refugee community. They each stepped out into rural America, mastered English, and left the trauma of childhood war and genocide firmly buried in the past, in order to prosper in the present. I wonder how they turned out so normal.

"Up monkey," Grady says, reaching for my hands, wanting to play his favorite game. He holds my hands as a brace and walks, step by step, up my body until he reaches the top, where he flings his arms around my neck and plants a big kiss on my lips. It's my favorite game, too.

As Amanda introduces me to her older brother, David, I recognize the Khmer phrases that follow, which explain that my husband and I adopted our son from Cambodia. As usual, it ends with Amanda saying his Cambodian name, Ratanak.

"Ratanak. Good name," David remarks. They always say that. Ratanak means "to be more precious than diamonds and gold," an appellation with which I easily agree. To the Cambodians, it means he'll have good fortune and become rich. Amanda's father, a devout Buddhist and former monk, has already studied the lines and lengths of Grady's fingers to confirm this prediction. Unfortunately, when he examined my hands, he found no riches at all. But he told me not to worry: My son will take good care of me when I'm old.

"He's a handsome boy," David says. "How much did you pay for him?"

The comment touches a raw nerve. I muster my toughest voice to answer, "Not enough!"

It's a Cambodian thing, I tell myself. They always ask me what I pay – for everything. In Cambodia, asking "money questions" is the way people exchange information to keep from getting ripped off. Understanding that, I've gotten used to questions I would otherwise find inexplicably rude, such as how much money I make, or how much I paid for my house. So why should I expect this situation to be any different? I guess I draw the line at asking the price of human life.

"Hey, it's Cambodia," David says, in a feigned jocular manner. "Come on honey, let's make a baby. We'll get rich!"

Amanda comes to my rescue. "He would have died. He lived in an orphanage."

David's mocking disgust is directed at the situation in Cambodia, the homeland he escaped 20 years ago, a place where human lives are cheap, poverty is the pawn of politics, corruption is a way of life, and the social fabric of family and community is tattered beyond repair. He's unaware of the cruelty of his words. And I've heard them before, harsh comments that cheapen adoption to a commercial endeavor. It's a common misconception fueled by news reports that often use economic terms in adoption-related stories. I've even seen such reputable papers as *The New York Times* print phrases such as "American demand for healthy babies" – implying that rich Americans support a Third World industry to buy babies from poverty-stricken women.

If only it were that simple. The global problem of dispossessed children and the tendency to reduce adoption to economic terms hides the more complex details of individual adoption stories, each one of which is multifaceted and heartbreaking. As in any other form of prejudice, a little bit of information is used to make a general judgment. It's much harder to navigate the convoluted and harsh realities of a poor country, and to find peace with your role in that world as an adoptive parent from a rich country.

Wham! M'yiey's cleaver strikes a hard green papaya. The fruit splits open instantly and spits a black seed onto my cheek. With a surprised, wide smile I wipe it away, and everyone laughs.

I'm used to papaya – its soft, sweet, orange-colored flesh – when it's ripe. Unripe and green, the Cambodians consider it a vegetable, the essential ingredient in Ngoam Lahong (green papaya salad). Julienned strips of papaya are mixed with bits of browned garlic and small, salt-dried shrimp. The whole lot is then made zesty with fish sauce, lime juice, salt, sugar and hot chilies. For the wedding feast twenty papayas need to be grated, so every woman in the room grabs her own hand grater. The restaurant professionals shred twice as fast as I can.

With the sudden whirl of a food processor, the smell of Kroeung filters into the air. I take a big whiff and try to discern the spectrum of spices in this exotic herb paste. Kroeung is the basis for many Cambodian dishes, but M'yeiy will never tell me the exact amounts of ingredients she blends into the mixture. She simply adds them by the handful, to taste. I'm left to guess at the measure. Shredded lemongrass stalks spread a smell like Lemon Pledge into the air. That acidic aroma mingles with the bitterness of kaffir lime leaves, the rich, rooty odors of galangal and turmeric, the hot, spicy scents of garlic and shallot, and the sweet, rotten vapor of shrimp paste. It's an exotic, intense smell, evoking deep memories for everyone present.

"At my wedding day we serve nine dishes," Savy recalls. Food is a big part of traditional Cambodian wedding rites, which can last three days or more. Usually the groom's family prepares half the food and the bride's family the other half, but in this case only the groom's family knows what to do. Amanda's youngest brother, John, is marrying a local Wyoming girl, so it's up to his family to prepare three or four traditional dishes for the reception, which will accompany an American buffet of sliced roast beef and potatoes.

"You'd better get used to it," I tell Amanda. "Your children will probably marry white people, too, and your grandchildren will look just like mine."

Then Amanda's sister Malis innocently asks the dreaded question: "How come you don't have your own?"

Every adoptive parent I know hates this question. No matter what the ethnic background of the person asking, or the complicated answer required to reply, the implication smacks the same. It's as if they don't recognize that my child is an integral part of me, and our life together is a real parent/child relationship. Do people think we're just a substitute for the "real thing"? The adoption journey is so complex and expansive, it's a very difficult question to answer.

While George and I waited for parenthood to begin, instead of reading *What to Expect When You're Expecting*, I read *First They Killed My Father: A Daughter of Cambodia Remembers* and *When the War Was Over: Cambodia and the Khmer Rouge Revolution*. Instead of gaining valuable child care knowledge, I confronted those conditions that defined the facts of life for the child growing in my heart. The world widened and shrunk at the same time, as the joy of a child entering my life brought with it the darkest side of humanity. My son was born into the legacy of Pol Pot's killing fields, into a country rife with poverty and dysfunction. Grady would lose his birth family and culture but he would gain me, and George, and a homeland filled with opportunity. Does a parent's love make up for the loss of everything else?

three

The Chicken House

*"The best index to a person's character is how he treats
people who can't do him any good, and how he
treats people who can't fight back."*

Abigail Van Buren

One thing definitely sets apart adoptive parenting
from the biological kind: We face the possibility that
our child will need to search for birth family one
day, in order to answer the basic questions of self. Raising an
adopted child is not only about giving him love to grow strong
and healthy and self-assured, it's also about giving him the truth.
For this reason, the trend in the United States has been toward
open adoption, in which adoptive families and birth families
communicate regularly. But in the international arena there are
cultural taboos to consider, a completely different set of logic to
follow, and economic and political forces that affect the quantity
and accuracy of record keeping. The information available to
us is speculative at best.

The good fortune of our family's acquaintance with Sovann
has been that he was able to interpret the story a nanny at the
orphanage told us about the day Ratanak arrived there. A woman
came to the door of the orphanage, alone, with three children in

tow – a baby, a little girl, and a ten-year-old boy. She was taking her oldest boy to the free hospital in Phnom Penh, and needed the orphanage to take care of her baby while she was gone. Two days later she returned with only the little girl; the ten-year-old had died. She begged the orphanage to keep the baby because she had no food for him. Her husband also was dead. A half-literate nanny had scratched the details onto a paper the size of a napkin. She handed us a copy and I pointed to the thumbprints at the bottom. One was hers; the other was the birthmother's. There was nothing exceptional about the circumstance.

"We have a million stories like that in Cambodia," Sovann said. But if this particular story was true, our son may have a sister.

The idea of that little girl made us fret. We'll help Grady search some day, if he wants to, but what might he find? The fate of destitute girls in Cambodia lurked in our thoughts and crept quietly into daily conversation. George narrowed the point to its essential question, and finally found the courage to utter what we'd both been thinking since we got home from Cambodia. "What if he were to find her in a brothel, and then ask us why we didn't do anything to help?"

The weeks George and I had spent riding on the back of Sovann's moto taxi had given us an experience of Cambodia that our Lonely Planet guidebook only glazed over. Although Sovann's tendency to move us around the city on his whim (so he could hustle another fare between transports) strained our patience, we remained loyal customers because the relationship seemed mutually beneficial. We appreciated his singular, independent mind – in contrast to the passive Asian servant most of his wealthy, foreign customers expected. Adoptive parents were a new and rare kind of client, and he wanted desperately to make us happy. He had a cryptic talent for prying open our perspective, and shifting the focus of our agenda.

"You want to eat real Khmer food?" he asked on the first night of our meeting. We knew better than to insist on the four-starred recommendation in the guidebook.

We crossed a bridge spanning the Tonle Sap River, and Sovann deposited us at the Heng Neak restaurant alongside the Mekong, where "real Khmer food" is served in traditional style. A large tin roof staked a claim to a patch of jungle beside the river and the tile floor hosted a hundred long tables neatly dressed for dinner but mostly unoccupied. A high-pitched kara-oke singer belted out a tune on the stage. The sun had set and the temperature had dropped from a sweltering 100 to a rela-tively cool 90 degrees. The riverside tables offered a refreshing breeze over a bamboo partition separating the seating area from the jungle.

A swarm of colorful, teenage girls greeted our table, each wearing a sash from shoulder to hip with the logo of a different beer company – red for Angkor, green for Hennessy, orange for Tiger. A girl in a black and gold uniform offered cigarettes and one in purple offered French wine. A small boy in dirty shorts pointed to my shoes, while a dutiful young girl held out a plate of white jasmine flowers. Their little faces were undeniably insistent, so George bought the flower necklace for me and I submitted my ripped Birkenstock sandals to their first polish.

The company representative of the local home-brew, Ang-kor Beer, kept a vigilant eye on our glasses throughout supper, refilling them as she moved around the table like a gentle breeze. George sought to equalize the awkward effect of her shy servi-tude with a generous tip.

"No pay her," Sovann said. "The company pay her to sell the product."

"How much do they pay?"

"Maybe one dollar per day," he said.

"Is that enough to live on?"

"No, sometimes the customers take her home, then she can make more," he answered nonchalantly, then quickly added, "Only Vietnamese girls do that." Yet among the rainbow of beer girls, every one looked and spoke Khmer. Several times I caught myself searching their features for a clue to the woman who birthed our son.

Steaming piles of rice arrived, alongside vegetables and soup that smelled at once sour and hot, salty and sweet. The smells overwhelmed my taste buds and the loud karaoke gave me a headache. I lost my appetite. The churn of Sovann's facial muscles, crunching food between high cheekbones and a sharp, square jawline mesmerized me. He's a thin man. Eyeing the cracks between the bamboo slats, I thought, with his waistbelt pulled tightly, he might just slip through. The sheer volume of food he ate amazed me. Watching him, with his head bowed over a plate of rice, precisely shoveling spoonful after spoonful into his small mouth, I finally had to ask, "Where do you put it all?"

He looked up at me with a squirrelish grin and mumbled without spitting, "It's in my cheeks." That it was. The pouches of both cheeks were filled to capacity with rice. He wiped the corner of his mouth and swallowed.

"During communist regime, not enough food," he said. "Save, eat later." Quickly he resumed eating as though he didn't know when the next meal would come.

Great sheets of heat lightning rumbled across the sky as we repositioned ourselves onto the moto for the return trip. Electric blue streaks outlined the storm clouds. With each flash, the clouds appeared as an explosion petrified by darkness. The night was alive. The traffic continued at its normal erratic pace over the Japanese Friendship Bridge and by the time we reached the other side, the dam of heaven itself had burst. Through the dense rain, it was hard to discern the headlights and tail lights of other vehicles – if they had lights at all. The tension from several close calls was softened by the wetness, more a shower than a drenching, a refreshing break from the dismal heat. For the first time, Phnom Penh struck me as beautiful. With the somber guise of its bruised buildings and impoverished people rinsed clean, it became another eye-popping capital city. Under the cover of darkness, flashy neon and loud music beckoned the rich and the weary to come out and play.

On the day Ratanak left the orphanage with us, Sovann had convinced George to rent a room at Phnom Penh's Hotel Sheraton (a rip-off version of the American brand), in close proximity to the slum where he lived, so he could easily service our every transportation need. The discothèque on the hotel's ground floor featured an arched doorway with concentric rows of blinking, white lights and slim figures gyrating under it to a bass beat emanating from within – boisterous and sexy, decidedly un-Khmer. With new babe in arms, nearly every morning we shared the elevator of the Hotel Sheraton with very young prostitutes. Their elliptical, brown eyes cast to the floor or the wall when we entered, their smallness filling the box with a presence of remarkable strength. The AIDS epidemic has sex shoppers pushing the demand for girls younger and younger, and Cambodia has become known on the international sex market as a pedophile's paradise. The going rate for a virgin for a week is $600; 16-, 15- and 14-year-old girls are common; many are as young as 12, some younger still.

When Sovann strode past the Hotel Sheraton's regular moto drivers hanging outside the entrance and greeted us with a handshake, the other drivers were visibly peeved. He was careful to park his motobike in full view, paying a street kid a few hundred riels to watch it. Sovann was a savvy street player, but George and I needed to determine if he was trustworthy. In a world where shyness is a virtue, saving face a matter of consequence, and obscurity prolongs survival, it is difficult to get a straight answer from anyone. By contrast, we sensed an unusual capacity for candor in Sovann. He was meeting us for a job interview, only he didn't know it.

"You look tired," I said.

"Last customer, man lady," he answered.

"A ladies' man?" I offered. The previous day, as it turned out, he'd driven us all day and returned us to the hotel at 10 p.m., then wrangled another customer and drove him to brothels and night-clubs all night. The traffic of outsized, foreign men – European, American, Middle Eastern, and Asian – in the company of two or three slender, young girls, tightly outfitted and lavishing sweet affection on their customers, busied every bar in the city.

"He take three different nightclub, buy lady three times," Sovann replied, rubbing his tired eyes, but visibly astounded by his customer's late-night stamina. If it were physically possible, I think Sovann would work around the clock.

Prostitution had given Sovann his start. He'd been a moto driver to the sex scene since 1992, the year the United Nations peacekeepers arrived. That year the ASEAN Hotel, auspiciously named for the Southeast Asian economic partners Cambodia hoped to join thanks to its new capitalist system, played host to a full house of U.N. soldiers. Sovann was their bellboy. His very first experience with foreigners quickly piqued his instinct for opportunity. As a quiet but keen observer, he formulated a plan to make the most of their unusual behavior.

The United Nations Transitional Authority in Cambodia (UNTAC) descended on Phnom Penh in 1992 with 20,000 sol-diers and civilian workers to oversee Cambodia's first national elections after more than two decades of war. The U.N. would spend 2.8 billion dollars on this mission, and equip a coalition of soldiers from around the world to keep the peace, paying each one a stipend of $145 per day. According to Sovann, most of the peacekeepers lodged at the ASEAN Hotel spent the money on drinking and whoring.

Sovann was keen to get in on the action, but astute enough to keep his day job in order to make friendly contact with soldiers. Meanwhile he wrote to a cousin who had fled to Paris in 1980, and asked him for a loan. Following the Cambodian custom of family financing, the cousin dutifully fronted him the cash. After Phnom Penh customs officers pilfered their share, Sovann ended up with $300 that he quickly converted into two grams of gold, the standard currency of the time. But two grams was not nearly enough to buy his goal – a motobike – so Sovann's mother chipped in a gold earring, and his aunt gave another two grams, until together they had amassed eight grams of gold. The haggling went on for days as Sovann drove hard for a bargain, finally settling on a used 50cc Honda, badly in need of new tires, spark plugs and brakes.

"Not original, secondhand," he said, laughing lightly as he recalled the vehicle. It was the first motorized transportation anyone in his family had ever owned.

He parked the bike proudly outside the ASEAN hotel, locked it, and took out the starter's spark plug as an additional anti-theft precaution. That evening, when an UNTAC soldier asked him, "Do you know where the Chicken House is?" the answer was one of those things that everyone knows.

"Yes! I take you tonight?" Sovann replied. If the soldier was generous, Sovann could earn in a single night what took him more than a month of hauling luggage and serving coffee at the ASEAN hotel. "I take you there, stay a couple of hours to wait for you, and come back." Sovann told the man. "You pay me $5." When a horny soldier was happily satisfied, sometimes he gave more. Sovann honed his eye carefully to select a lighter-skinned clientele – American, European, Australian and Japanese – because they tipped better, sometimes giving him $10 or $20 for the whole night.

The Chicken House is a brothel featuring 500 girls, mostly Vietnamese and Cambodian, in a section of town called Svay Pak. In the Cambodian prostitution market, various forms of sexual amusement can be purchased for between $2 and $30, depending on the time spent, cleanliness expected, and age of the female. As the age goes down, the price goes up.

That first time, Sovann kept himself focused on the tense business of negotiating his moto through darkened squalor in the sticky streets; his customer reveled in waves and whistles while choosing his consort. When the guy said he wanted a virgin, Sovann made a small attempt to discourage him. "The young one is very expensive, triple the price," he yelled over his shoulder. The peacekeeper didn't care; he was celebrating his birthday. Sovann put his head down and drove to a small, wooden hut glowing red with Christmas lights and expensive golden silk hanging from the door. He had to shout to be heard over the traditional string music pleading loudly from within. "You want I wait for you?" The soldier, slightly high on hashish and Hennessey, swung an arm about Sovann's shoulder and asked him to come in and negotiate the price. "Not allow, I can wait for you," he lied. It was a personal rule: He never entered kiddie corner.

While hanging around the competitive crowd of moto taxi drivers at The Chicken House, Sovann quickly deduced that speaking English would give him a practical edge. He spent a few dollars each week from his nighttime earnings to buy an English lesson book and begin studying. His strategy was good for business on two fronts, because many of the foreign English teachers around the city were also good brothel customers.

"Now the girl go down," Sovann explained, while shoveling spoonfuls of hot breakfast soup into his mouth. "During UNTAC time, two girls from good place cost $80 per night." He sighed, with a peculiar sense of knowing. "The girl, at the beginning she sell her virginity, she still have very high price, after one year, two year, then she go down." Bending back over the steamy bowl he added, "Not original, secondhand."

A hollow distance sometimes glazed over his eyes when a battle between memory and conscience was being fought. Detachment ultimately won, in a draw, when the impartial acceptance of a somber reality would lure Sovann back to the present. It is a hauntingly miraculous quality that most Cambodian people of his generation share.

The UNTAC elections took place in 1993 and on that festive day in Cambodian history, 90 percent of registered voters cast a ballot. Like almost everyone else, Sovann voted for Prince Norodom Rannaridh, the son of the old King, who won in a landslide. The United Nations Transitional Authority in Cambodia managed to keep peace during the election, but eventually the results of that election were upset by the acting communist party leader, Hun Sen. A former Khmer Rouge cadre leader, Hun Sen had been an appointed minister during the Vietnamese occupation. Soon after the 1993 election, a coalition government with two prime ministers – Norodom Rannaridh and Hun Sen – was formed. Their uneasy alliance disintegrated into a bloodless coup d'etat in 1997. Hun Sen emerged as head of state, and to this day, is still in power. The only lasting legacy of the UNTAC mission appears to be a thriving prostitution business.

Amid the corruption and sputtering violence that accompanied the political tension of the 1990s, Sovann had learned how and where to deliver any customer's pleasure – be it the nightclubs, the Chicken House, or the industrial-style sex stalls lining the muddy street of Tuol Kok Dy brothel, where a trick could be turned for $2. Sex tourists, and how they chose to spend their money, confused Sovann. Typically they would take two girls to their room every day and spend hours at the shooting range playing with Kalashnikovs, AK-47s and shoulder-mounted rocket launchers – not inexpensive pursuits. But then they would eat cheap food and stay in cheap guesthouses. Sovann couldn't figure out why.

An amiable personality and discrete style quickly won him faithful customers. The "man ladies" seemed to relish the homey feel of having a regular moto driver for whore hunting. Their attempts at camaraderie often required Sovann to refuse the offers of one prostitute or another. Even if his customer offered to

buy him "a clean one," Sovann declined with a polite challenge:
"If you have enough to buy me prostitute, then you have enough
for a good tip." He was in it for the money. Sex was irrelevant.
The hardest part of the job was staying awake all night, and he
caught his rest in fitful catnaps.

Asleep with his head cradled in the handlebars one night,
Sovann awoke suddenly to the high-pitched demands of a prostitute named Chea Chantra, who seemed ready to overturn his
moto. He'd become a de-facto interpreter in the sex trade, and
as such was often required to settle international disputes. That
particular evening, Sovann had negotiated a fair price with the
boss at The Chicken House for Chea Chantra to escort his customer for the whole night. He'd driven them to several nightclubs
and deposited them finally at the ASEAN hotel. It was all very
customary, but little Chantra was very upset.

"He no pay me!" she shouted in broken English, and then
Khmer, while pointing at the flustered man she had dragged
into the street. Sovann knew what to do; this had happened
many times before.

"You saw me pay the man!" the aghast Australian snapped.

"Sir, you have to give the girl a tip," Sovann explained, "Or
she not receive enough for the service." He went on to clarify the
system: The brothel owner charges $40 for the whole night, but
the girl receives only $5. Sovann figured the man would ante up,
once he understood; white men usually did, unlike his Indian
and Thai customers, who preferred the $2 dirty shack-style shag
and never tipped. The man apologized to Sovann and handed
Chea Chantra twenty dollars. She quickly pocketed the cash and
climbed onto the back of Sovann's moto. Chantra was one of
the most popular girls at The Chicken House, a pale, wide-eyed
beauty. Her name meant "the light of the moon." She was 16.

"How come you don't work freelance in a nightclub?" Sovann
inquired of Chantra over his shoulder, once they had cruised a
few blocks away, "That way you can keep the money yourself, rent
an apartment, and bring the whole family to live with you."

"My parents owe a debt to the boss from the time of my brother's funeral, and they give me to him to work it off," she replied. "But I cannot work it off because he has a high interest rate."

Sovann didn't blame the girl; a poor family mired in debt was easy prey. Buddhism and custom create the taboo: To die in debt precludes the soul from redeeming merit in the next life. Yet a soul cannot find safe passage to the spirit world without a properly festive three-day send-off. Borrowing from property-owning neighbors often finances funerals, weddings and medical bills for landless families with meager earnings. A pimp, preying on this cultural policy, walked into Chea Chantra's rural village one day and offered badly needed cash to her illiterate parents. He told them he had a friend in the city, a restaurant owner who would give their daughter a job, and with her beauty she could make the money to repay him. All family members expect to pitch in to pay off a debt, so Chantra went with the man, but once she reached the city there was no restaurant job. Chantra was beaten into submission and charged a 25-percent interest rate. She had no money to return to her village and even if she did, her shame would be too great. Debt service kept her family estranged and Chea Chantra, like so many others, became essentially a sex slave.

Sovann dropped Chantra back at The Chicken House and she handed him a dollar, thanking him for negotiating the tip. A simple, mutual courtesy exists among Phnom Penh's working class of prostitutes and moto taxi drivers. "You keep it and buy yourself some medicine," Sovann insisted, feeling pity as he noticed the "light of the moon" from this bright, young girl was beginning to look gray and sallow.

Perhaps Sovann saw his sister behind Chea Chantra's eyes. In the distant memory of childhood he remembered his oldest sister, Theary, cleaning house for a wealthy Chinese merchant to help pay off their mother's medical debts. Doctor Lim expected regular payments for the treatment he had given his father for tuberculosis. At six years old, Sovann didn't understand why they had to keep paying even after his father had died. He and his little sister sold lottery tickets alongside their mother, at the busy intersection of Monivong and Kampuchea Krom boulevards, sitting on the sidewalk with sad, silent smiles in front of a popular French restaurant. He collected 1,000 riels per lottery ticket, hoping with each sale for a nice French customer who might give him 2,000 riels and say, "Keep the change and go to school."

Sovann also sold cookies and bread to children in the schoolyard and dreamed that once the debt was paid he, too, could go to school. But before that day came, war engulfed Cambodia. When the Khmer Rouge emptied the city of Phnom Penh on April 17, 1975, Theary was visiting a cousin in Sihanoukville on the coast. Sovann never saw her again. Over the years he has questioned relatives, searched the coast, and written letters to the foreign embassies of every country that accepted Cambodian refugees – all without ever finding a shred of information about Theary. She's not even a number, just an estimate, somewhere between the 1.5 to 2.5 million Cambodian people who died or disappeared during the Pol Pot era. Unconsciously, he's always checking the brothel doorways for a familiar pair of eyes.

Other moto drivers in the Hotel Sheraton parking lot were eyeing Sovann's cherry-red 250cc Korean-built motorbike. He had come up in the world. Some of them operated secondhand motos; others had only a rickshaw-style cyclo to pedal. They all had a hundred stories just like his.

"Do you know the video *36 Sexual Position?* " Sovann asked me candidly. "It means they have many different way?" I really didn't want to hear it, but before I could steer the interview in another direction, Sovann shed his traditional Cambodian shyness to engage the memories repressed by years of head-down doggedness.

The video had been the brainchild of a Dutch customer who came for a two-week holiday in Phnom Penh, specifically for the purpose of independent film production. Sovann suspected Dutch

might not be worth the trouble but he hadn't had a customer for
five days, so he negotiated Dutch's deal with The Chicken House.
The last time a customer tried to make a video, an angry boss had
chased him from the brothel. You have to pay extra for that.

The girl was already naked when Sovann arrived at the hotel
room with his customer's baggage. The shy teenager quickly hid
her small, barely developed breasts. Dutch was loading a new
tape into his compact, digital video camera. "Here, you make the
video for me," Dutch said. He shoved a crumpled twenty-dollar
bill into Sovann's hand and began to unbutton his trousers.

"No, I cannot do like that," Sovann answered, dropping the
bill from his hand and averting his eyes to the floor to ease the
girl's embarrassment. He scurried down the hall while Dutch
was trying to find a good position for the camera to sit. Sovann
mumbled to himself all the way down the narrow staircase, "I
cannot do like that. My business just moto taxi driver."

Back at the ASEAN hotel, loud chortles punctuated the humid
haze of cigarette smoke in the Parisian café that fronted the hotel,
where comrades in arms held lively conversations fueled by bites
of marijuana pizza. Sovann was replacing the starter plug in
his moto when a Korean man at one table shouted, "Hey, moto-
driver, you know where is The Chicken House?"

Sovann nodded. "I take you there, five dollars." He was
sure to be back before Dutch had finished his video. By the
time he returned, however, Dutch and the girl were arguing in
the street.

"She pushed the camera away," Dutch shouted. "I already
paid her!"

"You not pay her, pay her boss," Sovann told him. "You pay
money for sex, no pay video. If the girl don't like, she can say no,
she have the human right." Sovann felt emboldened by the girl's
smear of garish pink lipstick, suspecting that she might have been
traded to the brothel by an uncle in exchange for a motobike or
television. "We have the Women's Crisis Center to protect the

girl, if they know you make the video picture of the young girl like this, they will put you in jail."

Dutch was doubtful of that idea. Cambodian police protecting the girls? They were some of the best brothel customers. Everyone knew that when the Women's Crisis Center tried to make a raid on kiddie corner, policemen tipped off the brothel owner ahead of time and the girls were gone before any heroics could take place. Dutch put away his video camera and straddled the back of Sovann's moto, demanding to go to the shooting range. He'd vent his frustration with an automatic assault rifle.

"You have heard of *36 Sexual Position?*" Sovann asked me again, while slurping the remainder of his soup from the bottom of the bowl, "It means they have different way?"

"No, I've never heard of it," I answered.

"You know, sometime, they make sex with the mouth." He looked at George and me aghast, his eyes round like saucers, adding for emphasis, "Yeah!"

"I've heard of that," George answered, trying not to smirk. At 37 years of age, married, father of three children, having serviced the prostitution industry for 10 years, Sovann still found the idea of oral sex an absurd perversion. The conservative innocence found in the old Khmer culture has somehow remained.

"How can the man take two girl, three girl, sometime two times per day?" He earnestly wanted to know. "How can they be that strong? Do they take drug?"

"Viagra," George answered.

"Can you get that here?" I asked.

"How you say dat?"

"VI – AG – RA," I sounded out the syllables slowly. Sovann handed me the *Cambodia Daily* so I can write "Viagra" above the masthead, but I doubted he'd find it in the dictionary.

"You know, sometime the customer tell me that in USA cannot do like that, because the girl under 18 years old, against the law," he whispered over the table, "But he still want younger, because they don't care; they think the girl living in brothel, not from a family."

George and I looked at each other across the table, quietly considering Sovann's history. "What do you think of the brothel business?" I finally asked. Sovann paused for a moment, formulating an opinion he'd never been asked to express.

"You ask me what is in my heart when they do like this, take the young girl, do different way, make the video?" Cleaning his teeth with a toothpick, he leaned back in his chair and muttered, *"Ot k'ma d'yum."* ("Selfish.") He thought about the hundreds of customers he had driven to The Chicken House and for the first time speculated aloud, "Where does that man come from, is his own mother female, does he have sister, or auntie?" He sighed. "They should be thinking of the human right, and respect the woman."

That clinched it. Sovann was hired.

We handed him a piece of paper with the name of a remote village scribbled on it, and a few names and thumbprints. It was all the information we had about our son's birth. We wanted him to investigate it. Knowing that a penchant for saving face could interfere with honesty, George demonstrated clearly how to say "I don't know" if a true answer could not be found. We asked him not to start the job until after we left the country. If Sovann could prove himself to be honest and trustworthy, then we might hire him for more meaningful work than driving seedy, foreign men to brothels.

It just didn't feel right to leave Cambodia with a baby and not do something for those left behind. The grim exploitation of children is inevitable when families make less than $300 per

year. We asked Sovann to join us for an important errand that
was to become his first opportunity to help his country, rather
than trying to run away from it.

American Assistance for Cambodia is a nongovernmental
organization with an ambitious program to build 200 rural
schools. On the wall of its office was a map of Cambodia with
thumbtacks placed where they already had built schools. Ours
would be number 81. We had raised $15,000 by selling photo-
graphs over the Internet to family, friends and colleagues; our aim
to build a school in our son's name. George pointed to the area of
the map with the least number of thumbtacks and said, "There."
Chrauk Tiek village in the Cardamom Mountains is near Mount
Aural, the highest mountain in Cambodia. It sounded like a perfect match for a family from Wyoming.

Sovann joined us, unpaid, for the six-hour journey to the village in a rented Land Rover. The dusty, potholed road took us
north from the town of Kampong Speu toward forest-covered
hills in the misty distance. Only one of the four small river cross-
ings we navigated had a makeshift bridge – a few planks of wood
pushed into place by young boys who dodged between the car
wheels. After we crossed, a child's blackened hand pawed at the
window for a tip. Our driver cracked the glass just enough for me
to pass a few hundred riel out the window; the wad was grabbed
by hands seemingly too fierce for a child. The touch of those tiny,
ravenous fingers remained on mine all the way to Chrauk Tiek,
where the schoolchildren were waiting.

School was being held in a dilapidated shack that had no walls
and a dirt floor, with table-sized holes in the poorly thatched roof.
Fifty children sat shoulder-to-shoulder on logs, sharing a few
newsprint books. Three teachers passed a single piece of chalk
between them, writing lessons on wooden boards they'd painted
black and nailed to a post. Looking up at the gaping holes in the
roof, I asked what they did during the rainy season. One brave
teacher answered, "No school."

We spent the afternoon talking to the children, with Sovann helping interpret. "What would you like to be when you grow up?" seemed such a stupid question, in a world with so little choice. With some coaching by Sovann, a few children tentatively stood up one at a time and answered. Almost every one wanted to be a teacher. Two or three students wanted to be a doctor or nurse. No one said that they wanted to be a farmer, which is what all of their parents were. We told the children that if they would show up for school, we would make sure they had what they needed to learn.

Before we left the dusty schoolyard, one brave, dirty girl in a mismatched green shirt and sarong stepped slowly forward. Staring at me in an unconvinced but inquisitive way, she put her hands together and bowed. She didn't believe me, but she hoped.

A new building site had already been selected by village leaders a few kilometers back toward the village, on the bank of the Kantout River, where a pile of cement blocks was already waiting. American Assistance planned to install a rooftop solar panel on the new building; it would power a computer they hoped might leapfrog the digital divide. But the children still didn't have shoes, uniforms, books or school supplies. A building would be just the beginning.

When we returned to Phnom Penh, we took Sovann to a bank because we needed a place to wire money for our own projects at the school. He'd never used a bank, so we donated the initial deposit of $100 to open an account in his name. As George instructed him how to fill out the forms, Sovann's lip started to twitch, then he started to pace, and soon perspiration rolled from his forehead, even in that cool, air-conditioned lobby. Opening a bank account was giving him an anxiety attack. We quickly left the building before he started to hyperventilate.

"What if the bank close, and the government throw away the money?" he stammered. He was dead serious. No matter how hard we tried to explain our business protocol, the boy in him could not release his adult body from a haunting memory. Sovann was seven years old when the victorious Khmer Rouge army marched into Phnom Penh and forcibly evacuated hundreds of thousands of city dwellers, closing all the banks and abolishing money. The useless currency was blowing in the streets as Sovann walked out of the city with his widowed mother, four sisters and brother toward the inescapable countryside and more than a decade of starvation. One family swept up in the frenetic movement of millions. He held on tight. From that day forward, no matter how hard he worked nor how much money he squirreled away, Sovann would never feel secure. He would never have enough.

Our altruistic designs were no match for his survival skill set. What could we expect, hiring a de facto interpreter in the sex trade for the delicate social work of a cross-cultural birth family search? Perhaps we should forgo hiring him to look for a needle in a haystack, we thought, and instead focus our efforts on the children attending our school, where a real difference could be made. I kept wondering what would happen to that girl in the mismatched green shirt if we didn't follow through on our promise.

four

Year Zero

*"We stand for self-reliance. We hope for foreign aid
but cannot be dependent on it; we depend on our
own efforts, on the creative power of the whole
army and the entire people."*

Mao Tse-Tung

"Sok sabai, kmouy?" Amanda asks Grady when we meet her at the kitchen door, removing our shoes in proper Asian fashion. My son hides between my legs, too shy to answer the Khmer question, "How are you, nephew?" I make him *sompeah* anyway, hands together and bow. Respect toward elders is one Cambodian value I hope to instill.

Grandma, M'yiey, is hunched over a bowl of long, green pods. "You want to try?" She holds up the fruit of the tamarind tree and I readily take the bait. With one hearty chomp into the fruit, my face puckers under the assault of sour juice. I've never learned my lesson about such temptation; once when I was a toddler I insisted on eating a whole spoonful of hot horseradish that my father was smacking his lips over, and my resulting bawl was family legend. Amanda and her mom laugh heartily until my face returns to normal. They offer me slices of fresh pineapple to cool it down.

The sweet pineapple throws a surprise punch, too – a hot sting in the throat, so painful it makes my ears burn. It has been dipped in a paste of salt and hot bird chilies. I'm still coughing as Amanda hands me a glass of water. I sip it between pounds on my chest. Sometimes I think half the reason they put up with my pestering to learn Cambodian cooking is that my stumbles over the Asian palate are so entertaining. It's the contrast that gets me, the extremes and the subtleties – a palate of flavors as foreign and complex as the layers of culture itself.

"The Asian like hot and sour," Amanda says. "That's real Khmer food."

"Real Khmer food:" a tender-loving expression that carries the weight of the centuries. The *oo* sound resonates deep satisfaction from the stomach. Food is precious, fondled with thought and desired by hunger pains, the love of it made more special by the longing for it. Cherished beyond money or gold, food connects people to each other.

As Amanda stirs the pot on the stove, a silver-gray fish head appears, floating in the salty lemon broth; the whole fish – head, bones and all – was tossed into the soup pot. *Sngow Chruak Trei* (Sour Fish Soup) evokes a Cambodian hominess akin to our chicken noodle with its childhood comforts and familiar smells in the kitchen. I'd like my son's olfactory memory to include the sour rootiness I inhale in this soup's steam.

"What's that?" I ask Amanda, as she peels leaves from small stems and tosses them into the pot for the final fragrance.

"Chi," she says.

"What's chi?" I ask.

"Herbs."

I can tell this is one secret she's not giving away easily. Chi is a fresh herb mixture that defines a Cambodian cook's personal style. It might include holy basil, saw-leaf herb, and cilantro, to name a few.

"What kind of herbs?"

"Barang herb," Amanda says. "Barang, that's my nickname. It means French lady." Her hearty giggle infuses the barang leaves with childhood memory as they fall into the soup. She remembers being two years old and running into her mother's kitchen one morning to tell her about an auspicious dream: She was a French lady falling out of an airplane! Buddhists are big believers in reincarnation, so from that day on everyone in her family called her Barang.

Grady blows ripples into his reflection in the soup and Amanda instinctively touches his cheek, whispering, "Lucky, very lucky." She is remembering days when the soup reflecting her image held nothing to ease the hunger pains in her stomach. I don't think that being abandoned at an orphanage with potentially fatal diarrhea, losing your birthparents and being separated from your birth culture is lucky at all. But to hear a Cambodian say "lucky" is to savor the full meaning of a word; the soulful sound floats off the tongue and lingers a while, revered.

I want my son to be proud of the country he was born into, and equally proud of the country he was adopted into, yet his fate seems inextricably linked to a relationship between our two nations that remains largely unexamined and unresolved. The Cambodian war started the year I was born and ended, supposedly, the year I entered high school, half the world away. Like the covert war that infertility waged inside me, this war and its ruin leave an eddy in which I'm adrift.

The smell of Sour Fish Soup worked its way into Amanda's past, stirring up memories best left unremembered. To glean the meaning of my son's "luck," we have to go back to where Cambodia's demise began – with bombs falling from American war planes. It started when Amanda was three.

*   *   *

Her real name was Ponluethida Chen So Maly, known to her family simply as Maly. She was the fifth child born to Sokun Prom and Neang Om in Battambang, a French colonial city in

the rice fields of northwest Cambodia. The year was 1970 and
the King had just been overthrown by a military general hardly
anyone knew, the former prime minister called Lon Nol. The
political havoc had given rise to a civil war. The United States,
believing that it would help win the war in Viet Nam, decided
to support Lon Nol with financial and military aid. The King,
meanwhile, sought an army to fight for his return. A small and
little known communist insurgency dubbed by the King as the
Khmer Rouges, or Red Khmer, had been his sworn enemy for a
decade. Yet a shared hatred for the imperialistic designs of foreign powers – both Viet Nam and the U.S. – forged an alliance
between the King and the Khmer Rouge guerillas. Switch-hitting
had been a classic power maneuver made by Cambodian kings
for centuries. Battle zones in the eastern provinces bordering
Viet Nam remained relatively obscured from life in the western
cities, where a middle class had been slowly but steadily finding
its economic footing. As the war edged closer, refugees from the
eastern provinces swelled the western cities. Battambang grew
to accommodate them and the Proms' family business – selling
snacks and dry goods by the roadside – grew with it. By 1974,
with the help of a wealthy friend, Maly's parents had purchased
a restaurant in Pailin, 60 kilometers to the west.

At four years old, Maly was oblivious to it all. She was concerned only with chasing after rubies. In the time before war,
Cambodia had been known as the Jewel of Asia. The resort city
of Pailin was its shining gemstone, a rich, mining boomtown
near the Thai border. The mountains around the city contained
crystallized minerals of all sorts: sapphires; emeralds; zircon;
and rubies. During the monsoon season, when rain flowed down
the forested mountainsides, an array of sparkling, colored stones
washed into the creek beds. Maly ran naked as fast as she could
through the water, picking up as many stones as her little hands
could carry. These forays always turned into a competition with
her brothers and sisters. A jar in her mother's kitchen displayed

their collection. For hours they contrived elaborate comparisons: Who had the most? The biggest? The prettiest?

Each morning after eating a bowl of her mother's sour-spiced "kuy tieu" noodle soup, Maly helped her older brother, Bon Louch, 9, and sister, Malis, 6, set up the tables in the restaurant on the ground floor of their home. Then they ran out the open front and into the street to play. Their father had selected a restaurant located across the street from a big hotel, Pum Sum Baht, or Pile of Treasure Hotel, a getaway for the rich and famous. When no one was looking, the children crossed the street, stepped on each other's shoulders to climb over the brick wall, and spied for hours on the glamorous people. Maly had never seen a movie, so she didn't know what a movie star was, but she admired their dazzling clothes and golden jewelry. The ladies' faces were pale and smooth, their hair like black silk, pinned up with bright flowers. She loved to gaze at them and dream of beauty.

Like most kids, Maly assumed that everyone lived the way she did. She knew the places where her mother hid money, squirreling away the means to educate her children. Maly's oldest brother, Dani, 13, could already speak French and read the newspaper, and now he was studying English, the language they heard on the radio at night when her father tuned in to Radio Free Asia. Dani and her second oldest brother, Bon Leoun,11, (not to be confused with Bon Louch), had remained in Battambang to run their small dry goods store with a cousin. Maly missed Dani; he had always been her protector and the leader of their little sibling gang. That April of 1975, she was excited that the New Year celebration was fast approaching and her brothers would join them in Pailin for the three-day festival. The whole family would dress up in new clothes, go to the mountains together, feast, dance and sing. It was the most exciting time of the year.

Maly was proud that her father always wore a business suit and talked with the glamorous people in the restaurant, but she never dared ask a question or even let her presence be noticed.

Whenever she was summoned from the kitchen to serve water or coconut juice, Maly silently took heed of the clandestine world of adult conversation. She heard men arguing about Lon Nol and the King – two mythical giants riding elephants, in Maly's mind. Her father and his friends were rooting for the King. No matter how many posters were plastered on the light poles in Battambang and Pailin, proclaiming that Lon Nol was the new leader of Cambodia, the people still liked the King. His shrill voice came over the radio daily, screaming "Freedom Cambodia!" Maly didn't know what *americ* was, but she had heard adults tell stories about the bombs from *americ* destroying homes in Kampong Cham, the rice-growing province where her grandparents lived.

In peaceful Pailin, the mid-April New Year celebration went on as usual in 1975. Maly couldn't believe the three days she'd been looking forward to for so long had already passed. Her family was together: Ma; Pa; Dani; Bon Leoun; Bon Louch; Malis; her younger sister, Srey Pau, and their baby brother, Atuit. They all sat around a table in the darkening restaurant, dipping chunks of crispy French bread into Num Ban-Chok Samla Curry and listening to the radio. In the sky above them a comet's tail emerged, pointing toward the east.

"A sign of war," Dani whispered.

"I need my sons to return to Battambang to run the business," Pa was arguing with Ma.

"No, let's wait to see what is happening," Maly's mother protested. She was worried.

A few days later, Maly was showing three-year-old Srey Pau how to crush the kroeung in a clay mortar on the kitchen floor while her mother chopped crisp stalks of morning glory. Suddenly people began shouting outside the restaurant. Maly quickly ran out the door. People were pouring into the streets, which were instantly jammed with the noxious noise of horns blaring and trucks rumbling past. Boys hung from the back of trucks, wielding guns with bayonets. They were all wearing black pajamas and red scarves. Maly thought, "Maybe they are playing a soldier game."

Some people were waving Cambodian flags, others cheering "Freedom Cambodia!" The smiling faces delighted Maly, but many were not smiling. A mixture of confusion and panic passed through the crowd as one of the older, black pajama soldiers started yelling into a bullhorn.

"Get out, everyone, you must get out now! We must clean the city. Take only food you can carry. You will return in three days."

Maly wondered, "Who is this boy shouting at us to get out?"

A crowd of excited children ran behind the trucks. Red, white and blue Cambodian flags waved, people shouted, guns pointed this way and that. Maly didn't know whether to be thrilled or scared. She wanted to run after the trucks, to find out what the big excitement was all about, but suddenly she was pulled by the hair back inside the restaurant. She hadn't heard her father shouting, "Get in! Get in!"

Tears rolling down her mother's cheeks and the strain in her father's voice forced the many questions burning in Maly's mind to retreat. Her mother was desperately trying to collect all the kids, handling baby Atuit with one hand and little Srey Pau with the other.

"Come, run to Thailand with us!" begged a friend who had slipped into the restaurant.

"No, we stay," Sokun Prom replied. "Do what they say, everything will be okay."

He snapped orders to the children: "Pack the food! Hide the pictures! Bury the jewelry!" Maly's mother quickly sewed all their gold baby jewelry into the waistband of her sarong. Her brothers buried money and photographs in the ground behind the house and her father stuffed paper money into three cloth bags. Maly did as she was told and piled into the neighbor's car. The rich man next door, a jewel merchant, was the only person Maly knew who owned a car. At his invitation, her family climbed into the four-door Mercedes sedan, beside the six members of the jewel merchant's family. Then the car slowly muscled its way onto the street to join a throng of people, in the exodus of Pailin.

Squished onto a pair of bench seats, the two families spoke very little. Maly was transfixed by the surreal scene, as if she were suspended in the windowpane between her and the impassable crowd. Everywhere people were running and yelling, some struggling to carry old people and young children, others pushing motobikes or carts full of household goods and food. One barefoot man was pushing a cyclo with pigs tied onto the canopied seat. Even the patients from the hospital were walking in the street, or being pushed on an oxcart, or carried by a relative. Hours passed. Old people too heavy to carry were left by the roadside. A toddler stood crying, her family lost in the crowd. The early morning excitement wore into somber distress, as the long flow of humanity moved on and on, as far as the eye could see.

The armed men directing traffic were young, ill-tempered and weary. "Go that way!" a teenage boy shouted, slamming his bayonet on the hood of the car and shoving his dirty head in the window. "Angka wants you to go to the countryside."

Maly couldn't believe his insolence, ordering her father around. He didn't even sompeah! She'd never seen a young person be rude to an elder. Things were getting strange. The boy-soldiers spoke in unfamiliar words, a rural dialect punctuated by rote revolutionary phrases such as, "Angka has defeated the Americ imperialists!" The restaurant customers had also used that word, *Americ*, but what was Angka? She knew better than to ask. Her father appeared to understand perfectly, and he followed the boy's orders without a word of protest. Complaints were met with a gun to the head.

Maly saw many people shot that day; after awhile it no longer shocked her to see a body crumpled on the ground. Government soldiers and civilian workers were ordered into the streets to surrender and greet the King. The Lon Nol soldiers had worn their dress uniforms. They were quickly escorted to the outskirts of town and executed. That's what Angka meant by "cleaning the city." The bodies lay in a pile where they had fallen alongside the human-jammed roadblock. At that point, Maly and her family and their neighbors were ordered out of the car.

"Everyone must walk!" a wild-eyed soldier shouted. "Angka will accept the car for revolutionary purposes!"

Without protest, the family grabbed some water, rice, and bags of money from the trunk, and slipped into the crowd. Maly's father and the jewel merchant exchanged a tense glance and then parted without a word, wishing well only with their eyes. The Angka soldiers led hundreds of evacuees into the forest, following a dirt road that quickly diminished to a cow path. The children struggled to stay close. In hushed tones, their parents chastened them never to speak to anyone about their background.

"Where are we going?" Maly cried. She had blisters on her feet. She was hungry. Her father picked her up and carried her a while. For a moment she felt like a normal five-year-old, until he put her down and she had to walk more. She tried not to cry for food. Her mother had already scolded her many times for asking and she didn't want to anger her further. Her little brother, Atuit, just 10 months old, cried for food. She was not a baby; she could do better than he.

Darkness fell as they reached the rural village of Don Meay; there the crowd of urban refugees set up a makeshift camp in a rice field. Maly's mother lit a small fire with sticks her brothers collected from the forest, then she boiled water for a small ration of rice. The rural villagers quickly learned to capitalize on the city dwellers' predicament. Maly's father returned with dried fish to add to the pot; it cost him four times the normal price but it produced a hearty, yet bland fish soup flavored with a pinch of salt and sour s'dao leaves picked from the forest. Maly was too tired to complain. She finished her soup and spooned in beside her sister, falling asleep while soldiers patrolled among the campfires.

The next day they walked again, 13 kilometers to Kampong Kohl, without food or water. Hour after hour they walked through the forest. The older children tried to help carry baby Atuit and Srey Pau, but no one carried Maly. Even the flip-flops on her feet were getting heavy. Guns, kicks and shouts from soldiers corralled and pushed the massive caravan of humans through the forest. Old people sat down to die and no one stopped to help them. Maly was scared. If she didn't move fast enough they might kill her, but she was too tired and thirsty to care. Once she knelt down on the path where cow prints had filled with rainwater. After a quick look for soldiers, she placed her lips to the puddle, the way her mother had, and slurped a quenching drink. She'd consumed several cow puddles by the time they reached Kampong Kohl; she wasn't the only one running into the forest to relieve herself.

"Angka has a place for you," barked the soldiers. Maly knew it had been more than three days. She had already learned not to trust anything Angka said. The soldiers were, in fact, waiting for orders, but Angka had no way to house and feed the massive population they had turned out to the fields and forests. Perhaps they were hoping to walk them into the grave.

Plodding on, the crowd descended upon Rung, a beautiful village alongside the Sangka River. As far as anyone knew, there were no other villages in this direction. Maly hoped the long trek was over. Rung had good, clean water and a market. Dani told Maly that the river meant the village would have a good supply of fish, but their father returned from the market empty-handed.

"The vendor tell me the soldier say Lon Nol money no good," Sokun exclaimed to his wife. "They outlaw it!" Her parents were very upset.

"How can money be no good?" Maly thought. Tears rolled down Dani's face. He had worked hard to earn money for the family. Now they were penniless.

"We just use it for toilet paper," Amanda says to me, stirring the soup pot on the stove. She shrugs. "Or burn it."

The family survived by harvesting watercress from ponds they passed on their trek through the forest, but the contamination from dead bodies floating in the water gave everyone diarrhea. Soon even the toilet paper was gone. Gold, watches, shirts and jewelry were the new currency. Maly's mother had stitched a cache into every hem of her clothing. The people of remote Rung were happy to trade for worldly goods.

Maly wanted to bite the armed boy who stood over them, telling everyone to cross the river. "Why can't we stay at the village and work?" her mind protested.

"Angka has a place for the new people across the river," the boy soldier announced, with a grand gesture of his gun toward the large forested hill in the distance. "T'oul S'nau Mountain." During the dry season, the river channel was shallow and easy to cross. When the faction of urban evacuees reached the other side there was no village, just endless forest.

"You will make a new village," the Angka soldier announced, "A revolutionary activity!"

"Out of what?" Maly heard her brother mumble. There wasn't even a rice paddy to cultivate. What were they supposed to eat?

Eating was the only revolutionary activity on everyone's mind. As soon as the soldiers left, the new people of Toul S'nau took to the forest in search of food. With bare hands the boys caught squirrels, mice, snakes, and spiders. Whatever they found was boiled into a thin soup with salt, and rationed among nine family members. Each day the soldiers came to supervise the felling of trees under gunpoint, and each night they returned to Rung for hearty meals in comfortable housing. Meanwhile Maly's family and the others worked to survive in the forest, catching what they could or harvesting wild roots and fruits. Some died from eating k'duit, a wild potato that is poisonous if not prepared properly. Having grown up a rural villager, Maly's mother knew what to do. She soaked the potatoes in water and forced her hungry children to wait. After three nights snails gathered on the roots, and only then was k'duit safe to consume. The snails added a little meat to the broth.

Hunger ate away at Maly's fear as she watched her brothers cross the river and disperse into the forest on their scavenging missions, taking longer each day to come back with food. The most abundant wild fruit trees, banana, mango and sugar palm, were being stripped bare. With the onset of the rainy season, the river began to swell. Her father and mother were starting to fear that if they stayed in the forest much longer, their children might not survive.

The only source of information about what was happening in Cambodia came over a small transistor radio, the signal from Thailand secretly tuned in at night. When Maly's mother decided to trade it, they were cut off from the outside world forever. Bribery, however, was not dead. The chief of Kampong Kohl, a sugarcane producing village, was less loyal to the ideas of Angka than to the perks of power. In exchange for the radio, he granted Maly's family permission to build a small hut in his village. Following the lead of Ma and Pa, who acted as though they knew what to do, Maly and her siblings helped fell the trees by hand, built a one-room structure, and weaved together palm leaves to make a thatched roof. The chief assigned her parents to tasks in sugarcane production. Finally, it seemed, they were done walking.

The communist militants known to the world by the King's nickname, the Khmer Rouge, were known to Maly as Angka. Angka meant, simply, "the organization," and it had a long list of rules Maly soon learned. Each day her parents and brothers went to the sugarcane fields to clear land, burn it, and plant more cane, while Maly and her sisters went to a child-care group called the "go ma." Old villagers were assigned to care for the children, teach revolutionary songs and serve one bowl of thin rice porridge per day. Maly quickly learned not to cry for her mother; when she did, she was hit with a bamboo switch until she stopped.

At daily meetings, Angka gave out the rules of the new society. Money and education became the enemy, and all foreign influence was banned. Jewelry, wristwatches, and books were suspect. City dwellers were to plant and harvest the fields. Teachers, doctors and nurses were ordered to "go to the school" to teach Angka their skill. News of their true fate quickly spread: They were tortured or executed, and buried in mass graves.

Maly dared not question her parents when they started calling her Gahing – "Fat Frog." She hated it. But taking up a rural form of Khmer speech was a strategy to hide the fact that they were educated city dwellers. Restaurant owners would be considered dangerous capitalists; their children, too.

"Do not call us Ma and Pa," her father ordered.

"Why? Why can't I call you Ma?" Maly's younger sister cried. Srey Pau was only three years old.

"You must call us Mai dop and A Pok," she said, using the more formal words of "Mother" and "Father."

"But I love to call you Ma," Srey Pau whined. Their mother held a hand over the child's mouth to keep her quiet.

"Shish. You ask too many questions. No more asking," her mother snapped.

Maly was so confused that she dwelled mostly in her mind. Words could not be spoken; no one knew whom to trust. Silence ate up most of the time.

One day the drone of daily silence was broken by a woman's scream. People came running to see what was the matter as the Angka leader pulled the woman from her hut. She was forced to publicly confess her crime: making love with a soldier. After the confession, she was shot. But she didn't die. While she was writhing in pain on the ground, no one spoke, but the Angka soldier whipped himself into a furious anger. He ordered her ankles bound to an oxen plow, with pots and pans tied to her arms. The woman cried for help, but the people in the crowd bowed their heads and stared at the ground. Everyone knew that to help would be a death sentence, possibly for their whole family.

As the oxen dragged the screaming woman toward the water, the leader announced, "It is a crime to love without the permission of Angka. Angka decides who will marry."

The crowd stood paralyzed. Maly thought, "How can they make you not fall in love?" Her heart sank as she watched the woman being dragged into the water and pulled down by the weight of pots and pans.

"If you live, there is no gain! If you die, there is no loss!" cried the soldier.

The crowd quietly dispersed and Maly stood frozen for a moment. She had seen many people killed by gunfire, but this woman was the first victim the soldiers had made to suffer. Now she knew why her parents told her not to ask questions. Eat what they give you. Don't ask for more. It was, as Angka declared, Year Zero. Love itself was outlawed.

"Fish food, that's what he called her," Amanda says, detaching from the memory as she hands me a bowl of the sour fish soup with its delicate, multilayered fragrance of barang herb. Grady climbs up on my lap, but refuses my attempts to spoon sour fish soup into his mouth. I don't even try to make him open up and swallow it.

five

Breakfast, Lunch, Dinner, Snack

"Where love rules there is no will to power;
and where power predominates, there love is lacking.
The one is the shadow of the other."

Carl Jung

While watching *Heaven and Earth*, the only movie we could find in the Lander Video Express featuring the Viet Nam War from a Vietnamese perspective, George and I heard a little voice behind us ask, "Why do the people run away from Cambodia?" Grady was supposed to be sleeping. How long had he been standing there watching rice fields explode, with people screaming and running for cover? We felt pleased that at three years old, Grady could already identify Southeast Asian faces on a television screen, but unnerved that they were associated with the images of war.

"Why the airplanes shoot the people?" Grady asked when I scooped him up to tuck him back into bed. Oh boy, I thought, surely I can't be having this conversation already. I tried my best to come up with an answer that would satisfy a three-year-old mind without leading to another question. But it was already too late.

"It's just a movie about a war." I said.

"What's a war?"

"A big fight."

"Why those guys fight?"

"Because the Commander-in-Chief told them to."

"The Chief tell them? " he repeated, with a yawn. That seemed to find the end of his logic road and he rolled over, content with my answer. But before I left the room I heard him whisper, "You have to say sorry when you fight."

"Yes, you do," I said, and closed the door.

Months pass with no more questions about Cambodia, until "bombs" burst into the air, exploding at random from hundreds of private driveways below us, 180 degrees in view. The city of Lander, Wyoming, encourages private firework displays within the city limits by granting a variance of the public fire code for one day, the Fourth of July. Showing our patriotism with reckless abandon, thousands of "rockets red glare" are sent gleaming skyward, showering a fairy dust of patriotic fervor over our small town of latter-day cowboys and Indians. Our festival of Independence has been celebrated in these parts, in this way, for a long, long time – a high holiday of pure Americana. From the back deck of Amanda's house, on a small hill above town, the panorama of iridescent explosions can be seen for three solid hours.

"It's my Freedom Day!" Amanda exclaims, hurrying to find her sneakers among the pile of flip-flops at her back door, so she can go shoot fireworks at a neighbor's house up the street. She likes to compete in fiery fervor with the rodeo arena. I decline the invitation to join her, gathering up the leftover beef satay skewers we've roasted on the grill next to the hotdogs all afternoon. My feelings about our freedom day are not quite as jubilant as they used to be.

While our family is walking home, giant blocks of firecrackers crackle through the streets, punctuated by M-80s, bottle rockets, roman candles, and the airborne boom of multicolored sprays. Lander, Wyoming is like Baghdad on the Fourth of July, chock full of shock and awe. Our dog, Huckleberry, a 100-pound Chesapeake Bay retriever, is panting and shaking from the pummeling her psyche receives in these retorts. There's no communicating the benign concept to her; I can see from the wild-eyed fear in my dog's eyes that she takes seriously the threat from fake bombs. Grady is swinging between our arms, jumping the cracks in the sidewalk, when the next M-80 explodes nearby. His eyes suddenly match the dog's panic, and he demands to be carried the rest of the way, clinging to Daddy's neck, insistent that we tell him when the next bomb is coming. The problem is that we don't know.

As soon as we get home, George drives Huck to the outskirts of town to calm her nerves and I tuck Grady into bed, assuring him the dog will be okay when the fireworks are over. He wants to know why the fireworks have come. "It's the way we celebrate being American," I explain.

"What's American?" he asks.

"An American is someone who lives in the United States of America, like you, and me, and Daddy," I say.

"I was born in Cambodia," he reminds me.

"Yes, you were, so you are Cambodian and American." I kiss him on the forehead. "And so am I." The concept of a country, our own or another, remains an abstract idea. For now, Cambodia, to him, means Amanda's house.

It will be several hours before George can return with the dog. Sitting alone on the front stoop, watching the explosions over the rodeo arena, I remember the day I first felt like an American: July 4, 1976. It was the Bicentennial year, celebrating the two-hundredth birthday of the United States of America. At the age of eight, I couldn't conceive of anything being 200 years old; that

seemed ancient. I didn't know then that a country and a culture
that had been in existence for two thousand years, on the other
side of the planet, were being obliterated forever. I ran around
in my red, white and blue halter top, holding a sparkler in each
hand, drinking soda pop and eating hot dogs and new-fangled
Dorito chips, while my dad streaked in his underwear across the
neighbor's yard to torch an Independence Day bonfire. I cheered.
I loved everything about America, and I believed in "the land of
the free and the home of the brave." I felt proud when I heard that
line sung in the national anthem, especially when the American
hockey team beat the Russians in the Olympic games. I believed
in the fight with the Evil Empire, the commies, the nukes, and
the *Battle Hymn of the Republic.*

Of course, at that time no one was talking to us kids about Viet
Nam, and Cambodia was no more than a word vaguely associated with it. I knew a couple of kids at school who had a brother
or uncle who died in Viet Nam; it sounded like a really scary
place. There was a town drunk who sat regularly on one of the
park benches wearing an Army jacket, homeless and alone. I was
scared of him, too. I first learned what a Viet Nam veteran was
when I saw the movie *Rambo.* They had to be so brave to fight
"gooks," I thought, but I didn't know what a gook was. I had no
idea that Viet Nam was linked to our national feelings about the
Soviet Union. And like most Cambodians who grew up under
the Khmer Rouge, Amanda had no idea how the events of her
childhood were spawned by the Cold War.

Now that I'm grown, that patriotic July Fourth celebration
of 1976 is a distant memory. But the Viet Nam War is no longer a thing of the past. It's still happening, and it's in *my* family.
Reading books about the war, I discovered those policies of the
Nixon administration that were never spoken about in school.
The peculiar brutality of the Cambodian part of the story is not
as unsettling as the fact that nobody around me even seems to
know it happened. Perhaps it is this new awareness that lures

me back to Cambodia, ostensibly to fill in the blanks of my son's family tree.

The Eva Air jetliner lowered out of the clouds and cruised over the South China Sea, headed for the coast of Viet Nam. Looking out the window, I hoped that my three-and-a-half-year-old would be content without me for a few weeks. I knew George could handle the daily agenda, but what if something happened and Mommy wasn't there?

George is a man of routine, married to a woman restless for answers. In the home we've made together, he's the steadfast foundation and I'm the renovation committee, habitually impatient for expansion. For more than two years since our adoption trip, I'd been raising money for the Grady Grossman School and deciphering cryptic e-mails from Sovann about the progress of our birth family investigation. During that time the U.S., government had suspended immigration visas for Cambodian orphans, bringing adoptions to a standstill. The reasons given were the same old accusations of corruption, visa fraud, and child trafficking. The truth seemed more important than ever, so I was returning to Cambodia – by myself, this time – to meet with Sovann.

Fifteen minutes later the airplane was crossing high over the Mekong Delta. A checkerboard pattern in shades of green, muddied and swollen from the seasonal rains, framed the shadow of the airplane as it reached from rice field to rice field, sugar palms rising from the water and waving in the wind. In all that bright green wetness, I couldn't tell where Viet Nam ended and Cambodia began. In fact, the border has been a matter of dispute for centuries. For the U.S. Army, fighting in Viet Nam thirty years ago, the lines on the map were clear enough but the cultural boundaries were impossible to comprehend.

Breakfast, Lunch, Dinner and Snack were the code names for
the targets of Operation Menu, the first secret bombing sorties
inside Cambodia made by American B-52s. They started in the
spring of 1969. I was one year old and Neang Prom was pregnant
with her daughter, Maly. American forces had been warring in
Viet Nam for the better half of a decade, and the newly elected
President Nixon had campaigned on the promise of ending the
conflict. After two months in office, the new administration
decided they would have to use Cambodia to keep that promise.
The North Vietnamese had established a supply route called the
Ho Chi Minh Trail along the Cambodian border, and it was the
nemesis of Nixon's desired "peace with honor."

Nixon's National Security Advisor, Henry Kissinger, was the
chief strategist in the peace process, and he argued that a respect-
able amount of time needed to pass before South Viet Nam was
defeated. The logic called for a new word, "Vietnamization,"
which meant that the South Vietnamese Army was supposed
to take over their war, so America could go home without
appearing to lose.

From my aerial view of the territory in question, the murky
border between Cambodia and Viet Nam, I drift into a surreal
daydream: We're flying through the cloudy mist together, Henry
Kissinger and I, as pilot and copilot of a B-52, and it's time to
drop the bombs. From their desks in Washington, our leaders
have a plan, but it doesn't make sense.

"Henry, Cambodians didn't put American lives in harm's way.
Our own politicians did," I shout over the roar of the engine.

"Cambodia isn't really neutral," he yells back, reaching for the
release lever. "The communists are using Indochina as a single
theatre of operation." In the case of Cambodia and Viet Nam,
that was a deadly assumption.

Until 1970, Cambodia's leader, King Norodom Sihanouk, had
been proclaiming neutrality for many years in the Indochinese
Wars between Viet Nam and first the French, then the Ameri-

cans. Border brokering and low-level warfare had stayed the balance of power and defined Cambodia between her domineering neighbors, Thailand and Viet Nam, for generations of the royal household. Under French colonial rule, educated Cambodians splintered into political factions as the ancient culture slowly emerged from agrarian feudalism to join a global economy. The Cambodian King maneuvered between a pro-Soviet, communist revolution in Viet Nam, and a pro-China, capitalist, military government in Thailand.

King Sihanouk held onto power by earning and maintaining the territorial tolerance of Cambodia's neighbors, thus quelling popular fears of their imperialistic designs. He believed the North Vietnamese would win their war with America. Thinking ahead, he made a secret alliance with North Viet Nam, allowing the creation of sanctuaries inside Cambodia along the Ho Chi Minh Trail, yet at the same time cracking down on Cambodian communists within his own borders.

Telling America to rid his country of Viet Cong made the King look good to his people, and secretly scheming with the communists in Hanoi would secure his border after a North Vietnamese victory. Into this dynamic of local, tribal history came Nixon's concept of "peace with honor," which held fast to the logic of a domino theory of communist proliferation; the Cambodian War became a corollary to the peace process with Viet Nam.

In 1970, while the King was traveling in France, he was overthrown by his own Prime Minister, a military general named Lon Nol, who was worried about Sihanouk's "secret alliance" with the North Vietnamese. The coup started a civil war and, with that, Khmer social fabric began to unravel.

"We were merely innocent spectators in this turn of events," Henry's voice claims, in my head. Lon Nol controlled the army and was pro-American. Despite speculation, no one has ever proved that the CIA orchestrated the coup. Yet the United States became the first country to recognize the Lon Nol government,

when Nixon proclaimed Sihanouk legally deposed and reestab-
lished diplomatic relations. A month later, U.S. troops began
to withdraw from South Viet Nam; two months later U.S. and
South Vietnamese forces made ground incursions into Cambodia. Within a year military aid was flowing to Phnom Penh.

Lon Nol's military government was a client of the United
States, with the embassy doling out military equipment, remu-
neration and advice. Many Lon Nol officers padded their pock-
ets with paychecks for fabricated "ghost soldiers," while others
traded arms and supplies with the enemy. Lon Nol's incompetent
leadership and superstitious religious beliefs led to outstanding
military blunders.

Inside Cambodia the coup set disaster into motion. "Nation,
Religion, King" is the pledge of allegiance in Khmer society.
Still today, homes, businesses, and public buildings prominently
display images of the king and queen. Every Cambodian school-
child memorizes the words of the national anthem:

> *Heaven protects our King*
> *And gives him happiness and glory*
> *To reign over our souls and our destinies,*
> *The one being, heir of the Sovereign builders,*
> *Guiding the proud old Kingdom.*

The voice of Amanda's oldest brother, Dani, enters my aerial
daydream, as he recalled the coup: "We know that Viet Nam
and America making war in Viet Nam, but not Cambodia." He
was 13 in 1970. The breakfast, lunch, dinner and snack bomb-
ings were far away from where they lived in Battambang. "But
after Sihanouk out of the country, the civil war started. When
Lon Nol took over, I remember a lot of people get upset, there
are strikes everywhere, people upset because we lose the king.
People like the King absolutely."

The North Vietnamese liked the King, too, and they were
willing to fight for him, believing that his leadership in Cambo-

dia would favor their conquest of South Viet Nam. American and South Vietnamese incursions into Cambodia to oust the North Vietnamese army pushed the conflict deeper into Cambodian territory. When that happened, Cambodia's own internal politics, rivalries and insecurities became engulfed and exaggerated.

The two years of war between Lon Nol and North Vietnamese forces, from 1970 to 1972, relieved military pressure on South Viet Nam, allowing Vietnamization to proceed. As U.S. forces slowly withdrew from Viet Nam, the Khmer Rouge, a small, homegrown, nationalist movement in its infancy gained expert military training, fighting alongside the North Vietnamese.

King Sihanouk had sought to crush the Cambodian communist movement since its inception in the early 1950s. Yet, after the coup, communist leaders quickly seized the opportunity to turn their cause into a national revolution, seeking widespread support from the populace with a battle cry to fight for the King against "the Lon Nol traitors and the American imperialists." Without another option, the King accepted this strategic alignment with the Khmer Rouge, and sealed the fate of Cambodia. People flocked to the Khmer Rouge when they heard the King screaming over the radio to fight for Cambodia's freedom. The U.S. bombing drove illiterate peasant boys from destroyed rural villages into the Khmer Rouge ranks.

"I read in the newspaper America bombing Cambodia but I really don't know why," Dani recalled of his last year at secondary school. Thirty years later he is still perplexed. "We know about the Khmer Rouge but they are small, not very many people. We don't really know who is fighting who. After Sihanouk lose power, more people support Khmer Rouge. My schoolteachers are sad for the King, so they go to Khmer Rouge. The soldiers who came in our restaurant were on the side of the King and then they switch to Lon Nol."

When the North Vietnamese withdrew from Cambodia in 1973 following the Paris Peace Accords, they left their side of the conflict in the hands of the now well-trained and armed Khmer

Rouge. The United States, in support of Lon Nol forces, resumed an intensive bombing campaign for 200 days and nights, from January to August 1973. More than 500,000 tons of explosives were unleashed over the Cambodian countryside. A tiny, undeveloped country pummeled by more bombs than fell on Japan in all of World War II. To this day, there is no accurate estimate of the number of innocent civilians killed – somewhere between several hundred thousand and one million.

Beneath my airplane, a small group of thatched-roof huts mark a farming village at the juncture of two dirt roads atop the dikes between rice paddies. Bombs explode in my head, demolishing the huts. I can hear Henry protest, "It's a myth that American bombing turned a group of progressive revolutionaries, the Khmer Rouge, into demented murderers." Perhaps. But how would you know? I look down at the book in my lap, entitled *When the War Was Over*. Its author is Elizabeth Becker, America's pre-eminent journalist on Cambodia. My finger holds the page with the passage I'm trying to digest. It says, "Behind the lines, the Khmer Rouge ordered everyone in their zones into cooperatives, fortresses that locked up the people, the harvest and all material possessions for the exclusive use of the party and revolution ... Money was abolished to make illegal sales worthless A system of terror was instituted ... With nearly complete control, they were able to coordinate work hours to the American bombs." The Khmer Rouge system of defense foreshadowed what was to come.

The flight attendant calls for the return of tray tables to an upright and locked position. In the shadow of our plane reaching across the watery landscape, I can picture the murky shadows of military helicopters in retreat from the embassy in April 1975, carrying the American Consulate to safety and leaving Cambodia to the crucible the war had created. Lon Nol would spend the rest of his days on a Hawaiian beach.

Breakfast. Lunch. Dinner. Snack. Did you choose those names, Henry? His image fades from my mind, lost in the shrouded mist.

Up here in the clouds, floating between our worlds, the wholeness of our family is safe from the patriotism of my childhood.

The knot returns to my stomach, remembering my senior class trip in 1986 and a visit to the Viet Nam Memorial on the National Mall in Washington, D.C. Our high school history classes hadn't taught us anything about the war in Viet Nam. Yet the painful ache of seeing more than 55,000 American names etched in stone on a black swath, like a scar on the land, stuck with me. Now, skimming low over the Mekong Delta, I feel the same painful ache, wondering where the names of three million Vietnamese and two million Cambodians are etched in stone, to be remembered.

After Cambodia's four years of international isolation and genocide, Viet Nam conquered the Khmer Rouge in 1979. But the subsequent Vietnamese occupation of Cambodia became a political problem for China, Thailand and the United States. Cambodian resistance fighters would be funded to contain Viet Nam; the uneasy coalition included the Khmer Rouge. Civil war in Cambodia resumed; reconstruction did not. Aid to the genocide's survivors was withheld because a pro-Soviet government ruled their country. For a decade, humanitarian, military and political support flowed to the Khmer Rouge in refugee camps along the Thai border.

I don't cry when I hear the last line of our national anthem anymore – the part about the land of the free and the home of the brave. Dropping bombs on the Cambodian countryside doesn't look very brave to me.

*   *   *

Heat and steam from the emotional cauldron of Cambodia smack my senses as soon as I step from the airplane into the sunshine. Twenty bucks and half a dozen rubber stamps later, I'm granted a visa for entry into the Kingdom. Sovann greets me with a wide smile and a new car, a used Toyota Camry featuring a left-hand steering wheel. He always opts for the American way. His English skills have paid off and now he's a bona fide taxi driver. A lifetime of daily struggle has not extinguished his entrepreneurial spirit; he has just spit-shined the car for the occasion, to impress me.

Sovann is anxious to know if I've made progress in securing him a travel visa to the United States, and I have unwelcome news to report. To cushion the blow of disappointment I tell him that since September eleventh, it has become very difficult to get visas because all the rules have changed.

"I just dream to touch my foot on that soil," Sovann tells me, damming the river of his frustration. "Americans can buy the wise people from everywhere, and take them to America with the good idea to make their country rich," he says. His communist geography teacher had told him that.

"America is a nation of immigrants," I say, sounding as empty as a politician. "People with good ideas come from everywhere on their own, because they want to see their idea grow in the fertile soil of opportunity." I start to tell Sovann how hard Amanda has worked to create a successful restaurant business in Lander, Wyoming, and he cuts me off.

"I can do like that! Oh, I will work very hard!" he assures me, with great enthusiasm. I don't doubt him. He's the very kind of immigrant our nation was built by, but we are not that kind of nation anymore. Quietly Sovann swallows his dream and drives in silence toward the tourist section of town.

Phnom Penh's riverfront promenade is alive with festive revelry. "It's the Festival of the Dead," Sovann says. "We must pay tribute to the ancestors for 15 days."

The atmosphere is similar to our Fourth of July celebrations, but the cultural motivation is completely different. This Cambodian high holiday strengthens their connection to the ancestors, while in America we celebrate our independence from them.

Sovann and I order Num Paing Sach from a riverside café and the vendor piles pickled vegetables and ground sausages into a fresh, hot, French baguette, a delicious East-meets-West style sandwich. We sit down to eat at a long rectangular table and are soon joined by three men at the opposite end. I hear the American Midwest in their accents as they order Angkor beer from the petite, young waitress. Her shy smile doesn't indicate that she understands their conversation about tight asses and little titties. One chum draws a magnanimous conclusion: "It's the firmness." His hands clench an imaginary ass in the air. "It hooks you."

Sovann's lips are moving but I can't hear him. Tourists walk into the café, a couple in their mid-sixties, perhaps of northern European stock. Both man and wife are wrinkled and overweight; the woman is proudly wearing a large swath of pink Cambodian silk over her shoulder. The men at our table seem amused. "I just don't know how you can fuck that," one says to the others, and they nod in solemn agreement. A warm flow of adrenaline pumps toward my arms, shoulders and ears. I'm incensed by the thought of a little girl who looks like my son lying under one of them.

Hearing my accent, one of the middle-aged pedophiles asks where I'm from and, after I tell him, wonders if I know the one person he knows in Wyoming.

"What are you doing in Cambodia?" I ask.

"Extended vacation," he smiles.

"Just make sure she's eighteen," I retort. "It's illegal here, too."

All along the promenade, food and festival offerings are for sale. A small Buddhist temple is adorned with the decorative interpretations of an abundant afterlife: lights; flowers; sticky rice cakes in woven banana-leaf cradles; and shiny, tin twinklers. I purchase a large and rather lavishly adorned coconut with incense sticks and lotus flowers stuck into the green flesh. The happy coconut vendor smiles, revealing red, betel nut-stained teeth inside her tanned and wrinkled face. It looks as though she has been punched in the mouth. Chewing betel nut and lime supposedly strengthens teeth and calms the nerves, but it seems an odd habit for old ladies in a country that prizes a shy and tender feminine beauty. I bow three times to the saffron-cloaked Buddha and offer him my pretty coconut.

The coconut vendor quietly takes my hand and leads me to the bird vendor. Inside a wire cage several dozen small, brown birds flit wildly, vying for escape. I pay my fee and the middle-aged woman selling the winged wishes hands me my messenger. The feathery little critter has thus been commissioned to take my hopes to Heaven. Tossing my bird into the air, I wish to find some truth about my son's past.

six

Half-moon Cake

*"In spite of everything, I still believe that people
are really good at heart."*

Anne Frank

Whipping around the bottom of a stainless steel bowl, a beaten egg is tinted bright orange-yellow by the addition of finely ground turmeric root. Fistfuls of rice flour are added, and the batter begins to thicken and foam. Coconut milk thins the mixture to the consistency of thick soup. Amanda then tosses in a pinch of salt and licks a finger to adjust the seasoning. It's almost ready. Her mother, meanwhile, stands at the counter grinding pork into a fine meal and tossing it into a hot wok perched over the flaming cauldron of an industrial-size, Asian-style kitchen. It's Sunday, Amanda's only day off, and we're making Cambodian food at her husband's work station. Andy is home watching football.

As the pork browns, julienned strips of onion are added and a ladle of batter is spread quickly over a hot, flat pan. Timing is everything. The easy, rhythmic movements of mother and daughter spontaneously orchestrate the kitchen, like a well-choreographed dance. When the batter is about to reach pan-cake consistency, a couple spoonfuls of cooked pork and bean sprouts are tossed on top. A minute later one side of the circle is folded over the other, omelet style, and it slides with ease onto a ceramic plate. Amanda hands it to me. "*Ban Cheow*, you call Half-moon Cake," she says. "That's the one my sister ask for before she die."

Yes, I remember. Srey Pau, three years old. Ban Cheow was her favorite. Watching my friend swirl the batter in the pan and quickly construct another bright yellow half-moon, I try to imagine what it would be like to be reminded of death every time you cook.

There are no pictures of Srey Pau; she exists only in the memory of her family. The memories are of a skinny little girl who complained too much, refused to follow directions, and incessantly demanded to wear pretty things. She was a perfectly normal three-year-old whose contrary toddler-ness intensified as she began to starve.

In the mornings before sunrise, Maly could hear her family waking in the dark. The bamboo plank floor where they slept bent under body movements, creaking a lonely invitation to outlive another day. Nine people in a single three-square-meter room, and no one said a word. That's what mystified Maly. Through the palm thatch wall she could hear the family in the next hut shuffling about, and they never talked either. No one did. Outside the sleeping quarters, chhlops were always lurking. Chhlops were peasant sons, usually nine or ten years old, sent to spy and tattle everything they saw and heard to the Angka leaders, a task which prepubescent boys naturally embraced with enthusiasm. Their job was to be mean. They spied for books, for watches, for radios, and they listened for foreign languages or the educated vernacular of Khmer. Seeking the rewards of power, they'd embellish their discoveries to gain the favor of their Angka big brothers. Maly hated them and it drove her crazy, listening for their footsteps under the floorboards.

Maly gazed silently at her mother in the dawn light and noticed that her face was getting darker and darker from the months of work in the field. She tried to imagine her beautiful mother chopping vegetables and stirring noodles in their restaurant's kitchen. It was painful to think of food. Her mother picked up the sleeping baby, Atuit, and tied him into a krama tightly bound to her back. Her shoulder bones and ribs poked through the hand-woven cloth. Feeling jealous of her baby brother, Maly rolled onto her back and examined her own skinny arms. Taut skin stretched over her distended belly. Why did her stomach look so full when she felt so hungry?

Srey Pau was still asleep when her mother and Atuit slipped out the door to join the women's work brigade, walking in a long line toward another hopeless, hot day in the sugarcane fields. Better to be gone before the girl started to complain; the chhlops were always listening.

Maly no longer lived in Cambodia. Now she lived in Democratic Kampuchea, according to the leader shouting at the crowd last night. Sitting in the rain, exhausted and dirty from a day in the field, the workers listened to the drone of Angka logic regarding food production. In unison, everyone pumped their fists into the air and repeated the familiar slogan, "Che'yo! Angka!" ("Victory, Angka!") They sang revolutionary songs about the greatness of Angka and listened to the commune chief rant, as if anyone needed to be reminded how to cut the sections of sugarcane properly: With a few inches of stalk on either side of the joint, plant it standing up, not sideways. Planting technique wasn't the reason for the failure.

"Today we work late in the moonlight instead of sleep. Why?" the boss shouted. "Because you did not finish one hectare!" He answered himself indignantly, with one finger saluting the sky. "Do not say the soil is too hard," he protested. "You must sacrifice for Angka to get one hectare done!" He pumped his fist to the heavens again.

"Che'yo! Angka! Che'yo!" the tired crowd repeated, with feigned enthusiasm. Dani pumped his fist and rolled his eyes, making Maly laugh.

"So now we work late and we finish!" The Angka leader made a proud salute and the crowd sang out in response.

"Che'yo, Angka, Che'yo!"

"You make Angka very happy," he screamed, with a black-toothed smile. "Tomorrow we make one hectare and a half!"

"Che'yo! Ankga! Che'yo!"

"Where is all the food going?" Maly whispered to her oldest brother.

"Always more and more," Dani whispered back, "They work us like machines but we never go to take care of what is at the back. Sugarcane grows all year. We cannot just plant more. We must harvest, too."

The economy of Democratic Kampuchea was flawed from the start. What was not used to feed Angka leaders and soldiers was traded to China in exchange for arms. Failure to produce the quota was easier to blame on the workers' lack of revolutionary spirit than "the organization." Some commune leaders simply lied in reports to the leadership about the amount of food produced.

Maly caught the eye of the chhlop staring at her from the end of their row. Rather than shyly cast her gaze to the ground, she stared back at him, taking in the full measure of power and darkness behind his eyes. Her own defiant eyes dared him to come drag her away. She felt empowered by the bloodstained welts on her big brother's hand.

"Comrade, why are you not working hard?" the chhlop had asked Dani earlier that day, when he caught Maly's brother sitting with his back against a jakfruit tree, taking a break after several hours of planting. "You are supposed to make 10 meters per day. If you don't make 10 meters a day, maybe you don't want to serve Angka good!" Dani had stood up slowly, with his head hanging. Two hot lashes from a bamboo switch burned his hand, and the small piece of sugarcane he'd been munching on fell to the ground.

Now, sitting in the evening commune meeting and staring at the boy who was just a few years older than herself, Maly thought, "I hate you more." The chhlop was the first to turn his gaze and leave. It was a small victory.

The meeting had droned on late into the night and the next morning Maly felt drugged by just a few hours of sleep. Propelled by hunger, she and her sister woke up Srey Pau and walked silently to "go ma." Like the ceremonial start to a school day, the children stood in perfectly straight lines, each with her hand on the shoulder of the child in front of her, and sang the new national anthem:

> *The red, red blood splatters the cities and plains*
> *of the Cambodian fatherland,*
> *The sublime blood of the workers and peasants,*
> *The blood of revolutionary combatants of both sexes,*
> *The blood spills out into great indignation*
> *and a resolute urge to fight,*
> *17 April, that day under the revolutionary flag,*
> *The blood certainly liberates us from slavery.*

Then they marched to the communal kitchen. Mit Bong, "Comrade Big Sister," was a middle-aged woman dressed in Angka black with a red krama tied at her neck. She poured one ladle of soup into Maly's bowl. In disbelief Maly stared at her reflection in the clear liquid – water again, with a just few grains of rice. The knot of hunger in her stomach ate more fiercely at her mind; a tear dropped from her eye and splashed in the broth. Watching the ripples, she fought the urge to throw it back in Mit Bong's face.

Srey Pau and Malis kept quiet, but Maly had a temper that often got the best of her ability to repress strong emotion. Her big sister pulled at her shirt-sleeve. Maly willed her feet to turn and followed Malis to a clear spot in the dirt, where they sat down to eat. She handed her bowl to Srey Pau and the younger girl grabbed it and poured its contents into her mouth. Maly thought of her mother at work in the sugarcane fields. Maybe she would bring home an insect to eat. The idea comforted Maly but even so, she quickly put a stop to her mind's imagining and wiped the wet streaks off her face. Kids who complained were hit with a bamboo switch. She'd learned that the hard way.

Padding along the soft ground, Maly's mother worked silently, bending over the furrowed row, placing small sections of sugarcane into the soft ground and packing loose dirt around the little green nub. When the chhlop wasn't looking, she quickly stuck one end of the cane into her mouth and bit down, sucking the cane juice as fast as she could. She prayed for the sweet nectar to keep milk in her breast for the baby sleeping on her back. Then a scorpion appeared from behind the furrow, and her quick hands grabbed it and shoved it into a pocket. Any nutritious morsel would bring a smile to one of her children's faces.

Late in the afternoon, she returned from the fields and pulled the scorpion from her pocket, secreted away just for Maly. After her frenzied chewing of the raw insect, Maly almost hugged her mother. She wanted to kiss her and thank her, but she didn't. She'd been living under Angka for almost a year, and she knew the rules. A chhlop could be watching.

"Mai! Mai! Hungry! Want Ban Cheow!" Srey Pau begged, twining her skinny little arms around her mother's tired legs.

"No, no, don't have," she scolded her youngest daughter. "Shh! Don't call me Mai!"

"Why don't call you Mai?" Srey Pau protested, scowling. "I love that." She had been told a hundred times not to use the city dweller word for Mommy, because if the chhlops heard that word they might report it to Angka.

"I want pretty clothes, I want a necklace, I want Ban Cheow!" She was screaming now, and crying, a true temper tantrum.

As the child grew more irate, neighbors tried to help. Angka called them the "old people," which meant a family who had lived in the rural village, farming the land for many generations. While the minds of "old people" in Kampong Kohl may not have been "corrupted" by city life, neither had the Angka's vengeful spirit consumed their hearts. Hearing the cries of a little girl from a family who worked hard and minded their own business, they reached out to help.

The old lady next door held Srey Pau on the steps of her hut, swaying back and forth, saying, "Shh! Shh! Why are you crying, Pau?" The old woman cried, too.

A childless couple living in a wooden house across the dirt alley went to work gathering the ingredients for Ban Cheow. Turmeric root grew in the forest surrounding the village, so that was easy to find. Someone shimmied up a coconut tree to get milk for the bowl, while others stole an egg from the duck that nested on the dike. The women quickly pounded some rice into flour. No one had pork to make the filling, but bean sprouts grew in the family garden. "Old people" were still allowed to privately harvest. In no time, the quiet neighbors in Kampong Kohl returned with enough half-moon cake to quiet Srey Pau, and share a little bit with the rest of the family.

Maly never thought anything tasted so good. She licked her fingers for every last morsel. It had been weeks since she'd eaten real food.

"Food, look, food, Mai!" Srey Pau beamed. "I like it." She ate and ate and ate. The old people smiled. Then the begging resumed. "Mai, I want a necklace." Srey Pau babbled about a necklace and earrings, while pulling at her mother's clothes. It was dangerous. What if the child gave away what was hidden in the seams of her mother's sarong? Tiny golden necklaces, anklets and earrings, the hidden jewels were totems of good luck and prosperity purchased at the time of each child's birth and blessed at the temple. A bolt of pretty, blue pamoung silk was stashed between the rafters and the roof thatch. Mai cut a small piece from it, wrapped it around her youngest daughter's puffed-out belly and tucked the ends through her tiny legs, tying them into a kben, the traditional dancer's pantaloon. She hoped the bright material would calm the girl.

"Pretty, pretty!" Srey Pau was delighted, but not finished. "I want necklace!" she screamed.

"Why does she want to look pretty?" Maly thought, looking down at her own soiled black trousers, a little mad that her mother was spoiling her sister, but still too happy about the half-moon cake to complain. "My sister has such a big mouth," Maly thought to herself. "She's going to get us in trouble."

More loudly Srey Pau cried, "Earring! I want earring!"

Finally her mother unbound a small gold earring from the bottom seam of her sarong, hedging the risk to quiet the toddler. The otherworldly object did the trick. Between sniffles and tears the child fell asleep, continuing to babble softly in the dark about all things pretty. In her fancy clothes with a tummy full of Ban Cheow, Srey Pau gave up. Perhaps somehow she knew that her temper tantrums put her family in danger. Drifting off, never to return, she allowed starvation to claim her soul.

When the child did not awaken in the morning, Maly's family mourned in silence. Someone fetched a monk to say a blessing. A funeral would call forth the ancestors to escort Srey Pau to the other side, but the monk could not go with them to a small hill at the edge of the village to bury the child. It was too dangerous. Rumors of ruined temples and forcibly defrocked monks laboring in the fields drove fear through compassion. He made a quick blessing over the body and wrapped it in a plain cloth; it was better than nothing. Maly's father said quiet prayers while carrying his daughter to their chosen gravesite. Two neighbors followed him, to help dig the hole. Her mother joined the woman's work brigade with Atuit on her back and tears falling silently onto the krama wrap. Her brothers went to the fields. Maly and Malis walked slowly to go ma. No one seemed to notice that Srey Pau was missing.

Maly sat in the dirt all day throwing stones at the confusion between happy and sad. Her sister had died: No more complaining, no more Srey Pau. But the half-moon cake was so good.

"Why did you die? Why did you die!" the old woman next door had cried, as the body of little Srey Pau passed by. Two days later, the old woman died, too. To honor her, her relatives rounded up a funeral feast in the customary fashion. From the familiar forest around the village, they harvested deer meat and palm juice, raccoon and rabbit. The chhlops who came were her own kin, temporarily departed from spying duties to join with the community of mourners. No one seemed to care about the repercussions, living for the moment in a traditional world that made sense, where fraternity through food was more than a painful memory. Maly and her family ate their fill.

"I was so happy," Amanda says, salty drops of guilt rolling down her cheeks and dripping onto her plate of half-moon cake. "I couldn't wait for the next person to die, so that I could eat."

One week later, Atuit died in his sleep. His last request – one of the only words he knew, at 18 months of age – was nom ba chok (rice noodle curry). It was the last meal the family had eaten together for the New Year celebration at their home in Pailin. For little Atuit, there was no blessing, no mourning, no feast, no burial. Two Angka soldiers came to the hut and took the boy's body away. A few days later Maly's mother saw her krama cloth hanging on a stalk of sugarcane. She wondered if a tiger had eaten her baby boy.

"I think my daughter die to help my family," Grandma says, releasing tears confined by the years. Spooning fish sauce and garlic onto my half-moon cake, she stops and holds my hand, as if she were touching the ghosts of her lost daughter and son. Then she chokes out the words stranded in her throat for nearly three decades.

"I think she traded her life for our family. That's why we can get a job and stay in Kampong Kohl. If she not die, maybe my whole family die." Grandma's eyes reach deeply through mine, trembling as she revisits her children's deaths. In her pained expression I can see into the heart of my son's birthmother and comprehend: In motherhood, we all are one.

Bewildered and lost in her incomplete memory, Grandma collects our plates and returns to the sink to start washing the dishes.

seven

The Festival of the Dead

"Life shrinks and expands in proportion to one's courage."

Anais Nin

I remember with regret how I had asked at the orphanage, more than two years before, why our legal adoption papers said "unknown" in the place for a birthparent name. We knew that wasn't true. They had a name and a thumbprint on a napkin-sized piece of paper. We weren't sure if the person who made the thumbprint really existed, but we knew that in the chaos of contemporary Cambodia, Grady's history would disappear forever if we did not find out now. As nervous new parents George and I had accepted the answer, "That's the way it's done here." But as time slowly passed, we realized we couldn't wait for our child to grow into his questions. By the time he was ready, the opportunity to find answers would be long lost. Why the lie was written on his paperwork, and who was benefiting from that lie, we didn't know.

We had chosen international adoption partly because we sensed a certain level of security in anonymity. We had all the usual adoptive parent fears of dealing with birthmothers: a chance encounter in the grocery store; our child being taken away from us; an "open adoption" and a lifelong relationship with an unwanted third wheel. Then there was my secret fear that my child would love his birthmother more than me. Now, I couldn't get her – and the gratitude I wished to express to her – out of my mind. Whoever had written "unknown" in the box on the adoption papers was not going to steal Grady's pre-adoption identity, not if we could help it.

Grady's first word, spoken in a whisper at 13 months old, was "Wow!" Pushing around his small Red Wing Flyer wagon, he toddled back and forth on the front lawn, often stopping to say "Wow!" at ordinary things: a gust of wind; the creak of a tree; a rock; my ear. His favorite word hit the nail on the head, pinpointing remarkably how my love had overcome my fear. As his vocabulary grew, so did the security of our bond. We had a few scraps of information given to us by the orphanage director. If the birthmother truly had left her name and a thumbprint before saying goodbye, clearly she wanted Grady to know who she was.

Once I was back in Cambodia, the reasons for tracking down my son's birth family didn't seem quite so clear. Grady would be turning four in a few months; I didn't want to miss a single magical moment of his emerging personality. The idea that truth was central to his well-being felt like a superfluous, intellectual luxury in the context of a world where five-year-old street children fight viciously over the smallest scrap of food scavenged from the Central Market's dirt floor. Our school project felt safer and more productive, expending energy to help many people versus finding one person. Our school lies to the northwest of Phnom Penh in Kampong Speu province but I felt pulled in the opposite direction, toward Takeo Province, which lies to the southeast. Sovann had uncovered some information there. I hoped to trace the movements of a landless farmer in Takeo, before traveling back north to the Cardamom Mountains to attend an opening ceremony at the school, which was being planned in my honor. Needles can't really be found in haystacks, I told myself. I didn't necessarily consider what would I do if we actually found a birthmother.

When I released my wishing bird on the riverfront promenade during the Festival of the Dead, in the presence of a dressed-up little Buddhist temple, the bird flew straight toward Heaven – but then it stopped short. Perched on the statuesque head of Naga, the serpent who protects the temple rooftop from evil spirits, the bird began to preen. I suspected its behavior might be the avian equivalent to saving face, a sign that once again Cambodia would divert my attention from my intended mission. The next morning Sovann met me on the promenade, freshly showered and waving from his Toyota Camry, honking his way through the oncoming traffic.

"Is okay my family come too?" Sovann asks. "Ngim want to see her mother for the Festival of the Dead." His wife, Ngim, had been pregnant with their second son when I met her the first time. Now she is again with child. In our e-mail communiqués, Sovann refers to Grady as his nephew, and now he considers me kin as well. He has relatives in Takeo province, and that's were we'll go now. Cambodia is like that: There's always a relative somewhere who will take you in.

Ngim and I stumble our way through a sisterly greeting in my limited Khmer. Sopheap, the oldest son, bows politely and then says "apple" in perfect English, followed by its spelling: "A-p-p-l-e." He has been studying at a special private school that is costly to his father, and he's pleased to show off his English skill, with six-year-old pride. I pat Sopheap on the head, to Ngim's horror, forgetting that the gesture is taboo in most Asian cultures. Then I tell Sovann that his son can come stay with my family to study on a student exchange, when he is in high school. Sovann likes the idea but when he translates this to Ngim, she scowls. "What about his father?" She doesn't understand that I have neither the power to grant a visa, nor the money to buy one. The complications of the Department of Homeland Security's new immigration rules are beyond the reach of our communication.

A crowd gathers as I hand out gifts: a purse for Ngim; a shirt and vitamins for Sovann; electric toothbrushes for his two sons; a baby outfit and teething toys for the bundle protruding from Ngim's belly. The Tasmanian Devil electric toothbrush causes great excitement and Ngim quickly shoves the contraption into her new purse – afraid, I think, that someone will steal it.

Sovann slowly maneuvers the car into the chaotic roadway, past the Royal Palace, and turns onto busy Monivong Boulevard, where generally accepted traffic flow patterns are somewhat respected. Suddenly, to my surprise, everyone stops at a red light. The intersection has an operable traffic signal, and the drivers from both motorized and foot-powered vehicles are actually obeying it. "When did Phnom Penh get stop lights?" I ask, in shock at the progress of just a few years.

"Have long time, no electricity, so not working," Sovann says. "Now have."

My delight at this small progress is oddly tinged with regret for the reining in of Cambodia's anarchical soul. Her freedom has unique features, and lawlessness is one of them. Our light turns green and three lanes of traffic begin to move forward simultaneously, while traffic cops standing in the middle of the intersection wave us by with – a video camera? Sovann answers before I even ask.

"The police make the video to show people from countryside how to drive, how to use stoplight, signal, everything." Sovann says. "They show that on the TV, so everybody can know what is the right way."

The traffic thins as we filter onto the shoulderless, two-lane, somewhat-paved National Road No. 2, heading toward Takeo province. Little plank shacks covered by sheets of galvanized steel with blue tarpaulin verandas line both sides of the road in the "suburb." We stop to purchase bottled water across the street from a large, Chinese-owned garment factory. The shopkeeper quickly insists that I sit down and eat Kuy Tieu Cha. This fried noodle dish is her medium to tell me she likes me, and the reliability of my greenbacks. It comes with a tasty drink: ice; condensed milk and Nescafe, served in a plastic baggie fastened by a rubber band around a straw. It's the Cambodian equivalent of a Starbucks latte, my beverage of choice. The vendor deftly uses a machete to hack open several cold, green coconuts for Sovann's wife and kids to share.

Several patrons have gathered at the noodle shop to watch TV on one small screen with one station, fed by one wire. It is powered by electricity pilfered from the garment factory. Between karaoke video love songs. a public service announcement plays. On screen, a sick young woman lying prone on a straw mat is barely able to swallow the coconut juice her mother is feeding her. The Khmer audio is simple to follow. "Don't die my daughter, don't die," the mother pleads and a little boy adds, "Don't die mommy, don't die." The sick young woman whispers that she's sorry she didn't believe all the stories about AIDS; she didn't know her husband went to prostitutes. She's sorry she didn't listen to her mother, and marry a good man. With her family sobbing around her, she dies. Then a staggering statistic appears on the screen: 250,000 HIV infections; 50,000 AIDS-related deaths; 20,000 AIDS-infected orphans – this year. I can't read the Khmer script that follows, but I recognize the condom.

Garment factory workers from the industrial complex across the street stream out the gated entrance. All are wearing matching light blue work shirts. Jet black hair is pulled into ponytails that swing freely down the backs of happy women released from a 15-hour shift. A girl in a blue uniform purchases fried crickets

from our eager noodle vendor and leaves before the AIDS commercial is over. There is a full box of condoms near the wall of
dry goods.

"How much are those?" I ask.

"Free," Sovann answers. "The NGO give them away to the
garment factory worker."

A truck pulls through the industrial gate. It's full of light blue-
uniformed girls, being hauled like cattle into the compound for
the night shift. At a wage of $3 per day, how many will take to
the streets this evening, working as prostitutes to help their families eat? The exploitation of women, whom I consider kin, makes
me cringe every time I zip my son into one of his fuzzy OshKosh
B'Gosh sleepers, with a label that says "Made in Cambodia." I
know the garment will be outgrown before it is worn out, but
the economics strong-arm my guilty conscience, forcing me to
accept what is true: It's better than nothing. If my son's birthmother had even a $3 per day job, she might have been able to
keep her children fed.

Sovann points to a long, white-tiled, cement structure under
construction across the street. Another speculative, commercial
housing block, built in the urban tradition of small business space
in front and living quarters at the back. Sovann wants to buy one
unit so that his wife can sell noodle soup, and his children won't
have to play in the noisy, narrow alleyway of his present squalid
neighborhood. I point out that nearly every small vendor lining
the street sells noodle soup, but Sovann doesn't seem to grasp
the idea of competing with diversification.

"You have $30,000 to borrow me?" he asks.

"Why don't you borrow from the bank?" I say, shocked that
he would ask to borrow such a large sum. Real estate investment
is not exactly what I had in mind when it comes to humanitarian aid. But there is no reasoning with Sovann's distrust of the
bank; he launches into an explanation of how he plans to repay
me in only three years. Ngim's sister is a garment factory worker,

and he can rent living space to her and her friends. Then we do the calculations.

Garment factory workers make $40 to $70 per month, and the company charges $25 for housing, so in order to compete, he needs to charge less – say, $15 per month. If he rents to five girls, he'll make $900 per year, and it would take over 33 years to repay the loan, interest free. He realizes his error and looks dejected. I try to frame the matter in terms of cultural difference.

"In America we don't usually borrow that kind of money from friends, or even our family," I tell him. "We get mortgages." But paying back twice as much in an amortized loan to get what you want today is not his idea of a good deal. Sovann is devoid of long-term perspective. Besides, he has no documented means to prove his income to a loan officer; taxi drivers work for cash. Once he applied for a legitimate job with the U.S. embassy, presenting a recommendation letter from an American diplomat he'd driven for, but the position was given to a doctor. Four hundred dollars per month, driving for the U.S. embassy, was a better salary than the doctor could find practicing medicine.

As we continue toward Takeo, the pace of National Road No. 2 is dangerously faster than the city streets, exacerbated by a continuous game of chicken. Sovann pulls out and blinks his lights a few times to communicate our position to oncoming vehicles. I grip the dash and pray as we miraculously avoid collision with both an oncoming lorry and – in the lane we return to – a moto carrying two girls and a pig. It'll be a long time before the video-recorded civility of Phnom Penh's Monivong Boulevard spreads to the countryside.

Eventually we turn onto a red-dirt, country lane and begin making our way through the patchwork landscape toward Tra Peang Veng village. Banana trees and sugar palms line the path, giving shade and a beguiling sense of tranquility to this land of contrasts. We pass ox carts and bicycles and houses on stilts where people are lazing away the hot afternoon in hammocks.

For a second, I can actually appreciate the idea of an "agrarian utopia" that the leaders of Democratic Kampuchea had in mind. Then again, people who didn't have to actually do the work created that four-year revolutionary plan.

In the paddies surrounding Ngim's mother's house, a group of women is planting rice seedlings. Their faces are obscured by checkered, homespun krama cloths tied tightly under the chin to protect head and face from the relentless heat of the equatorial sun. They work the land for Ngim's mother, who is too old to manage it, now that her children are grown and her husband dead. The women work steadily, swaying in unison in wet sarongs, moving six inches at a time, bent over a mud-soaked row, planting each thin green stalk with a swift plunge of the thumb into soft ground – step, swing, push, step, swing, push. I wonder if they have babies somewhere, waiting to be fed.

This is the life my son's birthmother might have led; she worked other people's land for a share of the crop, migrating with the seasons. Ratanak was three months old, malnourished and suffering from diarrhea when she brought him to the orphanage. It was October, the harvest season; perhaps working in the rice fields all day made her thin breast milk dry up. At nine months old, Grady came home still clenching his mouth shut at the sight of any form of food beyond the bottle. His nanny said he'd been left as an infant in a hammock most of the day; another child may have tried to shove rice in his mouth when he cried for food. We had to be patient until he learned to trust us; he didn't open his mouth to take in solid food for a long time.

Ngim's mother, Niat Nhaw, is embarrassed that I've come to her house, complaining to Sovann that she doesn't have a bathroom. A jumble of wooden planks frame a split bamboo floor under a good metal roof. The whole house is raised on stilts ten feet off the ground, a step up from the usual low-lying, disintegrated, palm thatch housing in the neighborhood. A land-owning widow strikes me as middle class, but Sovann assures me that in the countryside, there are only different levels of poor. Mrs. Nhaw hands me half a pomegranate so I can snack on the sour seeds and firmly suggests that I take a shower, sending one of her grandchildren scurrying off to fetch me a clean sarong. It would be rude to refuse. Climbing out of my clothes after pulling the elastic waistband of the sarong up over my breasts is a clumsy affair out here in the open. The adults respectfully leave me to my business while the children cannot help but watch and giggle. One wide-eyed boy pantomimes how to wash by pouring water over my head with a little plastic saucepan from a giant clay cistern. Between douses, I slap at the bites of little red ants cruising over my feet, to the children's delight. Hamming up the attack makes me fast friends with them.

A half dozen cousins are playing in the dirt yard around grandma's house, creating games out of sticks and nuts. In their laughter the difficulties of their world are forgotten, reminding me of both what Grady has sacrificed and what he has gained. What happened to his extended family?, I wonder. Surely if they were alive, someone would have taken his mother in. Only one answer becomes clear: Every child deserves to be a part of a family. Orphanages are not good enough.

Ngim is quick to catch one of her mother's fat hens and break its neck, deftly plucking out the feathers before returning to the small, thatched-roof cook shack behind and below the foundation stilts. Inside the kitchen, mother and daughter squat on the raised bamboo floor with children crawling all around while they clean the chicken and chop vegetables by candlelight, crushing kroeung in a stone mortar, and tossing everything into a soup pot. The smells remind me of Amanda's kitchen, but the distance between these women and me is so much farther. I'm relegated to the hammock and the company of men.

The sky darkens, and small wax candles are lit to offer fragments of light while Sovann and I sup on morning glory chicken soup, flavored with lime juice and a touch of mint. With no electricity in the village, a chorus of paddy frogs harmonizes the evening silence. "Can you see the seven stars in that constellation?" I ask Sovann, pointing to the speckled heavens.

"That one, the baby chicken stars," Sovann answers. "We have a story about that." The story goes something like this: Once upon a time, a mother hen was being sacrificed for the New Year soup and she asked God to make her a star so she could watch over her children from the night sky. The little chicks didn't want to be separated from their mother so they jumped into the boiling water with her, and God turned them all into stars. The seven chicken stars appear in the constellation we call Pleiades.

I'll take that story home to Grady to weave into his fantasies of flying among the stars. He's already the essential matter of a more human constellation – two families, one American and one Cambodian, drawn into shape by some invisible force in the Universe of souls, one by adoption and one by birth. No matter which star I stand on, the perspective may change but the shape remains the same, mysteriously held together by an inexplicable force.

Sovann insists that he escort me into the rice field so I can take a pee. For reasons beyond my comprehension, I am not allowed to walk alone into the darkness and be left to my own devices. My sarong displays its usefulness, providing easy cover for the elimination act. Sovann is mortified that I would simply squat near the side of the road, insisting instead that I wade into the flooded paddy for privacy. He kicks his plastic flip flops in my direction, so I can avoid soiling my leather sandals. My bladder is too full to argue his cultural interpretation of modesty. I put on the flip-flops and splash into the darkness, suppressing my fear of leeches and land mines that so many stories of Cambodia have planted in my head.

My foot completely misses the raised dike, and the silt-saturated rice bed quickly sucks the flip-flops off my feet, pitching my whole body to the ground with a splash. Yuck. I can't even take a

pee gracefully in this land. How will I manage the delicate work of relating to my son's birthmother? Perhaps I should just go home and concentrate on raising the best American kid I can.

Drenched from another wash at the cistern, I follow Niat Nhaw up the outer steps of the two-room, wooden plank house. She fusses with a kapok-stuffed pillow and drapes a mosquito net over her bamboo bed. Hospitality and deference to my presumed riches place me at the top of the social ladder, a pedestal I find small and uncomfortable. I've spent countless nights sleeping on the ground and peeing in the woods in Wyoming's mountains; there's no need to pamper me. Despite my feelings of kinship, I'm still a foreigner to them.

Lying on my back under a mosquito net, listening in the darkness to the whispers of a pregnant woman and her sixty-year-old mother sleeping on the floor beyond a thin partition, I long to cuddle my son. If Grady and I had both incarnated as Cambodians in this lifetime, maybe we would be together on the bamboo floor. Neither one of us would have survived well in Cambodia, I think. I'm too impatient, and he's too trusting. I'm convinced that our relationship was born this way for a reason, but I wonder if I will ever figure out what that reason is.

The dogs start barking at 4 a.m. People are shuffling through the darkness banging metal pots with wooden sticks, making an awful racket to roust the dead spirits lurking in the bushes. The roosters go nuts well before dawn. It's an important day in the Festival of the Dead, the day to pray for lost souls. In the pre-dawn darkness, villagers visit the pagoda with gifts for ancestors without family, bringing offerings of food and devotion. Hungry spirits are known to be troublemakers, bringing sickness to the houses and poor harvest to the land. The village community placates lonely souls to avoid such mishap.

On the cement wall surrounding the base of the pagoda, offerings of fruit, sticky rice balls and burning incense quickly attract biting ants, slugs and flies. Apparently the dead aren't bothered by

the crude realities of the physical world. Unhappy spirits inhabit
the netherworld in this land that has been gripped by violence,
starvation and disease for more than a quarter-century. How
many dead, no one will ever know; neither their births nor their
deaths were recorded. Fathom the number of offerings it would
take to feed all the souls who died of "no food" in the first place.
Even now, every morsel is needed to nourish the living.

Sovann has informed me that the village where my son was
born, Prey Che Teal, is not far from here. "The village chief told
me that the daughter is still alive," he says. But first we need to
pay our respects to his wife's ancestors. Sovann has little interest in the Buddhist religion; however, The Festival of the Dead
is too important for him to ignore.

At the pagoda, word quickly spreads that my presence is good
luck. A sea of worshippers parts at the top of the steep steps, so
I can follow Sovann and his family with our offerings of rice,
banana and water gourd soup. Lovingly escorted to the Buddha
by old women with shaved heads and betel-stained teeth who
touch me as I pass, I make my offering in small bills. Behind
blind eyes covered by thick, white cataracts, the blessing man
sings a tinny chant over the crackle of an old loudspeaker system. He says I have long legs, can travel very far. He wishes me
riches and a safe journey. Sovann leans over and whispers, "I
have short leg, cannot go everywhere."

Five incense sticks burn between my fingers as I bow on
my knees to the Buddha and pray for the first time to my ancestors and my son's, both the living and the dead. Staring at the
Buddha's enigmatic face through curling streams of incense
smoke, I plainly ask for his enlightenment. This culture vener-
ates its ancestors, looking to the dead for protection, yet seems
to sever the connection carelessly when it comes to placing children for adoption.

We thought we'd done our homework, asking many times
what causes the children to become parentless. Birthparents die
of disease and land mines; some children are abandoned because

of "no food." It's the definition of orphan that breeds dishonesty. U.S. immigration law governing adoption defines "orphan" as a child with birthparents dead or unknown, law based on wartime conditions rather than endemic poverty. Cambodian law allows living birthparents to relinquish a child, yet there are no birth and death certificates, no social workers, no counselors, no relinquishment forms, no law enforcement. The infrastructure for U.S.-style documentation simply doesn't exist in Cambodia. Someone has to create the documentation necessary to fulfill an immigration visa application.

Adoptive parents must pay fees for services rendered, and the vast difference in scale between our two economies invites greed and undermines truth, even when a child's orphan status is completely legitimate. Government ministers expect payment for their signatures on paperwork; orphanages need to make room for the constant flood of new arrivals, and adoption fees cover the expense of caring for those arrivals. "Does the end justify the means?" George likes to ask, and we've never been able to come up with a suitable answer. Why this complicated situation is reduced to accusations of birthparents selling and adoptive parents buying, I can't figure.

The Buddha puts a stop to the argument going on in my head. Through the incense smoke, his smiling face calms me. I hear a gentle inner voice: People have created a flawed adoption system, yes, but spirit has its own divine plan for the evolution of the human soul. The ancestors are tired of the conflict created by a limited definition of family and tribe. People need to know what *we all are One* looks like, and you got picked. "Okay Lord Buddha," I pray. "If our ancestors have arranged this relationship from the hereafter, I need them to guide us in how to live in the *now what?*" I place my incense sticks in the rice bowl and ask him to show me the way to make peace with what I know.

Rows of old people in black trousers and white shirts, future ancestors all, are curled up sleeping on the cement floor, living in the pagoda for the entire 15 days of the festival to pray for a good afterlife and rebirth. One bald woman strokes my arm and smiles with her red teeth. "S'at na," she says. "Very beautiful." Squeamish in my role as celebrity good luck totem, I pull out photographs of my family. I point to my husband, my mother and father, brothers, aunts, uncles and cousins, and, of course, my son, who is in every picture. The word "kruah-sah" ("family") passes around the crowd, touched by a sacred hush. Sovann explains that my husband and I adopted our son. I quickly add that he's beautiful and smart and we love him, to dispel any back-of-the-mind thoughts that he's our servant, a lingering cultural belief about the role of adopted children.

"Pros samnang," several people whisper. "Lucky boy." Everyone wants to touch the pictures. The bald nun asks if she can keep the photo of him, but I'm not ready to let his image be her good luck totem, not until I know if there is anyone related to him living nearby. A young boy points to my toe ring, carved with the phrase *Carpe Diem*. He wants to have it. Seize the day, my young friend, seize the day; it's yours.

"Now you need a daughter," the nun is making Sovann tell me, "To take care of you when you get old." In Cambodian families, daughters are desirable; they help with the housework and care for their parents in old age. In theory, this is the cultural reason why destitute mothers relinquish boys more often than girls. Boys are karmically bound to fulfill their destiny.

"Do you want her?" A two-year-old girl is being held out by a twenty-something woman in lovely green silk.

"Not to sell, to give." Sovann reassures me. "Because her husband disappear with another wife."

I can see that tender care has been taken to dress the child for temple; her mother clearly loves her. "Akun ot tay," I say. "No thank you." The mother's proposal seems heartless at first, but there is selfless strength in her desire, too. Her hope of giving the child a better life prevails over her claim to her daughter as her duty-bound caretaker. Sovann tells the woman that what she is proposing is illegal. Hopeless air is hard to breathe; my desire to change the circumstances sucks my soul dry. The tinny blessing chants fade as we descend the temple steps.

Left to make small talk in the shade of a house on stilts with people I barely know, in a language I can barely speak, I am stunned when Ngim's sister candidly asks me if I want another one, pointing to her six children running around the garden with their cousins. Is she joking? I can't tell, but will it ever stop? Half of the population is under 15; clearly the adults do not know what to do with all these children. Birth control is not culturally taboo, it's just expensive and inaccessible.

George Bush's first bold act as President of the United States, on January 21, 2001, was to re-enact a global gag rule preventing U.S. family planning assistance to foreign nongovernmental organizations that use non-U.S.-donated funds to engage in abortion-related activities, thus using the abortion issue to deny access to U.S.-donated contraceptives, including condoms. No wonder the orphanage director had been so thankful that French, German and Australian funds are not similarly inhibited.

Sovann ventures down a long, deeply rutted, dirt path in search of the headman at Prey Che Teal village. He insists on traveling alone, since my very presence will draw too much attention to the investigation. In a village made of thin, palm thatch walls, news of an American travels quickly, the opportunity to make money knocking.

The noise of a very loud generator thwarts my attempt to discern Sovann's in-laws' eager questions. His brother-in-law operates the village electric company, charging $3 to recharge corroded DC car batteries with his diesel-powered generator. In one afternoon, he can turn $10 worth of diesel fuel into a $50 profit, to supplement his $25-a-month salary as director of the village primary school. Neighbors who can afford this luxury will hook up one light bulb for a few hours, once the sun goes down around 7 p.m.

Brother-in-law has sliced his foot on a piece of rusted metal while stepping over the jumble of twenty long cables used to charge the batteries. He uses gasoline to clean his wound. Mortified, I rifle though my pack for the first aid kit I brought and insist upon administering antibacterial ointment to the wound. The entire family gathers around to see what my bag of goodies has to offer. Ngim's mother asks if I have something for her headache, and I give her two Tylenol. Sister insists I look at her youngest child's scalp, crusted by the scabs of lice bites. Suddenly I have turned into a makeshift first-aid station, administering to all kinds of ailments that I barely comprehend. My Ziplok bag of Band-Aids, painkillers, digestive aids and anti-bacterials is the only medical care available within walking distance.

I've exhausted my supplies by the time Sovann returns to the house in late afternoon. The headman of Prey Che Teal has come with him. "His wife helped deliver the baby during the sweat on the bamboo with the fire under it," Sovann relays.

In rural Cambodia, where temperatures naturally hover close to 100 degrees both day and night, sanitation and obstetrical care is achieved with even more extreme heat. Under a birthing bed made of bamboo slats, a fire is built and an enclosure of cloth creates a steam room of sorts. The heat is supposed to force the woman's body to produce more blood, thereby speeding the delivery and simultaneously cleaning her bloodstream. The service requires payment, and a poor woman would likely borrow the sum from a village chief, incurring a debt that might be impossible for her to repay. If birth complications occur, there is little anyone can do. Cambodia has only one doctor for every 6,000 people, and the transportation costs to reach a doctor incur even more debt. Consequently, roughly one in ten infants die at birth.

"The father disappear before the baby was born, and the mother was very hungry," Sovann says. "One child die of disease already, and then she go to the city and she sell the baby." That word punches me in the stomach. Sold to whom? We asked at the orphanage if they gave the mother money. The director said the birthmother begged for money for her other son's funeral and transportation back to her village. The director gave her assistance in the form of Cambodian reil equaling about $40. Who decides if that is humanitarian aid or commerce?

"The mother returned to his village to celebrate her son's funeral," Sovann translates. "Then she disappear." A heated argument ensues, and Sovann doesn't want to tell me what the village chief is saying. I make him tell me, anyway. "He says that she borrowed money for the birth. She owes him a debt of $80." Sovann doesn't want me to pay off the debt, but I do it anyway. The callousness of the headman's demeanor isn't even shocking to me anymore. So many Cambodian men are like that – walled off, untouchable. I wonder how much he was paid for his thumbprint on our documents? Yet no one has ever come to ask him about the woman we're looking for, so whose thumbprint was it next to the caption "village headman"?

Suddenly, the headman remembers additional information. The husband who ran off was not a real husband, just an elopement; they couldn't afford a wedding. Before him, the second husband died, and before him, the first husband she divorced. Prey Che Teal was not her home village; she worked for her husband's relative there. When her husband disappeared, her own mother would not take her back to her home village because she ran off with a man her mother didn't choose, and the marriage was illegitimate. She and her daughter were last seen begging in the Om Tassam Market. I don't know whether to be ecstatic or infuriated about the news of a biological grandmother who had *refused* to help.

I recall the napkin story, verified with a thumbprint; in that version, the birthmother had declared her husband was dead. Running off with another woman is apparently the same thing. Cambodia is a nation of dysfunctional men. The Khmer Rouge boy soldiers have grown up to become today's fathers, emotionally detached, unable or unwilling to support wives and children. Farming rice for subsistence is hard work. What can a single mother do? Scarce medical care, diseases, and land mines may cause parental deaths, but how often does the veil of shame from a deadbeat dad bury the histories of abandoned children?

I will tell my son what I believe to be true: His first mother loved him, and that love gave her the strength to do something extraordinary. She didn't have what she needed to take care of him, so she took him to the best place she could find, where she knew people would care for him and find what he needed to grow strong – a loving family. What she needed to happen, what he needed to happen, and what we needed to happen – happened.

eight

Sacred Cloth

*"What you are now is what you have been,
what you will be is what you are now."*

The Buddha

Beyond a bridge over the Popo Agie River in Lander's city park, a short Asian couple in their seventies
emerges from the undergrowth beneath a stand of
Russian olive trees that line the walking path. Wiping mud from
their wet flip-flops, they pick up a five-gallon bucket of greenery
and smile. Neang Om and Sokun Prom have been harvesting.
Amanda's parents have an amazing knack for locating a food
source. A keen eye for edibles in any environment has been honed
by the primal need to survive. I have walked by this place hundreds of times and I never saw the fresh watercress growing in a
little wetland that flows toward the river.

"Look good, very good." Grandma shows me her crop and
points to the place where healthy clusters of the dark greens are
growing in the marsh.

"Good for stir-fry with garlic," she says.

Borrowing her cleaver and a plastic bag, I hoist my pant legs
above my knees and let the cold mud slide between my toes as I
tread into the water to harvest some watercress for myself. Bent
over shin-deep in water, scanning the swamped land for food, a
sense trickles down my spine and reflects in the water – a picture

of me in their shoes. Could I even survive in my own environment, much less keep six of ten children alive, if the normal food source channels were severed? Looking up as the couple meanders down the path with their bucket of fresh greens swinging between them, small and unassuming, they strike me as two of the strongest people I know.

"If your dad was an entrepreneur, a store owner, and a capitalist," I ask Amanda, as she's showing me the proper insertion of red kroeung paste into de-boned chicken wings, "Why didn't they kill him?"

"Everybody always likes my dad, even the Khmer Rouge guy," she says. "My dad always had this cloth in his pocket. Every time the soldiers take him away, something strange would happen, and they did not kill him."

In the work camp village of Kampong Kohl, Maly's father was known as Chen Kmao, "The Black Chinese." No doubt his dark features and small stature contributed to the ruse that he naturally accepted – the role of obedient, uneducated peasant. He never resisted an order, proving himself a willing and hard worker at any task the Angka leaders demanded of him, laboring all day long in the sugarcane fields alongside everyone else. Among the "new people," mostly urban dwellers from Battambang and Pailin, his background was secretly known. When the revolutionaries outlawed family life and ordered all workers to eat together communally, Chen Kmao was selected to be their cook. To be trusted with the food supply gave him a small measure of power; he might even procure an extra handful of rice for his own family.

Against his better judgment, Chen Kmao followed leadership instructions, pouring just 40 kilograms of rice into a huge cook pot with 2000 liters of water from the pond. He let it steam, while adding small sticks to the cook fire to keep the water boiling. The result was not rice, but rather a thin gruel of rice water. How was he to feed 200 workers with just 40 kilos of rice? Group by group the emaciated workers came to receive their ration, a painful sadness lurking behind every eye, desperate for more nutrition. But Chen Kmao did not complain about the food rations. To question the Angka way might cast suspicion on the whole family. His own background was precarious. Like every other Cambodian living under the new Democratic Kampuchea, he had to play the game of keeping secrets. For Angka, on the outside, he was Chen Kmao. But for his ancestors he remained Sokun Prom on the inside.

Sokun Prom had moved to Battambang in 1961 and experimented with capitalism in increments. He first bought an ice-scratching machine so he could sell cold treats at the roadside. Ice shaved from a large block was served with toppings his young wife, Neang, prepared in their small hut under a banyan tree: sugared black beans; small chunks of banana; coconut; and sugarcane syrup. Sokun had been careful to select a busy road connecting the government's military base to the town. With well-paid soldiers traveling the hot road daily, business grew quickly, and he added a wooden room to the front of the hut which functioned as a little dry goods grocery, kitchen, and sleeping quarters for seven. In the new kitchen, Neang prepared kuy tieu, beef broth noodle soup, to sell by the bowl. Her skillful creations of kroeung and chi attracted a faithful clientele.

As the business grew, a tent was added to the front side of the store to provide shade for customers, sheltering friendly conversations from the afternoon heat. While Sokun argued politics, Neang's pleasant beauty and light humor cemented new friendships, and business ideas flourished among young entrepreneurs. By the end of 1974, with the help of a well-to-do customer, Sokun and Neang opened a second business, buying a restaurant in a sturdy two-story building in Pailin, 60 kilometers to the west. It even had a rare indoor bathroom. That, along with their cement brick house, made the Prom family young, upwardly mobile professionals.

The Khmer Rouge revolution turned the family dream house into a dangerous liability. In the rural work camps of Cambodia's Democratic Kampuchea, building materials were scarce and scavenging parties were often sent to collect materials from the abandoned towns. At work in the field one day, Chen Kmao quietly sidled up to a man called Bon whom he suspected he could trust. In hushed tones, he told Bon where the house and restaurant had stood, across from the Pile of Treasure Hotel in Pailin, and asked him to go have a look on his next foray. Upon Bon's return, Chen Kmao learned that the building had been looted down to the bare cement, yet a few family pictures still hung on the wall. Bon had quickly removed the pictures, destroying most but saving one. The picture was a black-and-white wedding portrait of Chen Kmao and his wife, evidence of a former life that could lead to dire consequences. Burying the memory of all they had worked for, his life no longer existed.

Practiced in the Buddhist faith of quelling the impulse for material desires, Chen Kmao found solace working in the fields, planting stubs of cane or cutting the mature stalks and stacking them onto the back of an ox cart to be transported to the processing factory. When ordered to continue working late into the night, Chen Kmao did so without complaint, manually turning the wheels of the sugarcane presses and watching the sweet juice run into large clay pots where it was boiled, then dried and ground into sugar. Bags of sugar and bags of rice were stacked in a storage building near the compound and then disappeared. Where was it all going? A stomach gnarled by hunger begged his mind to ask the question, but he couldn't. To utter the question in the presence of Angka, or even a coworker, could be a fatal mistake. Doubts and fears were easily twisted into a tale of counter-revolutionary plotting. Do not ask where the food is going. Do not say anything. If you ask, you'll be dead.

Teenage guards held the dynamic in place; hundreds of workers silently engaged in their back-breaking tasks lived in fear of one another. If one talked, another might talk in hopes of gaining food or favor, and when night fell, the suspect disappeared. Like everyone else, Chen Kmao fell asleep each night wondering who the Angka would come for next.

While Chen Kmao was being informed of his new duties as cook, he saw a newspaper sitting on the Angka leader's desk. Turning it around to read, he saw the headline "WE HAVE FREEDOM, WE ARE INDEPENDENT!" A small happiness leapt in him, for on this point he could easily agree with the Angka leadership. He, too, had always longed for Cambodia's freedom from domineering foreign powers. But the light of hope was quickly doused by the words in the article that followed.

"Why do they say that our country will become Indochina?" Chen Kmao asked the Angka leader. He knew that meant joining with Viet Nam, and he didn't trust Viet Nam.

"Don't think about that," the Angka snapped. "Don't talk about that!"

It was fair warning from an Angka commander who liked him, so he didn't talk about it further, but Chen Kmao went right on thinking. "If the Vietnamese government wants Cambodia and Laos to make Indochina, who is going to be the boss? Cambodia or Viet Nam? Who has more people? When they elect a leader, who is going to win?" He answered his own question: "Viet Nam – we've been under them for 1,000 years."

In the past, nothing would have satisfied Sokun Prom's pride in the land of the ancient Khmer more than independence for Cambodia. That sentiment is what made him strike out on his own in the first place, heading to the prosperous town of Battambang to try his hand at entrepreneurship. He'd had enough of French bosses, after four years as an accounting clerk for a rubber plantation in Kampong Cham. French bread, a French Lycee education and development of the rubber industry didn't trouble him, but the French attitude did. His King had gained Cambodia's independence from France in 1954, so why did they continue to treat Cambodian workers as low-class slaves, making them labor long hours in the fields for inconsistent biweekly pay and perform jobs the Frenchmen considered beneath themselves. As an idealistic twenty-something, Sokun hadn't been keen on the elitism of colonials.

If the Angka's revolution was based on independence, however poorly executed, he could see the merit in the sacrifice of their lives. But in his heart, Chen Kmao knew it was a lie. He needed to look no further than the houses surrounding the sugarcane factory where he labored day and night, to know the truth. Large brick houses, built to a western living standard, were constructed for Chinese men by Angka's Cambodian slave laborers.

"Why does Angka treat these foreign Chinese so good?" Chen Kmao wondered. "They have a beautiful house, plenty of food, wine and rice steamed with coconut water. These Chinese men did not live here before Angka; if they are not working, they must be a leader of something. Why do they have freedom?"

He could not approach a Chinese man to ask him. Angka soldiers kept guard all day, forcing the new people to walk across the street and steer clear of the Chinese houses. Smelling the good food cooking in those houses, Chen Kmao left the cane factory to collect his ration of rice gruel at the communal kitchen. He could not speak, but he knew.

"Every Cambodian leader borrows guns from everywhere," he thought. "So this is how they pay them back." The rice was going to China. The wealthy Chinese men were import-export merchants, keeping records of how many guns came in and how much rice and sugar went out.

Chen Kmao recognized the import-export business. As Sokun Prom, his very first job had been clerking for the King's Ministry of Economics in 1952, then administered by Khieu Sampan, who was now a Khmer Rouge leader. As an ambitious new member of the government work force, young Sokun dutifully filled out the customs forms required of import merchants, and passed them along to his superiors for their stamp of approval. But when the merchants came back to collect their merchandise for distribution, his boss frequently claimed that the forms had been lost. For a small fee, they could be found easily.

One day Sokun's Buddhist upbringing could no longer restrain emotion, and he lost his temper with the corrupt system. Hearing his boss deny the existence of the proper forms to a merchant, Sokun marched into his office outraged, abruptly pulled the form out of his boss's top drawer, slammed his fist on the desk and shouted, "It's right here!" His boss, a distant relative of the King, lost face and Sokun lost his job.

By the end of the second year of Angka rule, Chen Kmao remembered those times as the good old days, back when there were laws – rarely enforced, but laws nonetheless. He could vent his frustration openly when laws were broken. Angka, however, did not rule by law, or even royal favor; they ruled by killing. Daily executions made that clear.

With prison routine, each morning the workers at Kampong Kohl lined up in long rows for a meeting with Angka, to be counted and assigned a task. The big boss of the sugarcane factory shouted the rules into a loudspeaker.

"Everyone is either your enemy, "ka'mang," or your friend, "mit." Do not use the words mother and father, son and daughter – only enemy and friend." From the second row of downcast workers he picked one lady to stand up and shouted, "Is she ka'mang or mit?" No one answered. He shot her in the head with a small gun. Had she broken a rule? No one knew, and no one wanted to know. Why was not important. If you asked too much, they would put you in the truck.

"1, 2, 3, 4, 5," the Angka leader counted, picking people from the crowd. "You go to meeting to study." Everyone knew they would not come back. They watched the selected group of people load into the truck, their trousers soiled by emptied bladders. When the truck came back it held only empty clothes.

Practicing the Buddhist religion was against Angka rules, Chen Kmao knew, but he prayed anyway. With a few small candles and a cloth for the altar, he and his wife paid homage to the Buddha at night. As a boy, Sokun had received a Buddhist education in the customary fashion for his generation. He had studied Pali scripture at his village temple, along with astronomy and the auspicious dates of the calendar. As the events around him now turned ever more violent, he didn't want his thinking clouded by judgment. Day by day he focused on the Buddha's Eightfold Path toward right mind, right speech and right action. Luckily, his father had given him a sacred cloth just a few months before the revolution began.

Sokun had grown up in a rural village in Kampong Cham. He hoped his parents had been accorded the rights of "old people" to live in their own home and grow their own food. Communications across the country no longer existed, so he had no way of knowing what was happening to them in Kampong Cham. The last time he had visited his parents, their home had been spared the impact of U.S. bombs falling from the sky. Many plank houses in the village had been shattered. Sokun's father seemed to know that the fighting would engulf them soon. He tore a small piece of cloth from the krama he wore at his waist, rubbed his foot in the cold charcoal beneath the cook fire, and embedded his footprint onto the cloth. Then he folded it neatly and handed it to his son saying, "My spirit can go with you, to watch over my children and my grandchildren." Sokun had tucked the heirloom into his pocket and set out toward home, knowing he might never see his father again.

Maly was playing ghost spirits with her sister and the other children at "go ma" when she saw her father walking across the sugarcane field toward her mother, who was digging a new row for cane stalks with a hoe. Maly was pleased that her parents still talked to each other, when so many others did not. Two playmates were holding a clothesline taut, chest-high over the dirt, and Maly helped push a boy under it. He was thrashing about spasmodically, possessed by the imaginary devil spirit he entered after crossing the divide. The children ran to push the boy back under the rope for his exorcism, when Maly stopped short. Her sister stopped, too. Their hearts pounded loud and heavy as two black-pajama soldiers approached their parents in the sugarcane field. Maly's breath quickened as they led her father away toward the Angka leader's wooden house near the factory. She wanted to scream and run after him but she couldn't. When they rounded the corner out of sight, she closed her eyes and pictured her grandfather's footprint on the cloth in her father's pocket.

Chen Kmao knew that Mol, his supervisor, was eager to see him dead. Quietly in step behind the fifteen-year-old guards, he thought about their boyish desire to please high-ranking officials. "What have they whispered in my supervisor's ear?" he thought. "Something he wants to hear, that a rule has been broken?" Vengeance proved simpler than that. The source of rivalry was his bed.

Chuon, the village leader, and Chen Kmao were on good terms, sharing a quiet, mutual respect during these strange times. Chen Kmao worked hard and didn't ask any questions, molding quickly to the circumstances. Chuon had done the same, a teacher who had joined with the western Khmer Rouge cadre during the civil war. Chen Kmao rose early each morning to serve rice porridge to the workers on their way to the fields, and had taken up the task of teaching Chuon's young wife how to cook. One day while he was cleaning the dishes from the morning meal, he fell asleep standing up. Working the kitchen in the morning, the fields in the afternoon, and the factory at night was taking a toll of exhaustion on Chen Kmao.

"You have to sleep better, Mit," Chuon told his favorite worker. "Here, take this to sleep on." Chen Kmao bowed gratefully as he was handed a bamboo cot, a small act of kindness that was so rare. Supervisor Mol had summoned Chen Kmao to this meeting to protest.

"A new person cannot sleep in a bed," he demanded. "That is against the Angka rules." Mol was jealous.

Chuon whispered a warning in Chen Kmao's ear as he was leaving the house: "Go back to the factory ahead of him. I will delay." Walking back to the sugarcane presses with his bamboo bed, Sokun wondered when Mol would find the right excuse to kill him.

Maly was surprised and relieved to see her father walk up the steps to their hut that evening. She didn't hug him or let out the sobs in her heart, but when the sky darkened and he lit a small candle beside the sacred cloth and began to pray to the Buddha, she knelt down beside him and prayed, too.

In late 1977, almost two years after the revolution began, the first restructuring of Democratic Kampuchea started with a massive reassignment of Angka soldiers throughout the provinces. Believing that favoritism and corruption were undermining the revolution, the cadres were ordered to move. Suddenly, Angka soldiers from the south showed up in Kampong Kohl and took the western soldiers away to meetings. Only empty trucks returned. Chen Kmao was scared. The small measure of safety he had worked so carefully to achieve had been forged by a precarious relationship with the western soldiers. After all, they were boys from Battambang. He didn't know any of the new soldiers from the south. "Be smart, move fast, or you'll be killed," he thought. Quickly he joined with the southern soldiers, working hard in solidarity and support. Somehow Chuon also had made fast psychological footwork pay off, for he remained the leader of Kampong Kohl village.

Jealousy has always run deep in Cambodian culture, and in the Angka power structure it had become deadly. Chen Kmao's supervisor, Mol, had tried on several occasions to make him the subject of Angka accusations. Luckily his boss, Chuon, had deflected the suspicion. On the third attempt to make him disappear, Chen Kmao knew he had been lied to, as he walked past the Chinese houses and the sugarcane factory. He hadn't been summoned to Chuon for a meeting; he was following the guards toward a tool shed. Is this where Mol's jealousy was going to end? Would a hoe meet the back of his head? Suddenly, a different Angka soldier appeared, this one a bit older, and he ordered the guards to go meet with Chuon immediately. As he turned to leave, he pointed to Chen Kmao. "You go back to the factory!" Chen Kmao shoved his hand deep into his pocket and felt the small tattered cloth he always carried there. "Akun Apoke," he quietly whispered. "Thank you, father."

Not long after the third time Mol tried to get rid of him, Chen Kmao was assigned a new job. Chuon selected him to be the group leader of the carpenter's brigade, building houses for widows. Every day one full truckload of new women arrived. The 12 people in Chen Kmao's work team constructed long buildings divided coarsely into 15 rooms with just a few planks of wood, split bamboo, scavenged roof-thatch and galvanized steel. As soon as each room was complete, it became home to several widows and their children. "They kill her husband because he is a Lon Nol soldier, and then make a house for the widow. This makes no sense," Chen Kmao thought, but putting his head down, he went back to work. At lunchtime he allowed the carpenters in his brigade to catch small fish from the river. He brought rice and a little bit of sugarcane, and together they ate every morsel without saving a small ration for dinner. Generosity, as long as it was kept quiet, didn't bother his boss. Chen Kmao understood this, but Mol didn't. Mol complained to Chuon about Chen Kmao's liberal lunch breaks, and earned himself a demotion. After his meeting with Chuon, Mol discovered he no longer held the position of supervisor and reported to a new boss, Chen Kmao, in the carpenters' work brigade.

"After that, the soldiers come from the East and kill the South," Sokun says, with a shake of his head. "When the Easterners come, they are all Viet Nam soldiers, so I join with them, too. Chuon escape to the mountain. Mol, they kill him. North Viet Nam, South Viet Nam, I don't know which is enemy and which is friend."

All these many years later, I see in the eyes of a wizened old man a soul that still cannot answer that question. Sitting across from me at Amanda's kitchen table, grandpa Sokun looks to the floor for solace; his head swings vaguely, remembering what had been possible for Cambodia. His Cambodia had been a nation where patriarchal power was dedicated to family, education, religion and progress; now it is a nation of dysfunctional fathers.

Garlic sizzles in the hot cooking oil as I load the wok with fresh watercress for a quick stir-fry. Amanda removes the stuffed chicken wings from the deep fat fryer, trying to keep her voice low so her father cannot hear. "I tried so hard to get the monk to come," she says. "I want to surprise my parents for their fiftieth anniversary." A tear rolls down her cheek. She had met a monk at a temple in Kampong Cham on a recent visit to Cambodia and was impressed by his strict adherence to the Buddhist traditions. She knew her father would be pleased to have a particularly devout monk perform a blessing ceremony, with the family he had saved from extinction gathered all around him. Amanda wished to show the monk the wonders of Yellowstone National Park. Although she planned to sponsor the trip, and provided the Department of Homeland Security with full financial detail of her ability to do so, the United States Embassy in Phnom Penh denied the monk's one-month visa request. No reason was given.

Her tears compel me to spend the better part of an afternoon on the phone to Wyoming's lone representative in Congress, soliciting help to obtain the monk's visa.

"They don't have to give you a reason," I am told.

"I thought this was America, where our government is account-able to us," I reply. "Since when does a Buddhist monk pose a terrorist threat?"

The representative's aide assures me that she will e-mail the embassy in Phnom Penh and try to get an answer. I wish I could make her look at Amanda and see Maly, the little girl who watched her father hauled off by Khmer Rouge soldiers and prayed to the cloth in his pocket for help, which miraculously always came.

The next time the soldiers came, it was little Maly and her sister Malis who were taken away.

Don't Put Your Fertilizer in Someone Else's Rice Field

"There is no shame in not knowing,
the shame lies in not finding out."

Russian proverb

Why do you want to find the birth family?" Sovann asks me, not long after we rediscover the potholed pavement of National Road No. 2. We are on our way to the market town of Om Tassom, to investigate our next clue.

In the checkerboard fields that line the road, boys harvest golden rice stalks, slashing bundles with their machetes. Behind them a group of girls plants a second crop of vibrant green rice seedlings in the paddy, which is still fed by a dwindling irrigation ditch. One of the bent women works with a baby on her back.

"One day my son will ask why, Sovann," I answer. Hesitating, I add, "I want to him to know the truth."

Widely publicized accusations of visa fraud and child trafficking provided the official reason for the denial of U.S. immigration
visas to Cambodian children, starting in December 2001. That
action led to a complete adoption shutdown, a year after my son
came home. Yet after more than four years of State Department
investigations and ample gossip of brokering stories, no birthmother has come back to reclaim an illicitly procured child. The
women of Cambodia are poor, not stupid. Unsavory characters
peddle for brothels, servants and thieves in their unforgiving
world with its excessive number of mouths to feed and its dis-
proportionate number of defective fathers. The promise of an
orphanage, or of a middleman, to find a good home for a child
may feel like the best they can do to solve the problem of survival
for another day. Clearly, unwanted does not mean unloved.

"No mother should have to feel guilty for loving her son," I
whisper, still watching the women in the field.

"Your son is very lucky," Sovann replies earnestly. "More lucky
than my son. Your son will honor you, respect you, take care
of you when you are old, and bring good success to the family
when he grows up."

"Not without self-esteem, he won't," I answer, more to myself
than to Sovann.

"Steam," he repeats. "It means getting very hot?"

"No, e-steem," I answer, wiping my tears. "It means confidence
in your own merit as an individual."

He hands me a scrap of paper pulled from the bottom of his
shirt pocket. Various notes and phone numbers are jotted in
Khmer on the paper. I find a small space and spell out S-E-L-F
E-S-T-E-E-M.

"Good Cambodia kid, he put the family first," Sovann states.

"It doesn't matter if my son is Cambodian on the outside. He's
American on the inside, and I cannot expect him to be prepro-
grammed with the filial obligation of an Asian," I say. "Frankly,
I'm not sure I want him to be." I try to explain that family fealty

is not an obligation in America; it's a choice. Concepts of American social structure like self-expression, independence, and teenage rebellion draw a blank stare from Sovann.

"Okay, I know, someone give him away, but you give him a good life," Sovann says. "Tell him do not question good luck, or maybe it will run out. In Cambodia we have been through too much, we don't care," he continues. "No matter how you get a good life, don't ask question – just go."

It's late in the afternoon when we arrive at Om Tassam and most of the market vendors have packed up their shops. Sovann insists we wait until morning to probe the market; "Not safe for you after dark," he says. He has an uncle living nearby, just off National Road No. 2. A nervous panic races through my bones as we pass through the town: What if she is here? Would she want him back? Looking down at the sweaty palms folded in my lap I say a silent prayer, asking for the strength to trust what I fear the most.

An old man who's obviously proud of his thirty-something nephew making good in the city greets us. Sovann and his wife pay their respect to the oldest member of the family, and Uncle's face brightens into a toothless grin as he accepts the young couple's grateful bow and offering of food. Heads bent, they receive in return a chanted blessing from this living ancestor. Sovann is the only family member to own a car, and extended family and friends quickly gather around it to hear his news from the outside world.

A ubiquitous small plastic saucepan floats in the household cistern and Sovann uses it to hand wash his precious Toyota Camry. His uncle's cement brick house features an enclosed bathroom with a hole in the floor to squat over, and a cistern full of rainwater for washing. An electric car battery powers a single light bulb hanging from the ceiling and a small, black-and-white television. By local standards, cement walls are a mark of economic stature, but the continuous noise from the busy road and the accompanying grime on the walls erodes the peace of traditional palm-thatch village charm.

Sovann introduces me to his brothers and sisters, friends and neighbors, who keep showing up to check us out. With many children running about, I lose my ability to keep track of their relationships save one, a niece called Mien. She watches me intently for a while and then disappears. A few minutes later she returns and plops her English lesson book down on my lap. The newsprint pages are smudged by use in the humid air, but I can decipher long parallel rows of English print and Khmer script.

> *Ball*
> *Boat*
> *Boy*
> *Bathroom*

I read down the list of words, and Mien repeats them with a strong accent shaped deep in her throat, devoid of the shrill, quickstep cadence of a Chinese speaker. Written Khmer is not a pictorial language like Chinese, but instead derived from Sanskrit; the vowels attached to the consonants in beautiful, flowing lines and curves. The back of Mien's book provides a lesson on verb conjugations, yet next to each English word the Khmer script is exactly the same. The Khmer language functions in the present, with no verb conjugations. The addition of phrases such as "already" or " in the future" indicate time references where necessary. Listening and speaking requires thinking in the present; perhaps that's the Cambodian secret to persistence.

Mien has her Uncle Sovann's determination and ambition. She overcomes her fear of me to seize the opportunity – not for money like so many others, but for knowledge. Under a tarp canopy before the front door, she sits next to me on a bamboo bed frame. Her little body feels strong, and her voice is firm. While the other kids stand back and listen, sometimes quietly repeating the words, 12-year-old Mien focuses on my lips, hungrily repeating all the new sounds with fervor. She teaches me the

Khmer word for every English word I teach her, and our mistakes provide entertainment for the woman sitting across from us. Later, I find out that the old woman is her mother, and Mien is her thirteenth child.

Sovann relays my offer to sponsor Mien's English studies at a private secondary school.

Mien smiles shyly and bows her head. Her mother, meanwhile, seems unsure. She wants to accept, I think, but it's hard not to be suspicious when you're uneducated. I understand why she's secretly afraid when Mien unexpectedly takes my hand and calls me "mother," joining me to walk on the little path atop the dike. Sovann is leading us toward a group of palm thatch huts at the back of the village.

Two small rice paddies away, behind a wooden plank house on stilts, is a large, cement platform with a brightly painted, arched wall, marking the grave of Sovann's mother. He replaces dead flowers with fresh lotus, and cleans debris from the sticky palm fruit tree overhead. "She die immediately in the street," he says. "At her sister funeral she look into the eyes of the dead; the Chinese fortuneteller tell me that why she die." The Festival of the Dead is a time to make peace with fate.

*   *   *

Sovann had lived with his mom in this village after the Khmer Rouge kicked everybody out of the city, until the middle of 1976 when, as a nine-year-old boy, he was sent to work on a children's collective farm. Scooping water by hand from a small canal to irrigate the rice paddies, where thousands of children worked for Angka in silence, he wondered all the time, "Where is all the food going?"

Sovann felt lucky when he was assigned the job of tending the cattle. It was easier than scooping leech-filled water into leather sacks, or digging endless ditches. Yet walking behind the cattle, collecting the dung for compost, he had too much time to think – and all he thought about was his mother. How hungry she must be; the Angka only gave her porridge. One day, while picking up a cow chip next to the drying irrigation pond, he caught a glimpse of silver gray gleam below the surface and knew it must be a mudfish. Catching it with bare hands took all his concentration. He squatted silently at the water's edge and waited patiently to pounce when the edible beast drifted within arm's reach. With one swift snatch the treasure was his, and it thrashed hopelessly under a thicket while he covered it with banana leaves. When he looked up to make sure no one was watching, the cattle were gone. His Angka leader was not pleased to find cattle grazing on luscious green rice shoots in the field his child workers had just irrigated.

To demonstrate the punishment he received, Sovann pulls his elbows together behind his back, as though they're hogtied for a whipping. After the hot lashes were administered, he was ordered to dig a compost hole while everyone else slept. When the task was finished, he defiantly searched in the darkness for the fish he had hidden in the bush, but it had swollen and spoiled in the afternoon heat. His heart ached more than the welts on his arms, because he had no food to bring to his mother.

"A Kampuchea Krom little boy that live in my collectivity stole a sweet potato, about three kilo, and he cut some sugar-cane because he want to bring it to his mother," Sovann recalls. "The angry Angka kill him with a hoe to his head, then push him into that hole that I already dig for composting fertilizer." The Kampuchea Krom boy's Vietnamese accent had gained him the harsher punishment.

Sovann points to each palm thatch home in the village to describe in dispassionate detail how each of his neighbors died.

At the end of the lane he shimmies up the limbless trunk of a coconut tree to harvest fresh milk for our supper. On the way back down, he points to a tall jakfruit tree, saying, "I found one lady hanging right there, after Viet Nam invade Cambodia in 1979."

In the afternoon after farm chores, Sovann attended a school re-opened by the Vietnamese in 1981. Although he was 13, he lied about his age to enter the primary class, knowing that if he passed the tests for advancement, he could study; otherwise, he'd be conscripted into the army. One day, while leading his oxen home from the rice field with a net full of paddy frogs slung over his shoulder, he was practicing Russian vocabulary words when the cattle suddenly stopped and refused to move. Sovann saw feet dangling from a tree and slowly raised his gaze to the attached body. He recognized the woman as his neighbor, a single mother of three. Her body hung limply from a twisted vine at a crook in her neck. The Khmer Rouge murdered 75 percent of Cambodia's teachers. Her husband had been among them.

"She tell her nine-year-old son she go to collect sticks for the fire," Sovann says, pointing to a hut across the road where the woman had lived. "She give him instruction how to feed the baby when he cry. Why would she say that, unless she know she not coming back?"

After the Khmer Rouge regime ended, the remaining population was more than sixty-five percent female. Without men to remarry, widows struggled to feed their own children, as well as the orphans of missing relatives, whose disappearance had eliminated the traditional extended family support system. While the United States led the world in an economic embargo of Cambodia, blocking U.N. development aid from 1979 to 1992, in hopes of collapsing its Vietnamese government, thousands of Cambodian women committed suicide.

Hearing Sovann's sigh and feeling my own within, his mother's grave embraces our silent sorrow and releases it into the breeze.

Because she did not give up, her boy grew to become an educated man. If the orphanage had not been an option for my son's birthmother, would she have given up?

✳ ✳ ✳

By the time we return to Uncle's house, Sovann's family is engaged in a frenzied argument over what to serve us for dinner. Food is the nexus of relationship with both the living and the dead. The communist revolutionaries, in their effort to assert complete control, had attempted to eliminate all aspects of food beyond what was minimally necessary to sustain the body. No wonder their ideas never won the hearts and minds of their people.

"Satch go, satch go," Sovann's sister excitedly demands, certain that beef must be served to an American. Compared to the bounty of fish in the rivers and ponds, red meat from the market is a rare and expensive treat. Sovann's sister returns to the table with grilled, stuffed frogs, nothing but the head and entrails removed. My repulsion has nothing to do with the taste and everything to do with the shape. The beef is on the inside. Stuffed with spicy, green kroeung paste, the little frog body looks so small and helpless on the split bamboo skewer – slimy, green, croaking, is all I can think. My mouth just won't open. Everyone is staring at me.

Over-amplified karaoke from the open-air nightclub across the street, combined with fumes of diesel-scented dirt, do not make it easier to eat a stuffed frog. Sovann slides a small pile of finely sliced "satch go," atop a mound of stir-fried morning glory, in front of me. Then he helps himself to the frog, bones and all. A table and a bamboo bed are the only pieces of furniture in the room; clothing and dishes are piled neatly on the floor. Two motos with large wire baskets, the tools of the family pig hocking trade, are locked to the rail outside the front wall. Sovann's sister tucks four children into the single bed, where she will join them later.

"In the U.S.A., they have a very strict rule," Sovann says. "Children cannot sleep with the parent. In your country, the parent has a special room for the baby. Why they cannot sleep with the mother?" He's emphatically perplexed.

"It's not exactly a rule," I explain. "American parents usually give the child a separate bed, in a separate room, because they want him or her to grow independent. And they want to sleep."

"What if the bad spirit come in the middle of the night to scare them, and the mother cannot hear?" he says, with grave concern. "Why they do like that?"

"If the child cries in the middle of the night, the mother can go to him," I assure him. It's funny: In our adoption home study we were expected to show pictures of an additional bedroom for the child, yet in our son's birth country the idea is absurd. Actually our family sleeps a little in the style of both cultures: Bedtime starts out the American way, with Grady falling asleep in his own bed in his own room; then somewhere during the dreamtime we switch to the Asian-style family bed, making room to accommodate each other's curves. However, that adaptation required an upgrade to a king-size bed.

"If your family sleeps all together, how can you have sex with your wife?" I ask Sovann. "In front of the children?"

"Ahh," he sighs, with a knowing eye. "We go to the bathroom to put on sarong and scarf." He can tell I'm confused. "And we turn out the light. Do Americans keep the light on?"

"Never mind the light," I retort. "What about the noise? Aren't you afraid to disturb the children?"

It never occurred to him. "We are quiet," he says. "Americans make noise?"

"Yeah, most people probably make noise."

The children have fallen asleep, and Sovann's brother-in-law brings a neighbor to the table to talk. The fellow has news for Sovann, and the three men discuss it in grave, argumentative tones. It's a serious matter, I can tell. Once a conclusion has been reached, Sovann explains. Each week the neighbor drives a truck to the north, taking product from Takeo to the Thai border. "He tell me about two orphan children, 13 and 14. Their mother is dead, shot at the Thai border. Now they're parentless and he ask me if you want to adopt them," he says.

"I can't do that," I answer, knowing that stories abound of teenagers trafficked at the Thai border for prostitution, forced labor and begging. "You must take them to the authorities." Even if I wanted to, children more than eight years old cannot be adopted internationally; it's against Cambodian law. Yet somehow I suspect that if I said yes, the children would suddenly become eight years old. In the accusations of child trafficking that swirl around international adoption, is this what is meant by the term middleman? It could be a true story. It could be a trafficking story. All the men seem sincerely concerned, and I don't think the truck driver has asked for money, at least not in my presence.

"I will ask the director of Hungarian Friend Orphanage," Sovann says. "When I bring donation there, then I can see if she have a place for them."

"Donation of what?"

"Food, formula and clothes from the adoptive parents."

"Please tell me you do not exchange money," I say.

"No, only the bad people do that," he says. I have warned Sovann several times not to get involved in the adoption business. He's an honest and hardworking man whose survival is determined by his ability to exploit opportunity. The western world ethics of putting children first requires a brand of selflessness I don't think he can comprehend.

In the morning, temple chants for the Festival of the Dead are drowned out by engine noise and the business of setting up market at the center of Om Tassam town. Sellers of alien vegetables neatly pile their goods into multi-layered shapes, and the sweet smell of burned incense drifts on the morning air from the offerings in spirit houses. The market is divided into sections where every wooden stall in a block sells basically the same thing. Stepping over fetid vegetable scraps, we pass the vendors of Asian broccoli, bamboo shoot, water gourd, wing bean, fuzzy melon and fungi.

At the betel nut vendor we stop for a demonstration, at my insistence, of how this form of chew works. The woman squatting on her haunches looks twice my age. The deep, crevassed lines of her face, weathered by the stress of time, reveal an arduous life. A blue-checkered krama cloth folded on her head protects her from the sun, where her pyramid of leafy greens is constructed in the middle of the aisle. She smiles crimson red and splits a fist-sized, green betel nut with a cleaver. A few pinches of powdered lime are sprinkled on pieces of nut and rolled into a banana leaf, then she hands it to me. I touch it with my tongue and make a nasty face, eliciting laughter from the crowd while Sovann takes our picture. The betel nut vendor tells Sovann she has a brother in the United States; she wants me to send him her picture and a message: "Please send money." No address is given but she has his phone number memorized – another poor relative pinning her hopes on someone in America. Truthfully, my greatest fear is that if my son were to meet his birth family one day, they might expect him to give them money, too – utterly normal in their culture, utterly devastating in ours.

I've been staring at the coconut vendor a long time before she looks up. They're a mother-and-daughter team, surrounded by piles of hard green coconuts. The mother deftly splits the green flesh with two whacks of a cleaver, to reveal the inner core. Each half is then tossed into a pile beside the girl sitting near my feet. She squats on a pink, plastic step stool, quickly excavating the meat from the shell with a spinning metal coconut router that is powered by her foot. The spent end of her work is a scrap pile of cleaned shells. One lands at my feet and I pick it up, then catch the child's eye under the brim of her bright blue, crocheted cap. She smiles just a little and I lose myself in those dark, chocolate eyes – eyes like my son's.

Sovann is busy talking to the group of pig hockers where his sister works, and several people appear to be pointing to the alley behind the market stalls. When he catches up with me, the news is not good. "They say she live in the alley for a short time, while she beg the money with her daughter," he says, "But someone say she go to the temple in Phnom Penh to beg the monk."

I ask him to speak to the coconut vendor. The mother shakes her head no, and the daughter goes back to her work, unaware of the intense connection I feel to her. Maybe it was just wishful thinking that the people I am looking for might have the stable income of a coconut vendor.

The fresh rot in the aisles serves a dense collection of human needs: food; medicine; tools; lively conversation; and refreshment from the heat. At the ice-scratching stand everyone selects his or her own toppings – coconut palm jelly for me, sweet black sesame for Sovann, and the kids point to something that looks like green gummy worms. The ice-scratcher pours condensed milk over a little mound of shaved ice, to sweeten the concoction. "Amanda's father was an ice-scratching vendor in Battambang," I tell Sovann. "The business grew into a nice restaurant until the Khmer Rouge confiscated it."

"My wife, Ngim, do that, too, when she was young," he says. "That's why I fall in love with her."

Ngim was love at first sight for Sovann when he saw her face peek out from behind the rotating, cast-iron wheel she used to shave ice from a large block at a roadside stand. She didn't even remember him when Sovann's mother and uncle came to discuss a marriage proposal. When asked if she wanted to marry Sovann Ty, Ngim responded to her mother in the filial fashion of a dutiful daughter: "It's up to you, because I am your daughter. You decide what to do, and I have to follow you."

Ngim's mother visited Sovann's uncle to see their house and assess the suitability of a familial relationship. She would have preferred a more traditional third or second cousin as groom, but Sovann begged convincingly. He had a rare job with a salary to provide for her daughter, working as a gardener at the home of an Indonesian diplomat in Phnom Penh. Sovann didn't mention his nighttime brothel moto service, where he made the bulk of his income. When he arrived at Mrs. Nhaw's house for the engagement ceremony in the dry season of 1996, it was the first time Ngim got a good look at his face. She recognized that he loved her, but she wasn't sure how she felt about him.

Two weeks later, the wedding ceremony started at 7 a.m. and extended through the night for two days. Ngim's mother received the dowry from Sovann and his family in small cash and food: assorted fruits; some ducks and chickens; pork; and canned juice. The mothers knelt at the family shrine – which was adorned for the occasion with new candles, lotus and jasmine, blessed water and rice – to inform their ancestors, specifically their parents and dead husbands, about the celebration. They made an offering of fresh jakfruit and papaya under the family photographs and prayed, "We are having our children's wedding ceremony. Please accept this food and bless our children with a good future and a good life." Then the ceremonial dressmaker, who had costumed the bride and groom in shimmering pamoung silks with gold brocade, to make them look as resplendent as a King and Queen, changed their outfits to ones in shades of metallic red. Finally the feasting began.

Two white-masked clowns chased the bride and groom with scissors and combs, pretending to perform a ritual haircut – a cut, it is said, from their former lives. Guests sprayed holy water from a bronze bowl. Cool sprinkles, laughter, and spatters of white powder brought wishes of prosperity. A clergyman tied a red thread on each of their wrists, symbolizing their union, and relatives placed red packets filled with money into the cloth bag hanging from the end of a long pole festooned with jingle bells. The feast continued and the dressmaker changed their costumes again, this time to shades of bright purple. The dancing and singing lasted all night.

In the morning, before the breakfast feast, wedding guests showered the bride and groom with jasmine flowers, and the dressmaker changed their attire to shimmering green and gold silk. To take their oath, Sovann and Ngim lay on their stomachs on a bamboo bed before a clergyman, softly repeating his words to seal their promise, while the guests sprayed perfume and splashed more holy water. "We will love each other, we will not dispute, we will be patient, we will not argue, we will take care of each other. We will try to have a baby, and have many children."

The final costume change brought Ngim to her husband in western-style white, trailing a long white lace veil. It was time to consummate the marriage. Sovann bent his head and took hold of the veil, submissively following his teenage bride up the outdoor steps of the house to the bedroom. Below the floorboards, guests continued drinking palm juice wine and singing karaoke long into the hot night. When the rooster crowed at daybreak, all was finished.

"I was 31 years old, and she was 16," Sovann says. "She was like a lamb, and I was the wolf." Within a month, Ngim was pregnant, but their first child died in her womb at the beginning of the third trimester. It had been a girl.

In the back seat of Sovann's Toyota Camry, Ngim has fallen asleep with beads of sweat rolling off her forehead, a son under each arm, and the large, hot bundle protruding from her midsection where their third son is baking. She was hoping for a daughter, to take care of her in her old age.

In a low voice Sovann confides to me, "I told Ngim we can adopt a daughter from the orphanage, but she say no." Ngim never dreamed while growing up on a rice farm, leaving school after grade four to help her sister run an ice-scratching stand, that she'd one day live in the city and drive around with her husband in an air-conditioned car. Her man turned out to be both reliable and ambitious; she relishes the benefits of higher social status. Sovann, meanwhile, worries he won't have enough money to educate all his children if they keep trying for a daughter. His desire to adopt a daughter meets with resistance from an ancestral definition of family, in a relationship-oriented culture that is organized by nepotism.

"They say don't put your fertilizer in someone else's rice field," Sovann says. For this reason, mothers most often arrange marriages between distant relatives. In a society of large families, it doesn't take many generations to have agreeable selections for marriage partners among second and third cousins. Perhaps that's why my son's birthmother had no support from her mother when the going got tough. Filial defiance had cost her dearly. Sovann's initiative, choosing to marry outside the family, is only beginning to find acceptance as a marriage practice. Adoption beyond bloodlines remains rare.

"My wife think the reason the foreigners don't have their own children is because they don't sleep in the same bed," Sovann says. I almost choke on a half-swallowed scoop of scratched ice. Imagine the pillow talk these two have had on this subject, considering that the only foreigners they know are adoptive parents.

"Most people adopt because they are infertile," I say, "Some because they think the world doesn't need more people, and that all children deserve a family." For George and me, it's all of those reasons.

"Cambodia people poor, they cannot go to doctor," Sovann says. "If a couple get married and after five or six years no children, the man go get another wife."

"What if it's the problem of the man?" I ask, opting to forego the discussion of sperm donors, which I find too bizarre to communicate in broken English and Khmer to Sovann – no matter how chummy we've become.

Sovann points his index finger in the air and lets it curl over. "You mean his pole dead?" Oh brother, I think, is the whole damn world confused about reproduction?

"That's impotence," I tell him. "I'm talking about infertility. The mechanics of sex are quite distinct from the technical requirements for making babies."

"The parents of the mother want grandchildren, especially the granddaughter to take care of them. If the man not have enough sperm they say to her, 'His pole dead'," Sovann explains. "They tell her to sleep with another man, but sometimes if she have the child of another man, the family will treat them like illegitimate."

He asks me to write IMPOTENCE and INFERTILITY on his little scrap of note paper for later study. Then he tells me that his mother-in-law asked if I would build her a bathroom. A conventional cement outhouse with cistern and ceramic squat-bowl costs $75. I challenge him to build one for her himself; I know he has the money. He counter-challenges me: The private English studies at the secondary school in Om Tassom will cost $60 per year; why do I want to help Mien?

"She is not your family, not your nationality," Sovann says. It was a spontaneous gesture on my part; I hadn't really thought it through. Perhaps I was placating my concern that we may not find the people we're looking for, and my fantasy that we could somehow steer my son's birthsister into primary school. Mien, at least, would be educated enough to avoid the brothel trap.

"I'm choosing to put my fertilizer in someone else's rice field," I say. "That's what you do when you have plenty of fertilizer. "

ten

Daikon Camp

"Survival is a form of resistance."

Mandel Le Sueur

manda's eyes swell with childhood memory when I show her a shiny mound of sautéed Red Ants' Eggs, presented in the picture book on an orange clay platter. The following page features a recipe for deep-fried tarantulas. In this Cambodian cookbook, the chapter entitled *Insects* presents a smorgasbord of creepy critters to consume. The recipe for Porng Ang-Krang says that four cloves of garlic are crushed and browned in the wok before tossing in 150 grams of red ants and their eggs. After two minutes of stir-fry, the whole mess is seasoned with sugar and salt. It looks disgusting, yet the recipe assures me that each stage of the weaver ant's life cycle is entirely edible. I wonder how many Cambodians would be left on this planet if they hadn't already been accustomed to eating insects.

"The butt end is sour and the egg is white. When you want to make some soup you put that in, and it turns sour," Amanda says. "But I just eat it raw, unless I have a little salt to add for flavor." She was a tough little girl, willing to eat anything to survive and possessed by the ultimate fear factor – extreme hunger.

Maly watched a boy climb a tamarind tree to a weaver ant nest, and scoop eggs into a palm leaf basket. He then jumped down and poured them into a bucket of water to separate the ants from the eggs. Quickly, he shoved his catch into his mouth. "They don't feed us," Maly thought, "but there is plenty of tamarind tree." When she found another tree with weaver ants, she climbed it, stuck her hand in the nest, and shoved the eggs directly into her mouth. She didn't care if the bites on her arms and throat stung. The eggs were ripe, just before hatching, with an extra delicious sour flavor. The Khmer Rouge had been in power three years by the time Maly turned eight, and she was a keen student of survival. Her defiance was driven by a fierce duty to keep herself and her skinny older sister alive.

Many months had passed since the girls were taken away from their parents in Kampong Kohl. Maly had no idea where her brothers lived; they'd been sent off to teenage work camps long ago. She didn't know if Ma and Pa were alive or dead. The last time she saw them was the day that Mit Bong informed them it was time for the girls to work for Angka; they must go to another village and learn to read and write. Maly clung to her mother's leg and begged to stay, but her mother knew they had no choice. She peeled the child away, took her by the shoulders, and looked her straight in the eye. "You have to go. You are grown up now," she said. "Be strong and take care of your sister." Maly wrapped her impatient mind around her responsibility to look after Malis.

Mit Bong lied. There was no reading and writing at the children's collective, just sandy fields to plant and wild monkeys waiting in the trees to bite them. Each night the two sisters slept side by side on a wooden plank floor, in a row with several hundred girls their age. A large metal roof protected them from rain, but the open-air long house was defenseless against biting mosquitoes. Maly knew nothing about malaria but the buzzing drove her mad, until exhaustion consumed all perception.

Each morning began the same. The girls assembled into perfectly straight lines in front of the long house, hands to shoulders, waiting to be inspected. Young Angka guards, teenagers hand-picked by their Angka big brothers to supervise the children, walked up and down the rows with ruthless eyes for imperfection, wielding their unquestionable power.

Maly clenched anger between her teeth as she stiffened her back straight and stared into the shoulders before her with mechanic resolve, until the young Angka kicked her emaciated sister for slouching. Maly's spirit jumped out of her skin with desire to fight, but her wild eyes held fast to Malis, who burned a silent warning into her soul. "Don't you dare say a word," her steely eyes demanded. Maly obeyed her quiet counsel, for fear that their parents might be called out and killed if she fought against her sister's injustice. Malis straightened up and Maly watched a section of her sister's leg turning purple as they began to march.

In the field she had learned how to work fast while bent over. Move leaf, step, plant, move leaf, step, plant. The sand was hot and it burned the girls' bare feet as they moved up and down the rows planting daikon seeds. At night, Maly copied the older girls, sewing two large banana leaves to a branch to create a makeshift shoe. She had to move quick; if she worked too slow, the Angka guard expressed his displeasure with the butt of his gun in her back. The girls' work brigade spent all morning planting daikon root. The only relief from the equatorial sun came in the afternoon, from the spillage of a watering can.

Hunger made the distance to the mountain spring seem longer than two kilometers. Maly felt dizzy in the heat, carrying the bamboo pole over her shoulder with a bucket balanced on each end as she walked slowly down a steep embankment to the spring. She cupped her hands for water to drink and splashed her face as the buckets filled, then hoisted the heavy load to her shoulder. The buckets hung just a few inches off the ground, spilling half their contents over the edge as they grazed the earth. She was met at the top of the hill by a guard who slapped her head and ordered her back down the slope to fetch a full pail.

Up and down the daikon rows she walked, pouring water over the green shoots from the holes at the lip of each bucket, slowly enough to make the water last and sloppily enough to cool her feet. The technique took all her concentration. One eye had to stay sharp to spot any edible morsel that might appear on the ground: a lizard; snail; or piece of daikon root newly emerged from the sandy soil. Suddenly, the Angka guard started shouting for everyone to stop working, come to him, and bring a shovel. Maly gladly dropped the bamboo pole from her sore shoulder, picked up a hoe, and followed the familiar sound of his shrill voice toward the place where other girls were gathering.

"Dig!" the Angka boy ordered, and the girls began to dig but they didn't know why. He was furious and demanded a deep hole. "Faster!" he shouted. The faster they dug, the faster the sand slid back into the hole. Maly stopped. Another girl was being led toward them with her hands tied behind her back. She looked more terrified with each shove. Maly sensed the dreadful humiliating sting of a gun to the back, and then she knew. The Angka boy had devised a new punishment: They were going to put that girl in the hole. "Why you eat on the job?" the boy soldier shouted. "Angka don't feed you enough?" The little girl's head hung silent. The crowd shouted "Ja!" in unison, a show of enthusiastic agreement to distance them from the offense.

"Why are you so hungry?" he demanded. "Are you like an animal?"

"Ja!" sang the taunting chorus.

"Angka give you all this food already. Why are you stealing our food?"

"Ja!"

The prisoner did not answer. She had stolen a piece of daikon and eaten it raw in broad daylight. Hunger had usurped obedience. She was guilty.

"Bury her!" the Angka boy shouted, and pushed her into the hole. He grabbed a shovel and threw the first scoop of sand at her head. Either follow his lead or face the same punishment; there was no choice in the matter. Maly put her head down and began to shovel.

The hole was big enough for the ten-year-old detainee to stand under a rain of sand falling from her head to her feet, filling up the narrow space around her. The brusque sound of metal on sand slowed to a stop when the level reached her chin, but the Angka was not satisfied. He wanted her buried alive.

Maly didn't even look at the victim's face. She just did as she was told. If she cried or complained she would be beaten, or worse. Caring wasn't worth the price. Once the disobedient girl's head was partially buried, the Angka boy ordered water. A bucket brigade formed from the small pond where human waste from the outhouse was mixed with water to make fertilizer. Bucketful by bucketful the brown water poured over her head, filling the space around her mouth with a foul, sandy soup. "How can she breathe?" Maly thought. Small bits of sand blew away from the girl's little nose as she began to beg for mercy.

"I promise I will never disrespect Angka," she seemed to be saying, through the tears and sand in her mouth.

"Walk away!" ordered the Angka boy. The girls' brigade formed a straight line, hand to shoulder, and marched back to camp, leaving the daikon thief buried in sand up to her nose, to bake in the hot sun.

"Maybe someone went back and gave her a reed of grass to breathe," Maly thought, when she saw the girl walking through camp the next day. No one dared dig her out. She must have unburied herself. Maly wanted to say she was sorry, but what if that girl told Angka? Contrition was too risky; she put her head down and walked past. Guilt could not trump fear.

"I don't know how she lived," Amanda says, wiping away the memory as it falls in two big tears from her bewildered eyes. "I saw that girl again many years later in Denver, but I did not say anything to her. I am so ashamed of that; I had no choice."

When I can no longer absorb the pain in Amanda's eyes, my gaze yields to a benign bowl of thumb-sized quail eggs on the table between us. They are dipped in a sauce of salt, pepper and lime juice. Quietly we eat the soft-cooked yolks and allow silence to flush out the heartbreak. There is nothing to say; I can only listen and wish that the world knew. It seems to me that Cambodia had been laden with indigenous dynamite when American bombs inadvertently lit the fuse, completely ignorant of the complicated shadows of Khmer culture.

"You know I eat that tarantula, too, because we believe it can give you the strength of a man," Amanda says, the stillness reminding her. "When I eat that, it makes me so brave."

One evening, Maly was sitting on the ground at mealtime with her soup bowl cradled in her folded legs, when she caught a glimpse of her reflection in the translucent broth. A few kernels of rice floated below the image of her dirty face and straw-like hair. She couldn't remember the last time she had waded into the deep water of the river to wash her stained black shirt and pants, the same set of clothes she'd been wearing for almost three years. Tears dropped one by one into her soup, blurring her image with the question, "I work so hard all day growing daikon; where is all the food?" She looked up and saw clouds of black smoke in the distance, the smoke from burning sugarcane fields. She imagined the delightful taste of burned sugarcane, scheming for a way to get some. "Do they enjoy starving us?" Maly thought. "Angka has chickens and vegetables, but we never get to see them eat. You want me to starve, Angka?" She vowed, "Make me!" She shoved her bowl of watered-down porridge into her sister's hands and walked to the edge of the forest.

Kids from the boys' long house were gathered in a circle, taunting each other. They'd stolen tiny bird's eye chilies from Angka's kitchen garden and were daring each other to eat it. The chili oil spread a fierce burn through the mouth, but Maly didn't care. She jumped right into the circle and ate. When the boys dared her to eat a live grasshopper, she did it. A tarantula, a worm, she didn't care. Suddenly she heard her sister's voice yell, "That's enough!"

"No, I want the food!" Maly pushed her away. "Of course she say enough," she thought to herself. "I give all my food to her!"

That night Maly lay nervously awake beside her sister, thinking about the daikon on the roof. The girls had spent the afternoon splitting the white tubers and laying them out on the galvanized steel roof to dry in the sun. Food was just laying there, right overhead. The thought was more than she could bear. She tried not to wake Malis as she gently peeled the krama cloth off the girl sleeping beside her, quietly wiggling her way out from between them. Tiptoeing to the end of the row, she slipped down the steps and headed for the outhouse, then circled back around to the far end of the building, and shimmied up the roof post as though it were a palm tree.

She cursed the noisy flexibility of tin as she stepped gingerly across the roof, taking quick bites of daikon while shoving as much as a bundle would hold into the krama cloth. In the darkness, the sound of someone else on the roof set her heart racing. She silently scurried back to her climbing post. As she was lowering herself over the roof edge, a sharp piece of the steel tore a deep gash into her ankle. She slid hastily down the pole and landed with a thump. Then she buried the daikon under a nearby bush, swiftly tied the krama cloth around her ankle to hide the blood, and waited for someone to come. No one did. She heard other kids whisper in the darkness and when the coast was clear, she grabbed a piece of daikon root and snuck back to bed beside her sister.

Malis was awake and ready to scold her, but Maly shoved daikon in her mouth before she could protest.

"Give me your krama," Maly whispered.

"Why?" Malis said.

"Because I want to go see Ma."

"No, they'll kill you," she said.

"I don't care." Maly's adrenaline was running high. "I can bring food and rabbit poop to her."

They called Angka's medicine rabbit poop because that's exactly what it looked like – forest herbs and charcoal, rolled into small brown balls. It was an old peasant remedy for stomachache. Maly didn't know if it was real medicine or not but she got a delicious kick out of stealing it from Angka. The nervous rush of sneaking into the supply hut; the thrilling discovery of the medicine box; the triumph of a rebellious snatch: These were pleasures that broke the monotony of daily planting and watering. When Maly returned from the supply house with a handful of little brown pills, Malis pinched her arm and demanded, "Why'd you do that?"

"If I die stealing something from Angka, I'm happy!" Maly said, pulling her sore arm away.

Malis had a better idea. She cried and held her belly and complained about pain in her stomach to the Angka who served as nurse in their collective. The woman issued her two rabbit poop pills and Malis hid them in the waistband of her trousers, demonstrating to her little sister a safer way to steal. Together, they'd accumulated a small pile of rabbit poop and buried it secretly, in hopes of helping their mother.

Tonight was the night. Maly had already spilled blood, and with adrenaline pumping through her veins, she was ready to go. Malis couldn't stop her but she couldn't join her, either; she was too weak. Maly had run away once before in the night and discovered her mother outside the hut in Kampong Kohl, tending a small fire. Underneath that fire had been a pot of fresh cooked rice. Maly ate warm rice with dried fish, and brought some back to Malis.

Now Maly again crept quietly through the forest at the edge of the daikon fields, limping a little bit from the gash in her ankle, nervous and numb to the pain. With a tarantula's intrepid virility, she walked through rainforest, fearless of tigers and snakes, yet wary of ghosts. So many people had died, so many disembodied souls. Maly thought she heard them screaming in the treetops. She avoided the road, for fear of Angka soldiers on patrol, and followed a mental map for six kilometers, through newborn rice fields carved out of ancient forest, back to Kampong Kohl. Gripping the bundle of plunder on her shoulder, Maly fought her imagination's instinct. A sudden chill and the lingering sensation of a spirit presence gave her goose bumps, prickly heat that made her skin itch. She abruptly turned about, but nothing was there so she walked on, praying to her ancestors for protection. Dead people were everywhere; there was no avoiding them. The head of a wretched spirit flew from the treetops right down to the road, followed by a liver and trailed by a stream of bright white light. "If the Angka kills me then I can become a ghost to haunt them," Maly thought. She scanned the moon shadows for the creature she feared most, the blood-eating witch children always talked about.

The witch was not a ghost spirit, but a real person. She came out at night looking for houses where new babies had been born, and she crept under the floorboards to eat the blood of the afterbirth. Maly had never seen the witch, but everyone knew about her. The red stain of sap dripping like blood from a hole in the tamarind tree was living proof of her presence, they said.

The journey felt like hours, running and walking, guided by an internal navigation system that seemed to recognize a familiar tree or shadow. When Maly finally reached Kampong Kohl, she snuck quietly behind the long row of single-family palm thatch huts until she found the one where she had lived with her parents for two years. Was Pa still living there or not? She didn't know. Anticipating the taste of warm rice with dried fish, she tiptoed under the floorboards, but this time her mother was not lingering outside.

Maly crept up the steps outside the hut and spied a row of large banana leaves covering a small hole near the floor. She had to twist her body to get into that small hiding place; there she found several stalks of sugarcane waiting for her. Did Ma know that her daughter would come, or did she always leave a little something in there, just in case? Maly knew if she took the sugarcane and left the daikon and rabbit poop, her mother would know she had been there; the medicine was her mark. Malis was a good girl; she would never steal food and run away. Maly was the thief. She stuffed the sugarcane into her krama to take back to Malis, replaced it with her gifts, and left without seeing her mother. The secret exchange filled her heart with the quiet authority of filial duty, and it helped her navigate a dark world determined to exterminate conscience.

At daybreak Maly emerged from the forest, pretending to have been peeing, and joined the other girls in the daikon patch. She was exhausted from no sleep but energized by the sugarcane hiding in the krama on her head. It made life worth living one more day. She only hoped no one would notice the gash on her ankle, which she'd covered with s'dao leaves to protect against infection.

"Did you see Ma? Did you see Eline?" Malis whispered, when her sister hastily shoved the sugarcane into her fist.

"No," Maly said. She hadn't thought at all about Eline, their mother's new baby girl. In the ten months since she had been born, Maly had only see her once. That time, the baby had dark blisters all over her body. That's why Maly and Malis had doubled their efforts to procure medicine and sneak it home; home would always be where their mother lived. A few weeks later their brother Bon Leoun was working in a field nearby, and he relayed the message that their baby sister, Eline, had died.

On the day Mit Bong finally sent her older sister away to the Angka hospital, Maly didn't care anymore; she ran away in the daytime. She had to tell her mother about Malis. No one ever came back from Angka's hospital. Malis had been sick with dysentery for a week, vomiting and suffering diarrhea so bad that she could no longer move. The malnourished child was hauled off in an oxcart with a pile of other sick children.

Om Neang had already lost three children; she was not about to let another die without a fight. It was time to cash in on some favors from the Angka leader she and her husband had worked quietly and diligently to serve. Luckily Chuon was still in charge of the Kampong Kohl collective. He gave her written permission to visit her sick daughter in the hospital at Battambang. She hoped she wasn't too late. She quickly packed her krama with a little rice that Chuon had secretly slipped into her hand and some dead crickets from her pocket. Then she placed her hand tenderly on Maly's cheek and mustered a scolding tone to say, "Go back, now!"

It was a fake hospital, a place to die rather than heal. It occupied the same cement building in Battambang where the old hospital had been, but Neang hardly recognized it from the days when her roadside dessert bar served the relatives of patients being treated with western- style surgeries and antibiotics. Now the walls were stripped nearly bare and the fetid stench of urine, feces and death enveloped the building. Uneducated Angka cadre, chosen for the job by their party loyalty rather than medical credentials, understaffed the hospital. Room by room Neang scanned the bamboo beds and crowded floors full of skeletal bodies; she could hardly tell who was breathing and who wasn't. Malis' bony countenance was barely recognizable in the bed where she lay with five or six others, some of whom were already dead. When her mother picked her up, Malis moaned in agony and Neang knew there was still a chance.

She carried Malis to a less crowded corner of the cement room and coaxed some grains of rice into the child's mouth, washing it down with a few swallows of the water she had boiled and carried on her head for the three-day trip to Battambang. She soaked her soiled krama in a pond outside the building to

clean her daughter's feeble body and shit-stained clothes. She
scavenged the swamp area for shrimps, snails and insects to
feed the ailing child. She collected sour s'dao, bitter endive, and
guava bark to prepare a natural medicine she had learned from
her own mother, back on the farm in Kampong Cham. With
just a few days of care and nutrition, Malis was able to open her
eyes and speak well enough to tell the nurse that she was feeling
better. The overwhelmed nurse couldn't care less if the child's
mother took her away.

Om Neang carried her daughter's tiny, ailing body all the
way back to Kampong Kohl, where Chuon allowed the child to
stay while her mother nursed her back to health. At nine years
old, Malis was the size of a five-year-old; it would take months
before she could even sit up. During her recovery, her mother
kept squirreling bits of rice and sugarcane into the secret hiding
place below the little banana leaf doorway each night. Sometimes
in the morning it was gone. When she found more rabbit poop
pills in the hole, she knew that Maly must still be alive.

eleven

The Amputee Band

"Although the world is full of suffering,
it is also full of the overcoming of suffering."

Helen Keller

The communist movement in Cambodia was founded on the desire to level the disparity between urban wealth and rural poverty. In 2003, after more than 30 years of conflict, it appears to me that little has changed; the disparity remains. Returning to Phnom Penh from the countryside feels like a time warp forward two centuries, with the city's electric neon lights, cell phone vending kiosks, and high-speed Internet access for seventy-five cents an hour. Sovann would drive 20 minutes through chaos to find a cheaper place. But I liked the Lucky Tech Café, near my accommodations at the Bright Lotus guesthouse. It offered a chat with cheerful Samnang, the limbless boy on a wheeled pushcart who sat out front, with stubby arms touching prayerfully, and a large donation pocket sewn to the chest of his tank top. Besides, the Lucky Tech Café featured voice-over Internet protocol.

When our search at Om Tassom market failed, I started to lose heart. My intentions of finding my son's birthmother were beginning to look like a wild goose chase. My family, in the

meantime, was carrying on a life of bedtime stories and playground triumphs without me.

George is groggy when he answers the line, trying to digest
my story at 5 a.m. If Mien wants to study, he'll go along with
sponsorship, but he's surprised that Sovann asked me to sponsor
English classes for his son Sopheap, too. Sovann doesn't have any
relatives in America he can beseech for money; he has to rely on
the sympathy of foreign friends who don't quite understand the
logic. The tuition is only $80 a year, and he's not destitute.

"Follow up with the monk at the temple and be done with it,"
George says. "Maybe the birthmother doesn't want to be found."
He's learning for himself just how difficult single parenthood
can be. Then he adds, "Happy Anniversary." The nine-year
milestone of our union has passed without me; it's the only one
we've ever been apart.

Wat Lanka, on the south side of Phnom Penh, is an oasis of
quiet respite from the noisy tension of busy city streets. Squished
between the walls of a cement block fence, a white, red and gold
pagoda stacks skyward, sheltering a calm courtyard surrounded
by cloisters and tombstones, a space to reflect on the emotions
that prickly afternoon heat resurrects. My soul unshackles its
resistance as we enter, and the relief rekindles my hope.

"I know the head monk here," Sovann says. "He's from Takeo.
All the poor people from Takeo come to him for help." He asks
me to wait while he looks for his former teacher, and I gravitate
toward a drumbeat emanating from the opposite direction.

The strange wooden instruments are singing in a minor har-
mony, strangely beautiful and penetrating. The musicians are
seated beside a public meeting hall where lay people and clergy-
men are sharing a communal meal from bowls of blessed food on
the straw mats at the center of the floor. The music sounds like
playful crying. My hips begin to sway to the beat of the small
drum called a Skor, but stop suddenly, to check: The drummer
has no legs.

Two other players pull a bow between two strings on the Tror Sauch instrument, fingers extracting an unfamiliar range of tones. One man is missing an eye, the other a foot. Another player hammers the Tah Kay, which is like a dulcimer struck with bamboo mallets; this player has just one leg. The youngest band member, a boy about 13, bangs the chimes; he cannot see. Behind the band are several well-worn prosthetic legs leaning against the instrument cases. My god, but they can play! A poetic rhythm of bright, angst-ridden music conveys an ancient story. The beat informs my feet to dance and a song emerges from sultry air.

> *Are they happy, sitting five in a row, with incense burning,*
> *silver plate waiting, for money to fall, upon the elephant carving.*

> *To play a song or two, on instruments of string and bamboo,*
> *beating buffalo hide, and strings that whine like the voice of a*
> *lady, who is both laughing and crying.*

> *The beat begs hips and feet to dance, with faces staring at*
> *my knees, making smiles as the money falls, into the silver*
> *elephant carving.*

> *A leg is propped against the instrument case – detached*
> *from a body it cannot feel. It must be easier to sit and play*
> *without prosthesis.*

> *Circling behind the band, a row of limbs dismembered – a leg, a*
> *foot, an arm. Try to guess which part belongs to whom, while the*
> *singer croons an ancient tune, and smiles, when the money falls.*

> *The tune of the amputee band begs happy feet to dance, attached*
> *by blood, and muscle, and memory of a time when musicians*
> *played with limbs a plenty, a time before land mines.*

Was there a time before land mines? I'm thinking when the music stops. The smiling musicians start up another tune, encouraged by the alms generated in the offering plate. Were they musicians before they lost their limbs, or was it something they learned afterwards, from a United Nations-funded program to save Cambodian culture from extinction?

Most of Cambodia's artistic masters were killed during Khmer Rouge political purges of "bourgeois" urbanites. The threat of their profession is puzzling, given that the stories of the ancient kingdom, the glory days of the Angkor Empire the communists were professing to reclaim, are told through ancient Khmer songs. The regime sought for the peasantry the imperial greatness of the olden days, minus the influence of its traditions. The two decades of civil war that followed the Khmer Rouge ouster left millions of land mines in the ground on which an agrarian society was to rebuild. An amputee band seems oddly appropriate – a phantom limb recreating a culture complete.

A woman holding a baby on her hip has been watching me. She follows me back to the quiet courtyard like a ghost. Haunted by her presence I turn and she tries to push her baby into my arms begging "N'yum, n'yum," meaning, "eat, eat." Tears communicate her appeal to my discomfort and Sovann, returning from the cloister, simply ignores her. I pressure him to translate her plea.

"She says she need formula for the baby."

"How much is a can of formula?" I ask.

"Don't give," he says. Her small, dirty baby bottle is filled with water. She drops to her knees, crying, begging at my feet, and upholding the baby. Strangely, the child is chubby.

"She says she want you to take the baby."

"Ot-tay," I tell her – "No" – but her plea becomes more fervent.

"She says she can sell to the German lady for $500, but she want to give to you."

"How much is formula, Sovann!" I insist crossly, forgetting my rule to follow his lead.

"Five dollars."

When I hand the woman a five-dollar bill, she weeps and kisses my feet. Minutes later she and the baby are walking by with a bag full of food, and I smile in Sovann's direction, but he tells me the food was free, procured from the monk by the offerings for the Festival of the Dead. The frequent holy days in the Buddhist calendar double as a social welfare system.

"Some people, they use, you know," Sovann insists. "She can get the free food from the monk, but she see a white lady and she know she can make you feel sorry for her."

That's the problem of being a white woman with a brown heart in a desperate world where good intentions are easily misappropriated. Who will she sell that child to? Would it really be so bad if I took her, if the other choice is a brothel? I wonder if the baby is even really hers. I'm not sure if I've become cynical, or if I'm finally developing a healthy sense of tough love for the quintessence of this mysterious kinship.

"The old monk told me that the birthmother did not come here," Sovann says, and he can see that I'm dispirited. Another dead end.

Resting in the shade of a cotton fig tree, Sovann offers me a bundle of small, sweet bananas and perfectly sliced papaya, as if food will fix everything. But the speechless void makes him nervous, fearful that he has disappointed me.

"I know this monk long time, like a father. He not lie to me," Sovann says.

The head monk of Wat Lanka focuses his teachings on the impermanence of suffering, a lesson he tries to instill in the impoverished children he houses in his cloister, children who dream of a day when they won't be hungry. However, acceptance of impermanence never quite caught on in Sovann. When he lived in a room on the second story of the cloister, the monk's charity filled him with the hope of one day leaving Cambodia.

*   *   *

Sovann showed up at Wat Lanka in 1988 at the age of 21, after finishing his studies at high school, with nothing but two grams of gold his mother had pressed into his palm. Other mothers had to hide their sons in their rice barns, or under a palm leaf basket, when soldiers came searching for new recruits to drag off to the battlefield. But Sovann had dodged the draft with academic success. His completion of both secondary and high school was a rare feat under the Vietnamese occupation. Seeing his schoolmates return home from the battlefields with their limbs blown off was motivation enough to study every minute he was not working. Most boys lucky enough to attend one of the few schools that the Vietnamese reopened were conscripted after just two or three years of primary classes. Teenage soldiers didn't need to know how to read and write to lay landmines.

While Sovann struggled to regain a lost education in the 1980s, a strange coagulation of differences amassed on the Thai-Cambodian border. Cambodians set up resistance factions alongside and inside refugee camps, with the support of international humanitarian aid; their aim was to fight the Vietnamese occupation. The sentiment among Cambodians, communist and non-communist, remained a feeling of racial superiority to, and yet fear of annihilation by, Viet Nam.

China, the United States, and Thailand were united in their desire to contain Viet Nam and thus were willing to overlook the atrocities committed by the Khmer Rouge and its leader, Pol Pot, in favor of backing a coalition of Cambodian resistance forces that included them. As a result, Khmer Rouge military capacity was strengthened and its political life extended. Democratic Kampuchea retained Cambodia's seat at the United

Nations, while a government calling itself the People's Republic of Kampuchea actually controlled the country. A military stalemate between the Soviet and Vietnamese-supported PRK, and the U.S.-Thai-Chinese-supported Khmer Rouge, kept Cambodia engaged in a civil war for 12 more years. Land mines, supplied by their sponsors and designed to maim rather than kill, were a cheap and prolific weapon of choice on both sides of the conflict.

While I attended high school from 1982 to 1986, I received a large dose of Cold War threats, mostly in the form of nuclear fallout from the holocaust that would surely engulf us when the Russians hit the button. During those same years, Sovann was treading the waters of political tension as fast as he could, to steer clear of the final battleground where the Cold War actually was being fought – the war-ravaged rice fields of Cambodia, on the backs of people who were, at that time, the poorest people in the world. The violent military stalemate did not end until 1992, when the U.N. Transitional Authority in Cambodia took over, and an internal, political stalemate began. By then, over 12 million land mines lay buried in the ground in Cambodia – one for every man, woman and child.

"You know, sometime the people that lost their arm, their leg, their eye, they think they're worthless, so they kill themselves," Sovann says. "Some kill themselves by don't eat the food, or eat the poison mushroom, or some they use the knife, slash the stomach or the chest, we have many way for amputee to kill themselves. You have heard about that in the U.S.?"

"No, my friend, I'm afraid that Cambodia's land mine problem is not much talked about in the U.S.," I confess.

"Some amputee they lazy, they go to market to beg the money, drink alcohol, but I think they are uneducated because not all the disabled people work as the beggar," Sovann continues. "Most the same my age that study at the secondary school, they lost one leg or two arms, but they come from the educated family. The family don't want their children to be called *towk teap*, it means people look down on them; they should be embarrassed. The family tell their children to do something *th'lei th'no* that has ingenuity." For amputees willing to go on, prosthetics and wheelchairs designed for field work can be obtained from victims' aid organizations, where training in carpentry, handicrafts, computers, motorcycle and bicycle repair is tailored to the function of remaining limbs.

Outside the gates of Wat Lanka, four ladies are sitting against the wall politely begging. Coconut bowls sit on the ground before them, and each is softly chanting "n'yum, n'yum, n'yum." Three of them are amputees and one is a mother with two dirty children clinging to her. Where is her husband? Did he meet with a land mine, too? The local courtesy toward polite beggars is to give small bills, so I carry 100, 200, and 500 riel notes for these occasions when I cannot feign indifference and walk past limbless women. By the time I reach the end of the line, I've run out of the small riel notes that amount to 15 cents. The last woman is the most severely injured, having lost both an arm and a leg.

"Were you planting or harvesting the rice when it happened?" I want to ask. I dig into my pocket to find something, but the only paper there is a U.S. one dollar bill. Giving it to her might make her neighbors jealous, but I can't leave her bowl empty. I crumple the dollar small and drop it quickly, hoping she'll remove it before the others see. In the rearview mirror of the Camry I catch a glimpse of her toothless, ear-to-ear grin. Her one good hand has picked up my greenback, and she's smelling it.

✳   ✳   ✳

"Atmosphere." George had told me on voiceover Internet protocol that Grady said the word "atmosphere" – all three syllables. Our preschooler went on to tell his daddy that the reason the astronaut wears a space suit is because the moon doesn't have atmosphere. And then he asked why the lava from a volcano on Mars doesn't fall on Earth. He has been read to every day of his American life. What might have happened to his expansive little mind if he never had books? I have brought books to Cambodia, two duffle bags full, to deliver to the school built in his name. In the time I have remaining, I can keep searching for a needle in a haystack or deliver the books. My body is here, but my heart longs to be with my little boy. I'm counting the days until I return home. I've spent a month searching for his birthmother, while I'm missing out on precious days of being his mother. In the end, maybe the books are even more important than the truth.

Heading west from Phnom Penh, National Road No. 4 is the best in the country, smooth enough to gun it 50 miles per hour past the cattle trucks carrying women to garment factories before we collide with oncoming lorries full to the brim with logs. Sovann is proud of this road because it was built by the United States, but he can't understand why there is a tollbooth at either end. The 3,000 riel (75 cents) maintenance fee, he considers extortion.

Our fortunes change when we turn north at the town of Kampong Speu. As we encounter potholes at high speed, my head slams against the ceiling. A group of boys and girls is using hand-woven fishing baskets to fill in the potholes from a large pile of chipped rock. High school students building roads by hand.

"You don't have machinery to build roads?" I ask.

"We can have machine, but the government make bad corruption," Sovann says. "When we have donation from other country, the government say it will cost 10 million to build the road but when they build it, they buy cheap materials and only spend

5 million. The other 5 million go into the pocket." His incredulous eyebrows rise at the center, a familiar look of exasperation.

In the distance, rounded hills rise from the flatlands, shrouded by a humid filter of thick, tropical air. There it is, just out of reach, the Cambodia of my imagination: lush green hills; quiet villages; and the tranquil peace of the Cardamom Mountains. But to get there we have to pass through Dante's Inferno, the scene of a living hell. Barren, brown and dusty, scrappy palm thatch huts line the road where men, women and children covered in black soot are piling product onto various modes of encrusted transportation – mototrailers, vans, oxcarts, and lorries. It's the village of the charcoal families. Charcoal used for cooking fires is made right here on the road to Aural, in the kilns on the edge of the forest. Charcoal hockers fill up their vehicles and deliver daily to the markets, hotels and restaurants of Phnom Penh.

The hellish gauntlet has grown since the last time I was here, causing the same sinking feeling. Charcoal is one sector of the Cambodian economy that appears to be growing. The first few hills we come upon, where a jungle canopy once stood, are scarred black and brown. Acres upon acres have been burnt. The ugliness is a bad sign for Cambodia's future. What will hold the water when the monsoon rains come, if not ancient root systems? Trees moderate the endless cycle of flood and drought and secure the soil for rice farmers. Charcoal is a small man's game; the real money is in timber, a resource reserved for the military.

A bit farther down the road we pass two brand new government buildings, one freshly painted green and white, the other blue. Their respective signs, both in English, say Ministry of Environment and Ministry of Agriculture. "When the government building go up, the tree go down," Sovann says, as we pass.

*   *   *

Finally we reach Aural, a pocket of peace still surrounded by lush forest at the base of the Cardamom Mountain range. I'm surprised by the growth of this sleepy town in just two and a half years. The main intersection of two dirt roads now features a roundabout with a crude cement statue of hill tribe villagers and elephants in the center. There's a new billboard, roughly painted to impart a message to those who cannot read: A child hammers an unexploded ordinance with a big, red X over it. Shacks have sprung up in all four directions, with blue plastic tarps covering the commercial spaces that front the roadway. The dusty atmosphere has a lawless, frontier flavor to it, like the tent cities of the Gold Rush era in the late 19th century. There is just one two-story cement building in town. Behind it, I can hear the buzz of band saws milling wood.

"Whose house is that?" I ask.

"The District Chief of Education," Sovann answers. The District Chief's standard of living appears quite extraordinary, given the fact that our teachers are paid $13 per month and sleep on the cement floor of the school. The last time I was here, the District Chief wore the camouflage cap of a combat soldier and hardly spoke; he walked away when I asked the teachers if they taught Khmer Rouge history.

The Grady Grossman School never had a proper opening ceremony when it was built in 2001, so this time I agreed to something lavish. The teachers' residence is finished, but the paint is still wet when Sovann and I arrive at Chrauk Tiek village for the grand opening. There is a big red ribbon to cut, and everything. Parents have gathered with 300 students, seven monks, and four teenage girls costumed in glittering pamoung silk brocades for a show of officialdom. The District Chief of Education, the Provincial Governor, and I parade side by side down an aisle of clapping children, bowing for our jasmine flower necklaces and taking our places under a ceremonial canopy of blue tarpaulin and palm fronds. We kneel together before the head monk to be blessed with jasmine petals while the entourage chants. Speeches follow. A sea of children squat in the sun, sweat pouring off their heads, as the politicians drone on.

I listen to the District Chief of Education admonish the crowd of children to turn up for school, study and work in cooperation. I hear my name, "Madame Curry," repeated over and over. "*Make her happy,*" is his point. I smile as I'm supposed to, feeling satisfied that we accomplished the goal, yet oddly suspicious of the District Chief. What took him so long to finish the teachers' residence? We paid him six months ago. Sovann was right: Hosting a public event got the job done faster than a temper tantrum. That's why I agreed to fork out eighty bucks for this ceremony to thank myself.

The new five-room school is the only cement structure in the village of Chrauk Tiek, and the wooden, four-room teacher house is a premium residence. It cost $3,000 to build. The school building has a solar panel powering one computer, and enough wooden desks for all 300 students to sit two-by-two, on bench seats. Almost half of the students are girls. The four 16-year-old beauties holding the red ribbon are repeating the sixth grade because there is no secondary school to attend. The addition of an English and computer class was reason enough for the girls to convince their parents to allow them to continue their studies.

The teachers had been sleeping on the cement floor of the school because they couldn't afford housing. A ten-month school year pays $130, less than half the national average. Since everyone here is illiterate, the teachers come from Kampong Speu, three hours away. Sometimes they travel home to get food from their families and don't come back for awhile. Sending a child to school, rather than work, is a sacrifice for a farm family. George and I have tried to ensure that someone will be there to teach the children by sending a food stipend to the teachers each month.

Someone scrounges up a rusty old pair of scissors that tear the red cloth in small increments made by, first the head monk, then the Provincial Governor, then the District Chief, then Sovann. I struggle with the dull blades to make the last cut. Everyone cheers as the red ribbon falls. The 20 brand new pairs of scissors in my duffel bags, along with a bilingual library and art supplies, remain my little secret.

The celebration continues with a feast. Women have prepared kroeung fried chicken, sour fried vegetables and a spicy hot, curried coconut fish stew. For my benefit, they've kept the real delicacies – pig's liver, snails, and bone marrow – to a minimum. In the gathering darkness community leaders take a seat in a circle of straw mats. The District Chief of Education supplies the beer, eager to keep my glass cold and full. He lifts his glass repeatedly to toast me: "Lok kau li!" Everyone drinks, casting curious smiles my way. I'm one of only three women in the room, and the only foreigner ever to have come here. The English teacher, a shy twenty-year-old who was trained at the Phnom Penh orphanage where he grew up, tells me with a wide-eyed smile, "I've never met a donor before."

I can feel the District Chief staring at me across the divide of our differences. "I tell him what you say about our business," Sovann relays. "Jealousy is bad, competition is okay, but love is number one."

Sovann holds up his index finger, and the District Chief raises his love-is-number-one finger, too, clinking his glass with mine. "Lok kau li!"

"Lok kau li!"

The District Chief is particularly interested in my library materials. We have maps of the world and Cambodia, a globe and a simple English-language atlas, toys, puzzles, and 42 preschool English books I collected from home. In Phnom Penh, I purchased 23 Khmer story books – all I could find in the capital city. I couldn't find a world atlas and reference encyclopedias printed in Khmer.

The District Chief points to the school's only cabinet, with a small globe locked inside which he's proud to take out and show me. I look at it, and I'm speechless. In a room full of teachers, no one appears to notice that the Earth on this globe is upside down. Cambodia is in the Northern Hemisphere. Rules of face-saving etiquette be damned, I turn the globe over to demonstrate to the entire room the proper orientation of the North Pole. The District Chief can see that I'm frustrated and finally rights the Earth, handing it back to me with an irritated *"Are you happy now?"* smirk.

"Lok kau li!" I say.

"Lok kau li!"

Before the District Chief will leave, a shrewd negotiation ensues over who will be protecting me overnight. He's not exactly pleased that I intend to sleep in the teachers' residence. We compromise by hiring some nighttime bodyguards. Two uniformed policemen cost one dollar. The men tie two hammocks outside my door and then leave on their shiny, well-equipped police motorcycle for the evening rounds. The ox cart caravans will be passing by soon. When they return I'm lying within on the hard bamboo bed, trying to fall asleep under a bright pink mosquito net, with two men snoring outside my door and an AK-47 propped against the wall under my window. I'm thinking, all I really came here for was to give the kids some books.

The roosters wake me early. The sun rises fat and lazy through the morning steam that hovers just above the trees as children walking from all directions begin to appear in the schoolyard. They're surprised to find me still here, giggling and running away when I walk by, curious but afraid. There is much work to do before school starts: cleaning up the yard; weeding and watering the garden. The hand pump on the water well has broken from overuse by the villagers, so the children must haul five-gallon buckets from the nearby, low-flowing Kantout River to fill the cistern in the outhouse and water the plants. I make a mental note to fix the well; less hauling, more reading.

When the work is finally finished, two teachers shout the order for the children to gather. They line up by class, in perfectly straight lines, hand to shoulder, like spokes of a wheel around the flag pole to sing the national anthem. The words of allegiance to the grand old King have been resurrected, even though the office itself is now nothing more than a ceremonial post, in a Kingdom officially designated a constitutional monarchy. The children stand at attention with stiff arms at their sides, while a girl and boy raise the flag. At the head teacher's command they all filter into the classrooms, to assume the position of learning by rote.

A young, authoritarian teacher stands at the front of the class loudly calling out the lesson, and the 60 children in grade one repeat back in unison. As the students' ages go up, their numbers appear to go down. A quiet room of 45 fourth graders is busily copying down complicated Khmer script from the blackboard. They copy and memorize, not question. The 25 students in grades five and six share a single classroom, half of them facing west and copying down a lesson about forest conservation, the other half facing east and copying down the lesson about AIDS. I'm anxious to get out the library books, but the school director has other plans.

"Mr. Bun want to take you to see the hermit living under the tree," Sovann says. Mr. Bun already has hired a dark-skinned boy he trusts, nicknamed India, to transport me on his moto. There's no refusing. I assume the sidesaddle position of a Cambodian lady behind India, and we follow Sovann and Mr. Bun down a single-track path through the trees behind the school.

I'm surprised to find the head monk who blessed me with jasmine flowers the day before. He has constructed a small thatch temple out of long grass and palm leaves. He lives here primarily alone; a couple of Buddhist nuns attend to his physical needs. He introduces himself as Cheat, meaning "nature," and says he's happy I've come. I try to bow to his feet three times, as the Cambodians do, but he won't let me, and when my gaze meets his, it settles with strange familiarity. I feel instantly at ease in his presence.

The bareheaded, soft-spoken monk walks barefoot through the forest in his saffron robe, with four humans and four wild peacocks following him. The peacocks sleep in his temple or roost in the trees outside. Cheat hands me the brilliant tail feathers of another one that was killed by hunters. Several wild monkeys climb around the little tree fort that serves as his sleeping hut. Cheat tells me that elusive creatures like leopard, sun bear, and gibbons visit his realm at night. He exhibits the carcass of a small wildcat that came to his temple to die, after being shot. A wild green parrot alights on his shoulder as he shows me the signs he has painted by hand and nailed to the trees. He has printed words in both Khmer and a rough translation of English:

WE ARE THE ECOLOGY MONKS, HAVE COMPASSION
    FOR ALL BEINGS,
WE ARE THE ENVIRONMENTAL GIBBONS AND BEARS,
    WE SALUTE THE HUMAN AND BEG FOR MERCY.
OH HUMAN BEINGS, WE ARE THE FORESTS AND
    WILD ANIMALS, MAY WE SHARE THE EARTH FOR
    OUR HARMONY.
THE DHARMA IS UNIVERSAL LOVE, UNIVERSAL
    COMPASSION, I NOT TAKE RELIGION FOR FIGHTING,
    I WANT THIS WORLD TO GREEN PEACE.
PLEASE DO NOT CUT DOWN THE TREE.

This Buddhist St. Francis of Assisi has never heard of Greenpeace, the environmental group. "He hopes you can give him paint and brushes to make more signs." Sovann says.

"I have four gibbon living here," Monk Cheat tells me in a soft and shy pronunciation of English. "I want to protect a place for them three kilometer square."

As I follow him deep into the old-growth forest, the dry jungle turns heavy and cool under the weight of tall trees, with a thick canopy blocking out most of the light. He moves quickly, like a forest spirit, until we stop suddenly at a clearing. The ground and the trees are blackened by fire, and hot sunbeams drill through the hole in the canopy, scorching the earth like that pitiful hole in the dilapidated roof thatch where the children used to study. The saffron robe picks through it, a sacred color gliding through the midst of ruin. With mountain goat strides, the monk scales a hill to a rocky outcrop and sits down in the lotus position. Perched above the trees, he begins to chant Pali, repeating in English for my ears. His prayer for peace and compassion for all beings floats onto the thick air while the buzz of chainsaws and smell of burning trees rises to meet it from the distance below.

I've often wondered why Cambodia has such a grip on my soul. Looking up from my camera, I ask monk Cheat how long he's been doing this. "Four years," he says. That explains everything. Four years ago we prayed in a sweat lodge for a child, and Grady was born not long after that. Of course I will buy the forest monk his paints.

That evening, Mr. Bun and his wife invite me into their floorless wooden hut at the northwest corner of the schoolyard for a meal. The teachers' residence is upscale by comparison. A straw mat is spread on a bamboo bed that serves as a table, and simple country cooking is served: fried chicken; plain rice; and peeled cucumber. Sovann, Mr. Bun and two teachers encircle the mat, cross-legged, and politely wait for me to gather bits of meat and vegetable into my rice bowl. The group appears pleasantly amazed that I can eat their food with hot condiments and fish sauce, easing the tension of a foreign dinner guest and inviting more intimate conversation, cobbled together by my broken Khmer and the English instructor's elementary command of the language he teaches.

The tin roof is just big enough to cover the eating area in front of the little building that 24-year-old Mr. Bun built by hand six months ago, after bringing home his sweet, 18-year-old bride, whom he didn't want sleeping on the cement floor of the school.

She has set up a little storefront selling shoes and clothing she makes or mends with her old-fashioned, treadle-powered, black Singer sewing machine – the kind regarded as quaint decoration in American antique shops.

"He depend upon his wife to live," Sovann conveys. The director's salary is $25 per month for teaching grade one, maintaining the school grounds, and managing homeless teachers.

"He want to tell you how grateful he is for the food stipend you send," Sovann continues. "But sometimes they don't get all. When the District Chief pick up in Kampong Speu, then the teachers get only half." I suspected this was happening, and I turn a weary eye to Sovann, who had assured me that the food was being delivered.

"What does he do with the rest?" I ask. They presume it works like the rest of the bribery system, requiring a payment of rice to staff at the district office.

"When he buy something for the school, the chalkboard, the soccer ball, something like that," Sovann relays, "Then he deduct from the teachers' pay, so maybe they just get $8 or $9 per month." The dejected countenance of these honest but weary men worries me; I wonder why they even bother teaching. Why do I care more about the children's education than the District Chief of Education does? How much does he make? No one can tell me. I want to go above his head and discuss it with the Minister of Education.

"I cannot tell you about the power man," Sovann argues, "You cannot protest. You only understand Cambodia fifty percent. Please do not put my life in danger." I don't know if his fear is warranted or paranoid, but I was raised to believe in transparency and the accountability of government. From the perspective of a heady American, the powerlessness of this situation is difficult to swallow. How can they just put their heads down and go on?

The sun is setting as a long caravan of ox carts approaches, each one carrying a pile of large tree trunks, driven by young men in dirty caps and T-shirts. The teachers stare silently at the primeval logging train as it stops right in front of the school. The ox cart drivers are soldiers, they tell me. Each one climbs down and gathers around the man at the karaoke shop three doors down. The blaring establishment is owned by the chief of police, a fat man in a brown uniform like the ones my bodyguards wear. He collects his bribe payments from each ox cart driver in broad daylight. I can see him counting the cash.

"How much do they pay?" I ask.

"Twenty or thirty thousand reil, I think. Depend upon how much he have to pay above him," Sovann says. Five to seven dollars each, from eight ox cart drivers: One bribe payment is more than three times a teacher's monthly salary.

The Grady Grossman School is located inside the Aural Wildlife Sanctuary, a biological World Heritage Site designated for protection in 1997, one year before Pol Pot died of mysterious causes (reportedly a heart attack) at his encampment in the forest to the north. Aural Mountain is Cambodia's highest peak – 1,700 meters of endangered old-growth tumloap forest and one of the last remaining habitats for Asian tigers, clouded leopards, sun bear, gibbons and tree sloths. The Cambodian government exercised only marginal control over the area when they drew the conservation zone onto the map. Logging funded the conflict through the 1980s and '90s; it staved off commercial development but destroyed precious forest habitat, in the process. Cambodia's prime minister Hun Sen, an ex-Khmer Rouge cadre himself, declared logging illegal in 1998, but even so there is little hope for this forest if the law is not enforced.

The non-uniformed soldiers return to their ox carts and give the weary animals a crack with the reins. They'll drive all night long to the lumber mills in Kampong Speu and return in the morning with empty ox carts, just as the children are gathering for school. Military commanders orchestrate the harvest of endangered old-growth tumloap, selling it to luxury timber traders who export to Viet Nam, where it is fashioned into fancy garden furniture for shops in China, the U.S. and Europe. Institutionalized corruption is nothing new in Cambodia, a canker since the turmoil of the early 1970s. Today a rogue military structure continues to fund itself the way the Khmer Rouge did for two decades. The reason for the delay in building our teachers a home was that the District Chief of Education, who also provides lumber and construction services, had been preoccupied with his lucrative business in the illegal timber trade. His meetings to trade timber in Kampong Speu also made him available to pick up and pilfer the food stipend I send. Even my desire to take action seems like a naïve, first world luxury.

Bun's wife, Sothea, serves us sweet, sticky rice, palm jelly and fruit. A couple of community leaders drop by to share the dessert. The head of community hands me a stack of photos and his handwritten letter, asking me to tell someone about the forest destruction. In one photo, a huge pile of timber is stacked behind a band saw operator, who is processing lumber in the middle of the forest with impunity. In another photo, the parents from yesterday's ceremony are sitting at the children's desks having a forest protection meeting in our school. He says he represents 437 families.

I tell everyone I'll do my best. Swallowing the weight of responsibility, I sigh to the warm night and wish that I had just sent the books.

"Do you teach the children about history, about the Khmer Rouge regime?" I ask the teachers. Before anyone can answer, the man who owns the little lumber mill across the road interrupts.

"We need to forget about that bad time," he says, with a wave of his cigarette. "I was a Khmer Rouge soldier, too." I visited this man's carpenter shop this morning to discuss building library shelves. On my way out the door, he had pointed to a small wooden cross, painted red and nailed to the front of his building, to show me he was a Christian; he had converted in a Thai refugee camp. He hands me a plastic bag containing a letter and photos of his daughters and asks me to send them to the address on the tattered envelope – his brother, who lives in New Jersey. The quiet flow of the Kantout River is drowned out by karaoke from a corrupt policeman and candlelight throws a soft glow on a former Khmer Rouge killer, turned Christian with humanitarian aid, now an illegal timber trader, hoping his brother in New Jersey will send money.

Sovann's exasperated eyebrows knit together again, and I think mine do the same. We all continue eating sweet, sticky rice and palm jelly in dizzy silence.

In the morning, I spread toys and puzzles on straw mats on the cement floor of the school. The books are laid atop two rows of wooden desks. Students age five to 16 wash their hands in the river and line up to experience their very first library hour. Their smiling faces, teeth blackened by decay, encircle the piles of school supplies. A teacher explains how to take care of the books, and then all hell breaks loose. The noise of the children bounces off the cement walls with deafening excess. The youngest ones discover blocks, Legos, cars, airplanes, dolls, and astronauts, and the older ones read aloud, two or three to a book, as fast as they can. I don't think anyone explained that the books are staying.

I dump the puzzle pieces onto the floor and give everyone a lesson, including the teachers; no one has ever seen a puzzle. Two children creep into my lap with a book, shocked when they suddenly realize they are touching me, but we smile at each other and they nestle in, knowing they are welcome to stay. Their body odor is strong; mine frighteningly clean. The book they've chosen is about farm animals, clearly relevant. Page by page I point to the pictures, and as the children shout out the Khmer words, laughing when I repeat them with a butchered pronunciation, they repeat the English words with amazing clarity. Soon a crowd of little people has gathered around me. On the chicken page there is a hard-to-decipher gray larvae; I start picking at my hair, and the children sneer in unison with the Khmer word for lice. They all know what that is.

As I watch the feeding frenzy, tears cloud my vision of children starved for books, appeasing their hunger for the first time. My own college-bound, public school education at once seems severely elite and profoundly underappreciated. A woman watching through the window says something to Sovann that he's reluctant to translate.

"She said that you bring the library, now you want to take the children to America, but I told her, no, you are humanitarian." The embarrassed woman walks away from the window, leaving me with awkward insight: Unlike the villages closer to Phnom Penh, no one here has tried to give me a child.

The children didn't want to leave school that day, and among the last to go was a boy in a black shirt and pants; he had no blue-and-white school uniform. He was piling the books one by one, straightening the corners with obsessive gentleness, as if they were the most precious objects he'd ever touched. He didn't want to stop touching them. He gave me a drawing of me standing in front of the school, with mountains and sunshine in the background, signed De Na. I have great hope that De Na will succeed in getting an education, yet my hope is tempered by the knowledge of what he's up against.

Half of the students at the Grady Grossman School are children of illegal loggers. Their fathers are typically illiterate, demobilized soldiers who were stolen from their homes and conscripted as teenagers. With no other opportunity for work, they follow their former chain of command, felling trees and driving ox carts through the night for $2 per day. The other half of our students are the children of Souy villagers. The Souy are a minority hill tribe of forest dwellers who have lived in the mountains for centuries, even while the Khmer Rouge occupied their forest until 1997. The Souy villagers often go hungry, Some grow enough rice for three months, some for six months. Most make less then

$10 per month selling charcoal; some make nothing. De Na is one of them.

Library hour is over, and the English teacher continues flipping excitedly through the preschool books. With a shy smile he divulges, "I have so much to learn!" His colleague, 23-year-old Son Sarith, sits at the end of the table, engrossed in his very first puzzle. A few lingering children lean over his shoulder and cheer his success. In a little under an hour, he has finished a 50-piece floor puzzle meant for four- to six-year-olds. I have also brought 100-, 500-, and 1,000-piece puzzles, but he's not ready to tackle a harder one.

"Puzzles help children learn problem-solving skills," I tell him. Mr. Sarith nods and promises to encourage the children to do the puzzles. If there ever were a country that needs problem solvers, it's Cambodia.

What a relief to get in the car finally and leave. We travel back down the dirt road and through the charcoal gauntlet, with Mr. Bun and his wife in the back seat. They're coming with us to Phnom Penh to bring back new parts for the water well, pipes for an irrigation system, and enough seeds to create a substantial school garden.

My real purpose for being here stares back from my reflection in the car window, and it brings with it a compelling urge to walk away. Once they graduate from grade six, the children here have two possible futures. They can work in the rice fields and barely subsist, or they can cut down trees and destroy their future for a monthly wage that is five times greater than a teacher's salary. I close my eyes and imagine that somewhere, out there, is a child with potential to be the leader who can define a different future. Perhaps that person is De Na. If he won't give up, how can I?

A caravan of ox carts passes by, each one carrying stacks of enormous tree trunks, and the tune of the amputee band ambles into my head. The forest recedes like a phantom limb, signaling a culture that is hellbent on amputating its future.

twelve

Same Bus, Different Driver

*"A communist is like a crocodile:
When it opens its mouth you cannot tell whether it is
trying to smile or preparing to eat you."*

Winston Churchill

iles of freshly washed vegetables adorn the table: Asian broccoli; water convolvulus; bean sprouts; enoki mushroom bundles and sprigs of holy basil. Mounds of quail eggs and thin slices of raw beef cover another plate, beside narrow strips of squid sliced with a cross hair to make it curl as it cooks. Amanda places an electric skillet in the middle of the table and pours in Yaw Han, a soup of tangy hot coconut milk, tamarind-flavored shrimp paste, chicken broth and sour lime juice. Into the coconut barbecue each person can toss the vegetables and meats he chooses to flash cook and then spoon onto a bowl of num pra chot, soft rice vermicelli. Cambodian family-style is a noisy affair; teasing makes up the bulk of easy dinner conversation. My preference for the hot condiment of crushed chili, garlic and fish sauce draws a few jests from my friends, who seem to find it peculiar that I can tolerate the spice but my little boy cannot. My acquired palate is the result of many unusual sorties into the strangely sapid world of Cambodian cuisine.

What lucky adoptive parents we are to have this multigenerational family welcome us into their lives, to experience with our son what it means to be Cambodian American. Is it coincidence or a divine construction that they survived and found their way to Wyoming, of all places? This is another spot on the planet that has inherited the dark side of American history, in the form of an Indian reservation peopled by the impoverished survivors of our own failed genocide. Bound in our friendship is the knowledge of Cambodia's confused suffering which seems so unnecessary and, at times, self-inflicted. We've left it behind but it will never leave us. Tied into the mystery of how our lives became entwined is this pile of international mistakes. The question is who, if anyone, is learning from them? More than 2,500 years ago the Buddha preached a philosophy called the Middle Way, a secure place to walk between joy and sorrow, righteousness and ruthlessness, past and future. It is a practice I hope to learn one day; it worked well for Amanda's father to guide his family through the misfortunes of incurable politics.

"My dad is smart. Without my dad I think I would not be here right now," Amanda's brother, Dani, admits when I ask how they made it out alive.

Provoked by Pol Pot's arrogance at starting renewed border disputes, Viet Nam invaded Cambodia in January 1979 – with the inadvertent result of releasing the long-suffering Cambodian people from Angka's cruel agrarian utopia.

"All of a sudden word spread around the daikon camp that Youn is coming," Amanda says. She was almost nine by then. "I've been in that village for so long, I feel brainwashed, and I can't remember if Youn is enemy or friend, so I just grab Malis and run. Run as fast as we can to find my mom."

The front lines moved quickly across the country. In the chaos of Vietnamese advance and Khmer Rouge retreat, the victimized work force of Democratic Kampuchea took to the roads and footpaths in search of family. Maly had made the journey enough

times in the dark to push her way through distraught people clog-
ging the pathways toward Kampong Kohl. The girls arrived
in the late afternoon, but their brothers had not yet appeared
when the Khmer Rouge cadre began yelling for everyone to
evacuate the village.

Adding more leafy greens to the hot skillet between us, Amanda's aged father recalls that fateful day. "When the Vietnamese
come to occupy, Chuon say to me, quickly get in the truck and
go to the mountain." To avoid being shot on the spot, Sokun
made a quick lie. "I like your law, brother, but I must wait for
my sons to come and we will go with you together to fight for
Angka." Convinced of his revolutionary zeal, the Angka leader
gave Chen Kmao a small portion of dried fish, repeating a tired
slogan about Youn determination to destroy the Khmer race.
When the sun went down, Sokun hid his family in a cave at the
base of the mountain to wait and see what happened. In the
night, Angka soldiers descended from the forested mountain to
discover a group of 10 or 20 families looting their storehouse of
rice, chickens, beer and wine. A massacre unfolded in the screams
of dark shadows as the enraged Angka unleashed the last vengeance of their dwindling power, killing the starved civilians as
fast as they could on the final eve of their domination. From the
safety of their cave, Sokun could only hope that his sons were
not among them.

Maly waited with her mother and sister inside the cave while
her father went searching for the boys the next morning. The
village was eerily empty, and the sounds of fighting edged closer
by the hour as the powerful Vietnamese army approached.
Maly breathed quietly, listening to flies buzz in the village and
the painful gurgle of hunger. "We waited in that cave for two
days, and we are thinking that we are going to have to leave,"
Amanda remembers. "When my dad finally show up with my
three brothers, we are happy but we don't know what to say to
each other because it has been so long. I think if we had stayed

another hour or so, we would all be dead, because we hear the big battle like fireworks after we get to the river."

To escape Angka, they ran toward the fighting. At Rung, a small village at the edge of the Sangkar River, the family met a crowd of three or four hundred refugees facing an impassable body of water. The river had swollen deep behind the dam Angka laborers had constructed downstream in the dry season of 1977. The conical palm hats peering from the thick bushes beyond signified that Vietnamese soldiers were positioned on the other side, but the Khmer Rouge were closing from behind, threatening to kill anyone who dared to cross. Maly clung to her sister and mother as they crouched in a muddy trench, steeling her psyche against the piercing retorts of gunfire overhead. The fighting went on for hours. By the time the morning fog had cleared, the Khmer Rouge cadre were once again in retreat from their fearsome enemy. Suddenly, the quiet lull erupted into a panicked surge for the river.

"Everyone run fast and jump in the water, hundreds of people," Dani says. "Some people fight over the banana tree trunk they cut down to float on, because many don't know how to swim. Some use empty bucket to float, whatever it takes to get to the other side, we just grab the old people and children and just run across the front line, don't look back, just keep running until nighttime."

By nightfall, the Prom family found themselves walking on a road with a column of Vietnamese trucks and tanks, blazing a dusty path westward against the current of weary stragglers moving slowly eastward. The Youn soldiers didn't seem to care where the people went, as long as they stayed out of the way.

"The road was noisy with chickens and cows, screaming and crying, all kinds of panic," Dani says. "Vietnam keep telling us that Khmer Rouge is coming back, so we want to keep walking as fast as we can."

For two or three days they moved with the flow of humanity, sleeping on the road only when necessary. No one dared venture into the forest to pee or scavenge food because land mines had been planted everywhere. Someone found a grenade and threw it into a small pond; the explosion sent a shock through the crowd. Dead fish soon floated to the surface and a crowd of rabid children jumped into the pond in a frenzied food grab, the Prom kids successfully hoarding enough for their mother to prepare fish soup.

"I cook, I happy, my kid have good food to eat, have fish. I put water, put salt, put tamarind, don't have lemon, don't have soy sauce, but my kid eat all, I say oh very, very good," Neang recalls, with a contented smile that quickly withers. "But I scare too, sometime people eat, eat, eat like that, they full but they keep eating, eat too much, they die. too."

Battambang was filled with migrant refugees when they arrived; the country to the west, toward Pailin, remained in the possession of Khmer Rouge guerrillas. The family went searching for food at the site of their old roadside business. Nothing was left, the wooden walls and steel roof long since dismantled and taken away. Sokun kicked dirt off the severed foundation beams that remained in the ground where the humble dwelling he had built by hand once stood. The children gathered sticks for a cook fire and water from a nearby pond, to prepare a single package of ramen noodles they found, sharing it evenly among seven family members. Sitting together on the hard-packed clay floor, no one knew what to do next.

Black market commerce quickly took shape on the ravaged streets of Battambang, the historical commercial center of Cambodia's rice bowl province. Maly's mother still had enough gold jewelry stashed in seams of her sarong to do business. Once the Vietnamese soldiers had taken the town of Saophoan to the north, a brisk flow of foot traffic set the transport of trade goods from Thailand in motion. Sokun Prom and his sons were among them, taking the flakes of gold that his wife cut stingily from her remaining jewelry, and venturing north on National Road No. 5 to trade for light commodities: dried noodle packets; sugar; rice; or baht, the hard currency of Thailand. Gold and rice were both viable currencies, and water brought the highest price, so Sokun sent his sons to scavenge unhulled grain from fields and his daughters to search for water bottles.

The boys were gone for two weeks at a time, walking round-trip to the Thai border, while Maly and Malis remained in Battambang to look after their pregnant mother. They never told her about the dangers of scavenging water. The supply came from a well in the remains of a cement block home that Youn soldiers had commandeered for living quarters. Maly and Malis had learned to follow older teenage girls to that place, so they could sneak in to steal the water while the soldiers were distracted. Within earshot of the screams from rape victims, Maly quietly filled her bottles as fast as she could, trying hard not to splash any precious cargo as she ran out the door.

With the road to Saophoan secured, more Vietnamese soldiers encamped in Battambang patrolled the roads, setting up roadblocks to control the migration of Khmers northward and demanding payment from the fledgling foot merchants. Rumor spread that the Vietnamese would soon cut off access to the Thai border. Like many Khmers, Sokun Prom harbored an ancient fear of the Vietnamese, and seeing their numbers steadily increase, he presumed they would, in the end, be worse than the Khmer Rouge. The Vietnamese occupation force fancied itself the victorious revolutionaries of Indochinese communism. Sokun had long resisted the concept of Indochina; the handwriting was on the wall.

"*Lan ta mouy, takong pseng knea* – the same bus, different driver," he told his oldest son as they approached the Youn soldiers' newest checkpoint. To avoid the shakedown of their meager earnings,

Sokun and his son stepped gingerly through a forest littered with land mines. They'd been liberated from the work camps for six months when Sokun decided to escape his beloved Cambodia, before the border closed.

"When we are walking to Thailand on the road, my dad lie to the guard, because my mom is seven months pregnant, and he say that she need to go this way to her mother's house to have the baby. The guard believed him, and let us pass," Amanda says. "We have to step over a lot of dead people blocking the road, and one lady is oily and puffed up, dead maybe three days; it smelled so bad."

Maly plugged her nose and bravely walked past the corpses, helping her mother carry a small sack of rice and some water, until they came to an encampment in the forest near the mountainous border with Thailand. The migration was choked by the Thai government's refusal to allow refugees across the border. The squalid stopping place soon became known as Camp 007. Each day porters brought a few bags of rice over the mountain, sent by international relief organizations desperately trying to secure permissions and supplies to accommodate a large influx of refugees in Thailand. A humanitarian crisis was at hand, as hundreds of migrant families lined up daily for one condensed milk can full of rice. A few weeks passed and desperation grew, until an announcement came over Radio Free Asia that a refugee camp called Khau I Dang was accepting Khmers; the migration immediately resumed. Alongside hundreds of their ravenous countrymen, the Prom family walked barefoot over the mountains in search of a haven.

As people emerged from the forest onto a dirt road in Thailand, soldiers corralled them onto buses with gun barrels poked into their backs. Siblings strained their grips on each other to be shoved through the same open door. A few miles down the dusty road, the bus drove into a fenced compound where a white and blue U.N. flag snapped in the wind next to a Red Cross banner.

Hundreds of skinny Khmers filed off the buses and into the registration lines, where the relief workers looked like giants among the stunned newcomers.

The woman asking Maly her name was the most astonishing human she'd ever seen. Maly stood mesmerized by her freckled white skin, blue eyes, and an amazing, sweet smell. "Why does she smell so different than us?" Maly thought. Instinctively she grabbed the apple the woman handed her and viciously bit into it, sucking the juice as though she would never let it go; it tasted so good. For the first time in many years, Maly saw other children playing. The tension around her 10-year-old mind released enough to allow a new thought to enter: "Maybe I am safe," it whispered.

With a hundred families already established in Sangket 1, Station 1, the Proms were assigned with the next 100 families to construct living quarters in Station 2 with a 5 by 5 meter piece of plastic and a small pile of bamboo. They would be issued a free food stipend: one kilo per person per day of salt-dried fish; dry milk; rice and cabbage. It wasn't a lot, but enough. On the advice of previously settled refugees, Sokun Prom set himself immediately to writing letters to every country open to Cambodian exiles, hoping to find a sponsor in France, Australia or the United States. It would take two years to get a reply.

Khau I Dang refugee camp evolved as a world unto itself inside a tall, barbed perimeter fence. Refugees crowded into the little tent city fashioned their existence from scarce resources and pinned their hopes on an uncertain future. Sponsorships came quickly for those with a relative living abroad, but the Proms knew no one living in a distant land far away from the fighting. Worried by the prospect of being sent back to Cambodia when the camp closed, each family member exploited his or her talents to earn food and money for their mother to stash.

The U.N. doctors needed translators to help communicate medical information to new refugees, so Dani and Bon Leoun set their sights on learning English. Anyone with knowledge of the language could operate a private school with many students eager to learn if they had the money to pay. The Prom brothers could not afford a place in the crowded classroom, so they stood quietly outside the open-air windows and listened, copying down every word the teacher wrote on the chalkboard.

"Can money buy you happiness?" Dani wrote the phrase in a notebook his father procured from the school supply room. Money would have been nice, but Dani was willing to work for sardines. In just a few months he had mastered enough English to translate prescription instructions to the new refugees at the camp hospital. His work earned him two cans of sardines per day and a T-shirt.

Sokun's business background and knowledge of French landed him a job as quartermaster of the U.N. school supplies, carefully doling out the exact limit of books, pencils, paper, chalk and slates allocated to each class. He often encouraged his own children to sell their supplies, trading his lofty values of education to gain more immediately tangible security. As a result, Maly never learned to read and write Khmer, but then she was not much interested in attending primary school classes, anyway. What use was learning Khmer if they were going to America? She determined to put her Angka education to good use, for she had highly honed stealing skills.

"When my brothers study English they come home hungry, but there is no food left, so I sneak out to steal vegetable for my mom to make for them," Amanda says, while tossing the last of the vegetables and meat into the coconut barbecue sauce. No such thing as leftovers at this dinner table.

With her face pressed up against the woven wire fence, Maly had been admiring the luscious garden at the Thai schoolhouse across the road for months. Once she discovered a route, she acted on impulse, crawling through the sewer pipe under the road to escape the camp. She pulled as many green stalks of morning glory, cucumbers and taro root as her little arms could carry, before returning through the sewer pipe under the cover of early evening darkness. Those impudent preteen escapades antagonized her mother, even while she accepted the stolen vegetables with pleasure.

"When children come home with food, sometime I happy, sometime I scare, because maybe the people will take my children to jail," Neang says, still shaking at the worry. "When my son go to jail in Thailand, I cry, very cry."

Maly's brother, Bon Louch, had been sneaking out the perimeter fence nearly every night to procure produce from Thai vendors and sell it at the camp market each morning. On the day he got caught, Thai soldiers tied the 13-year-old boy's hands behind his back, beat him, and threw him in jail overnight. While his mother lay awake wondering if the soldiers would kill him, Bon Louch spent the night nursing his wounds and stewing over the good food and money the soldiers had confiscated from him and thrown away. The hardheaded boy never snuck out again, but he could not curb his obsession with stealing food. If someone else's chicken wandered near their little shelter, Bon Louch quickly killed it, or captured it alive and sold it in the market.

His mother never scolded him for his thieving; with a new baby boy born just weeks after they arrived in Khau I Dang, she now had eight mouths to feed. Each chicken the boy brought her could last a whole month if she boiled it whole, deboned the meat, and packed it tightly into a glass jar. Each day she added one spoonful of chicken to a pot of vegetable soup, giving her children a taste of protein to add muscle little by little to their skinny bones.

At least once every day, the children went to the camp post office, sometimes alone and sometimes together. Each day they anxiously scanned the long list of names on the big white board. "Maybe this will be the day," Maly always hoped, but each day only blank white space appeared next to the name Prom, Sokun.

Another joyous family jumped up and down and Maly walked away more dejected than before. Busloads of people left Khau I Dang for new lives in foreign lands every day. She was twelve years old and waiting her life away. Youthful desire turned hope into action as she began checking out the churches.

"I go to church because I heard from my friend that you got paid twenty baht if you go to church." Dani laughs. "I see the cross sign but I don't understand what they are saying. It's new religion to me, but I don't care. I'm not thinking about Christian or Buddha. I'm thinking about the twenty baht."

"I go to a different church where they are baptizing people by spraying holy water from a hose," Amanda says. " I didn't know anything about twenty baht. I just know that if I believe in baptizing, then I can come to America."

"Please give us a Superpower country, but not a communist one," Maly prayed. After two years, Khau I Dang Refugee Camp felt like a prison. Daily disappointment from the sponsorship board was beginning to erode even her dream of freedom, until the evening her father walked home from the schoolhouse and sat them down together. "Guess what?" he announced, with a forced smile. "I have found a teacher who has an extra place because one of his children die. He can take one of you to America!"

He had been mulling the possibility of splitting up the family for a long time, struggling to square his Buddhist belief in destiny with the torment of giving a child away. Whoever went would have a better chance at life, but would be alone in the world, without family and estranged from their ancestors. He took measure of his six children; they were all survivors. Maly was only twelve. Besides the baby, she was the youngest, and he reasoned she had the best chance to learn English well enough to get a good job. She was strong and likeable. She was also his favorite.

"I want Maly to go," he said.

"I'm not afraid a-pok," Maly answered, with tears welling up in her eyes. "When I get to America I will work hard and send money to you." Her father held her shoulders tight and fixed his eyes on hers to swallow his own lament.

"Go!" he told her. "Just go to America!"

Her mind would not rest that night, as Maly thought about the picture of America in her schoolbook: A lady pushed a cart in the sparkling clean grocery store where piles of beautiful food lined the aisles. She was going to heaven. She hoped she would remember not to spit on the floor; her teacher said it was against the law.

For two weeks, Maly had been studying everything she needed to know about the new family to pass the exit interview. She was being drilled on the details by her father when Dani ran toward them shouting. "We got a sponsor!"

The whole family ran and gathered around the big white board in the post office, their hearts pounding. Tears of joy sprang from every eye when they saw a name written in the blank next to Prom, Sokun. The children had no idea who belonged to that name, but their parents did; he was a military policeman from Battambang, a customer from long ago, in the early days of the Lon Nol regime. How did he survive? Their letter had reached him in a place called Denver, Colorado. The letters U.S.A. hung like gold in the air; there was no containing the excitement.

With every ounce of gold saved for two years in the bank of their mother's bosom, the children ate and ate in preparation for their exit interview and physical exam. "My parents were afraid that if we have a disease or look too skinny, the Americans will not accept us. So my dad would crack an egg and beat it up in club soda with condensed milk for us to drink, like an energy drink to pump us up, so we look healthy for the interview," Amanda says. "And he drilled us on all this information we need to know, our T number, how to spell our name, birthday, how many student in the class room, how big is an M16, how many bullet in an AK47 magazine." The rumor mill had churned out a fearsome set of questions, which her parents made them learn but they were never asked. The physical exam, however, was unpleasant.

The doctor was a Thai man, and Maly couldn't believe she was going to have to strip down in front of him. She had never seen a doctor in her life and had to line up naked with her sister and the other girls, crying and embarrassed by the first experience of having their private parts exposed. While being poked and prodded for the germs she might bring to America, she thought about her little brother. Sey Ma was almost two and he was their little fortuneteller. Each time she asked him if she will pass the test, he responded, "Baat, baat – yes, yes." His tender little voice was like a blessing from heaven.

On the day they finally left Khau I Dang to begin a nine-month journey to America, the children were dressed to the nines in new school uniforms, pressed by hand for hours to make perfect crease lines. Everyone was excited to get on that bus, proudly smiling to the crowd and nervously shaking. What if the next camp had another barbed wire fence? How long would they live there?

"On the way from Khau I Dang to Mi Rot, the bus stopped in the middle of nowhere to let us go out to pee, and a Chinese lady dropped a bag of gold." Amanda remembers. "My stupid brother get scared and give it back to that lady! I was so mad, I yell at him because I want to keep it. I am a thief, and I needed to learn again how to be honest."

After passing two months in transit camps called Mi Rot and Chunburi, when the family was finally called to board an airplane they were flat broke, having spent everything they had on fattening up the children for the exit interviews and examinations. Maly walked onto the tarmac and gasped at the outrageous sight of a giant 747 jet. "The airplane is on the sky," she whispered, the only English phrase she knew.

Maly felt tiny in the big, soft seat; the smell of disinfected stale air made her want to vomit. The nervous pulse of eagerness and fear altered the boarding procedures into a theatre of the surreal, fraught with adventure, danger, and Thai policemen – who were making another family get off the plane! "Oh, please don't take us," Maly sobbed, as she fumbled nervously to make the metal plates fasten around her waist.

With a deafening roar, the airplane left the cruel ground and its horror forever. Airplane: The word rolled gloriously off Maly's tongue, and within minutes she was retching into the airsick bag. Most of the passengers were motion sick. Green-faced mothers rubbed silver coins on the skin of their children to free the blocked life force. In the bathroom, Maly braved the fear of being sucked out the disposal hole, having never seen a flush toilet before, and ran back to her seat. A beautiful Filipino flight attendant with flawless, light brown skin set a tray of food in front of her. "That's what I will look like when I go to America," she dreamed. She examined the juice box and soft foil triangles of cheese with a smiling cow on top and thought, "What do I do with this?" Her brothers and sister were wondering the same thing. At least the French bread looked familiar.

Traveling through both air and time, the Cambodians were on route to the Philippines, where they would spend six months learning how to function in the modern world. It was 1982. Telephones, toilets, television, traffic lights, electricity, and running water would all be new and startling experiences.

Maly's childhood resurfaced at the Refugee Processing Center in Battan, Philippines, a paradise full of promise. There was food and freedom, beautiful country and beautiful people. She could breathe deep and laugh hard. They lived in a two-room cement block apartment with a hard roof and floor, a lush green creek to play in, and she attended a schoolroom complete with books and a television. Rice was plentiful and they could walk where they pleased. She couldn't imagine how America could be better than this. She only wished that her brother, Bon Louch, would stop stealing food. He was obsessed. "What if they catch you and send us back?" she thought, when the police came looking for her brother after he stole bamboo shoots from the farmer's field. He ran in the door soaking wet, stripped off his clothes and ran up the steps to hide on the roof. They had to bury his clothes in a rhododendron tree and lie to the red-faced officer. Maly was tired of the familiar surges of fear in her blood. The teacher had made it clear that you are not allowed to steal in America. She liked going to the RPC School. They taught important things you need to know about how to live in America: how to use the toilet; how to wash your hands and brush your teeth; how to push a grocery cart; and play a game called Super Bowl.

Sitting in the classroom one day, the teacher explained that they were going to watch something called a movie, a popular American pastime. Associated words were film, cinema, and theatre. Maly wrote the words as neatly as she could in her composition book before the lights dimmed and the startling music began, grabbing her chest and nearly lifting her out of her seat.

The giant, perfectly sculpted, red-caped man on the screen was called *Superman*. He was a hero. She felt instantly in love – and immediately betrayed. Devoted to the flicking light in the darkness, she kept wondering, "Why didn't he save me?"

thirteen

Bones That Float

"The pure and simple truth is rarely pure and never simple."

Oscar Wilde

S ovann and I are exhausted from an afternoon spent
pleading our villagers' case about the illegal logging
in Aural to the *Cambodia Daily* newspaper and Conservation International, where the Brit in charge handed me a
human rights report by Global Witness, entitled: *Taking A Cut,
Institutionalized Corruption and Illegal Logging in the Aural Wildlife
Sanctuary*. The activities of our District Chief of Education are
detailed in section fourteen. The diagram of a vast web of con-
spirators includes Prime Minister Hun Sen.

As we honk our way through Phnom Penh's chaotic traffic, I'm
impatient and annoyed at Sovann for insisting we head for the
city dump; we pass dozens of western-style tourist restaurants by
the riverfront. I made the mistake of teasing him after we bought
the new water pump and irrigation pipes for Mr. Bun, saying I
don't think he would like America because he eats only Cambodian food. Now he's going to prove that I should sponsor his
visa by eating a massive bowl of spaghetti bolognese.

The Smile of a Child restaurant is located next to the city dump
and is run by a charitable French chef who provides showers and
schooling, hygiene lessons and the skills of the culinary trade to
more than 3,000 children who live in the Phnom Penh city dump.

207

The western-style fare is cooked up and served by his protégés. The smiling child who takes our order looks to be about 12, with several deep scars on her arms and neck. Children scavenging the dump are sometimes plowed over by bulldozers. Cambodia has exhausted my compassion; the scars don't faze me any more. "Life is a struggle," Sovann often says, and I've come to accept it also. Yet I believe the promise made by the monk of Wat Lanka: This, too, shall be impermanent.

"Maybe I should just walk away; illegal logging is really none of my business," I say.

"But if you walk away, what will the people do?" Sovann replies. He's afraid to speak out against corruption himself, and yet he pins their hopes on me. I'm guessing he thinks that either my whiteness, my foreignness, or my dollars – maybe all three – gives me reprieve from the Cambodian system that he has learned to accept. But there is a limit to the amount of my meddling that will be tolerated, I'm sure.

"Look, Sovann, the guy at Conservation International told us that he just got word from the highest level – that means the prime minister – that nothing was going to be done about the logging. What do you want me to do, get myself killed?" The Brit actually told me to write a reproach to Mok Marith, the Minister of Environment, who he says possesses a monarchical sense of bureaucratic influence. He's a "power man," albeit a lower power man than the Minister of Finance, and the Minister of Defense, so there's probably not much he can do.

"Now I think you understand Cambodia 80 percent," Sovann says. He's familiar with the relationship between the government and the trees.

When Sovann graduated from the Phnom Penh accounting school in 1989, he passed a government exam for a job at the Budget Bureau of the Ministry of Economy and Finance in Koh Kong, a port town near the Thai border. There, at the western edge of the Cardamom Mountains, he began his career as a communist accountant. Following a Vietnamese model, commune officials levied a rice tax according to the size of a farmer's family, 16 kilograms of rice per person. At the Budget Bureau, Sovann tallied the rice sacks on a state budget form and submitted the report to his department director. He then loaded the sacks onto government boats enroute to Phnom Penh, to be traded on the international market for weapons and ammunition.

He was paid monthly in government rations: a 16-kilo bag of rice; four packets of cigarettes; four flashlight batteries; and two bars of soap, which he bartered to subsist. The benefit of his government position came from Thai fishermen who needed to apply for a business license. A packet of cigarettes or several cans of beer usually accompanied their request to contact provincial officials above him. These petty bribes increased his trading supply.

Each morning he traded rice to a dessert vendor for a small bowl of string bean and sticky rice with sugar and coconut milk. He traded soap and cigarettes to rent a hand cart and compete with porters hauling supplies from the boat docks. With the 400 or 500 Thai baht he earned, he bought 200 grams of pork to fry and eat for two days, or a large case of spicy, canned crayfish imported from Thailand, which could be stretched for a month.

Life was a struggle, but unthreatened, until the Ministry of Economy and Finance sent its entire staff to the mountains to chop down trees. Khmer Rouge forces had set up bases on the other side of the mountains from Koh Kong. In turn, the PRK government sent its civilian staff to the mountains with machetes, handsaws and hammocks to hack down the forest and deny the Khmer Rouge its hiding place and funding resource.

Skinny and coughing, Sovann labored alongside the rest of the office staff, pulling one handle of a dull tin blade back and forth to cut through thick tumloap trunks. It was harder work than anything Angka had dished out ten years earlier, but at least they were fed. Curious but unsuspecting monkeys were caught and roasted on sight. Sovann wrapped two krama cloths about his head as feeble defense from the swarm of mosquitoes that plagued his sweaty body day and night. Eventually he stopped swatting them, and let the blood from their bites simply trickle down his neck. The officers provided plenty of cigarettes, beer and palm wine to the workers, and each night Sovann passed out in his hammock, a drunken stupor the only substitute for a mosquito net. The real vipers in the trees overhead would slither into his nightmares in the early morning, when the numbing effects finally wore off.

One day, while hacking at a mound of thick brush with his machete, Sovann pulled up a clump of tender fig vines and dry bamboo stalks to find a cobra staring at him, hood flared and ready to strike. He tried to suck in air but his lungs had no capacity to breathe. He stood frozen, the blood draining from his head until he blacked out. The snake was slashed to pieces by the men in his brigade. When Sovann awoke, he was coughing blood into his krama cloth.

He emerged from the forest two months later, dizzy with malarial fever. The only doctor in Koh Kong had no medicine for either tuberculosis or malaria so he put Sovann, coughing and burning, on a boat for Phnom Penh and stuck a few hundred Thai baht in his pocket. Through the muffled haze of delirium, Sovann thought he heard the man say, "Go find the hospital."

He awoke to an unbearable stench, having no idea how he made his way to the only hospital in Phnom Penh. The five nurses on the ward did their best to clean up copious amounts of blood and excrement, but they were severely understaffed. Sovann made his feeble body walk to the bathroom and found it full to the brim with human waste. Plugging his nose, he vaguely wondered how long he would survive.

Sovann's mother visited the Phnom Penh hospital daily with bowls of rice porridge and morning glory soup. His sister hocked a pig and a chicken to buy natural remedies in the market, to supplement what she collected from the forest. They boiled endive and elephant trunk leaves with guava bark peeled from the tree for its quinine. The bitter brew worked well to bring down his daily fever spikes, while he waited and hoped for a cure to reach him in time. He put little faith in the single white pill he received from the nurse each day with red Russian characters printed on it. Still too weak to hold a pencil, he regained enough mental faculty to dictate a letter to a scribe his mother hired with a quarter-gram of gold. The letter asked his cousin in Paris to send French medicine for malaria and TB.

A delirious month passed before the life-saving chloroquine arrived. When he returned to the Budget Bureau in Koh Kong four months later, Sovann discovered that his employment dossier had been transferred to the Department of Social Affairs. Payment was expected if he wanted his old position to reopen. He could borrow the money and then use his position to garner bribes to repay it, but he would always have to pay for advancement, and the only way to attain it would be to participate in the endless system of corruption. He had had enough of communist accounting. He collected his five months' salary, 80 kilos of rice, and sold it. The profit afforded a boat ride back to Phnom Penh, where he found a job at the newly constructed ASEAN Hotel. There was talk that the Viet Nam soldiers were leaving and that United Nations soldiers would replace them; there was to be an election, and there was a chance that Cambodia's war would finally succumb to impermanence.

The fever had forced Sovann to stop running and look at the direction in which he was going – a circle defined by Cambodia's quarrelsome borders. The foreigners who descended on Phnom Penh during UNTAC came from a world where prosperity was more than a wish on incense smoke. He sunk his teeth into the idea of freedom, vowing never to let it go, and started befriending every single English-speaking person who would let him, no matter what their purpose for being in his God-forsaken country. For 15 years he has held on to that dream.

I've helped Amanda submit visa applications for several female cousins she has arranged to marry American men. Even after a legitimate, three-day Cambodian wedding ceremony, they wait two years or more for a fiancé visa to be granted. Sovann hasn't a chance. He has no bank account or record of income. So why am I suggesting that we apply for NGO status and create a business to support the Grady Grossman School, to give him a job, or to make the forest around our school more valuable alive than dead? The villagers make camphor tea from the bark of cardamom trees; how do we turn that light and flowery essence, boiled from one-inch pieces of bark, into a profitable commodity?

Sovann shovels strings of spaghetti bolognese with his fork onto his spoon. As with most beginners, half the sauce ends up on his chin. "Bopha Prey Phnom," he says, between slurps. "Flower Mountain Tea." The villagers can harvest the bark and cover the denuded sections of trunk with mud until the bark regrows. We can package the product in bamboo tubes. His eyes are bright with creative thoughts bigger than the bounds of his country's misfortunes.

A heavy sigh. I can't even look at him. Am I getting his hopes up again? I have a child to raise, a mortgage to pay, mountains to ski, Christmases to celebrate, movies to watch and books to write. We have labeling laws, import tariffs and liability insurance to consider. What is this persistence Cambodia has for sucking the ease out of my American life?

Sovann promises to go back to Prey Che Teal village in Takeo and ask the headman about Ratanak's birthfather – where he worked and how he disappeared. Perhaps a relative can be found. Sovann is much more anxious to earn the $25 per day I've agreed to pay him, than to actually solve the mystery. But the rationale for my being here is no longer about my son and his truth; maybe it never has been. He was just a little soul who stood waving a neon light in the direction of my heart's desire

– to do something less selfish than my culture tells me I should. It's impossible to go about my American life and pretend the suffering is not here. It's always here. Sometimes I think if we changed our national anthem from *The Star-Spangled Banner* to *America the Beautiful,* baseball games and Olympic medals might actually shed enough grace on me to see how brotherhood beyond the shining sea will make my life better.

"When should I apply for a passport?" Sovann says, on our way to the airport. Like the traffic, his whole life has been a battle, never a moment's peace, always fighting for position, exhausting. He's confident that the U.S. embassy will agree to a tourist visa for business training. "I already save the money for fly-ticket," he says.

I want to keep my promise, but flying away will lessen the strength of my conviction. "I really do understand why you want to leave, Sovann. I love this place and I can't wait to get out of here, so that I can breathe," I say.

"You are the boat and I am the dock," he says, with eyes that penetrate my soul, holding the steering wheel more tightly than usual, steeling his countenance so that I cannot see the tears behind his eyes. I feel like I'm abandoning a shipwrecked boy adrift in the ocean. The only lifeline I can throw him is the hope that I will find a market for tea brewed from bark. The grip of his hope follows me into the airport.

It took him six months to find her. Sovann had more determination than I thought, and the information flowed more easily when I wasn't around. A one-page letter arrived in Khmer script, with two pictures. George and I held up the photo and gazed at a little girl who was the spitting image of our son. There was no question of its authenticity; the girl could be his twin. We held each other in that unsteady moment, knowing that the tide was pulling us into uncharted cross-cultural waters. If there is pain in not knowing, there is equal pain in knowing.

Sovann had followed a trail of maybes to Kampong Chhnang, and found Grady's birthmother scrubbing laundry in the river by hand for 15 cents per day. She gasped when he handed her the picture and read her the note I left with him, telling her what had happened to her son. Her lips swollen and blistered from the sun, her skin pale and yellow from malnourishment, she bowed to Sovann and called him "Pu," for uncle. She was living under a palm thatch lean-to with her brother, who lay coughing on a bamboo bed, the tuberculosis virus destroying his lung cells. Could we send money for his funeral? Her daughter scavenged the market; she'd never been to school. Unable to write a letter in return, the birthmother dictated one to a scribe. Using the highest vernacular it began: "Gracious big brother and gracious big sister..."

Amanda continues the translation, deciphering the meaning with the help of her husband, Andy, who had enough schooling in Cambodia to learn the Khmer script; she's Khmer illiterate. "She says her son is so lucky to find you, a good family to take care of him, because she cannot take care of him. She was afraid that he will die. Now she know that he must have done something good in a past lifetime, to find a good parent and have a good life." Big tears form in Amanda's eyes as she struggles to find the English words to explain the meaning of the next phrase. "She say that he have *ch'ung un deahdt* ... it's a very high word ... it means he has *bones that float*, like a sacred thing that rise up above all the bad things, and float away."

Bones that float – a physical explanation of God's favor, like incense smoke, impermanent and drifting. Grady has them, Amanda has them, and Sovann wishes he did. The unsmiling mother and daughter in the picture were not blessed with bones that float, either.

My little boy is too young to understand this now, but I finally feel entitled to love him completely, to be his mom. It will take a lifetime to comprehend this truth, but now we can confidently answer the claims of adoption opponents. He was not stolen or bought. His birthmother loved him enough to find for him a more secure place than her own arms; she trusted his bones to float.

Amanda holds me in her strong embrace. "I'm sad and I'm happy," I sob. "I feel guilty because I'm so thankful that my son is not growing up there."

"I know," Amanda says. "I feel that way, too."

Adoption love is wider than most. It includes people you don't even know, and may even fear. "Can you love a child not born to you?" is a silly question. Loving the child is profoundly easy. The question is, "Can you love the people your child was born to?" Loving birthparents is complicated. Someday, when my son grieves the loss of his birthparents, will I forgive myself for being the beneficiary of his grief? The only antidote to guilt is to love everyone involved, and that means throwing my arms and heart wide open, as wide as they will go, and then even wider. Forgiveness is not so hard when both joy and pain share the need for it; that's what makes adoption love endure.

There is solace in the smell of kroeung meeting my nose in Amanda's kitchen. Lemongrass, lime leaf and madaeng, deep-fried into fish meat for *prahet* cakes. Dipping the hot patties into a sauce of ground pepper, garlic and lime juice, I look to my friend for help in navigating emotions through a vast ocean of cross-cultural psychology. I have no idea how to relate to a Third World birth family, or even if we should. George and I don't want to obligate Grady to a relationship he may not want. Adoptive relationships are not secondary to biological ones; about half of all adoptees are interested in their birth family, and the other half are not. But everyone hates stupid questions such as, "Who's your REAL mother?" We're all real. Protecting real information for my son helps empower him in a world fraught with prejudice toward the two things we want him to feel proud of – being Cambodian and being adopted. We don't want to set our son up for disillusionment but the cultural reality is that, in Cambodia, if one family member is blessed with bones that float, the others expect to benefit.

The birthmother's letter etches a complex awareness onto my heart, with the attendant difficulty of facing true disparity; world poverty now lives with us. Should we do something to help the birth family or not? I know how good intentions can be misconstrued. Generosity will not draw compassion for a homeless migrant woman who has already lost one child to disease and another one to *no food*. Sadly, it's a common story. Contact with us could put their lives in danger. In a desperate world with palm thatch walls, generosity draws jealousy.

"What is the right thing to do?" I ask Amanda, the only person who could possibly understand.

"I don't think you can do something to help them, because if other people know, they will try to take advantage of you," she says. Amanda has learned this lesson the hard way, both as a refugee and a returnee. "My family always think here in America that money grow on the tree, they think I am their rich relative, but they do not understand how hard I work, waiting table in a restaurant seven days a week. They have no idea what we went through to make it here, either."

"Sovann has found a piece of land in Kampong Chhnang, and he talked to the birthmother about growing vegetables," I tell Amanda. "What do you think?"

"Grady is your son now. I think you are not responsible for them," she tells me, with her even lawyer tone. "The other children are not your children."

That's true but it's not easy to live with the fact that our son has a sister who could be sold into prostitution, or die of diarrhea, or remain illiterate. The idea of anonymously buying a piece of land, securing them a place to live, grow food, and have a roof over their heads, seems like the least we can do. U.S. immigration law forbids foreign birthparents from receiving anything from a child's relinquishment. So is it an act of civil disobedience to help them? A home would make schooling for my son's sister more feasible, and it would give Grady a place to find them in the future, if he's interested. As his mom, I feel blessed that I can even make the choice possible.

Sovann followed our directions precisely, picking out a choice piece of farmland and negotiating with the headman a fair local price of $350 for a measured hectare, never mentioning our involvement. But the birthmother bragged to her neighbors that American relatives were helping her, and the price suddenly tripled. The village headman justified the price increase because the landowner's son owed him $1,200 in gambling debts, and we were his opportunity to redeem them. We told Sovann to walk away; if the birthmother could not respect our privacy, we could not help her.

Predictably, in the months that followed Sovann received threatening phone calls from people claiming to be relatives and demanding money. It was not until her daughter nearly died from typhoid fever that the birthmother showed up on Sovann's doorstep and agreed to go wherever he might find her a suitable place to live. This time a man was with her; having heard of his ex-wife's good fortune, the father had risen from the dead. Unfortunately, she was again with child.

Savvy Sovann enlisted the help of his brother-in-law, who lived in a small village near the sea, where no one would know the family. He negotiated a fair price for a small piece of land with young fruit trees and a palm thatch hut, the humble beginnings of their opportunity to build a better life. We were not going to just give it to them; they would have to work together to build a home and a farm. If they were successful, ownership of the land would transfer to the birthmother's name after three years. Sovann personally drove the family to their new home, eliciting the help of their new neighbors to gather cooking pots, kerosene, and a few sacks of rice, for they came with nothing but the clothes on their backs. He even found the father a job on a road-building crew.

Once settled into a place where they were not servants, with enough ground to grow food to eat and surplus to sell, it seemed like human ingenuity would prevail, a better life was possible, and the school uniform we sent would be put to good use. I even started to daydream about the day we would take Grady to meet his birth family, although they never asked about him. George and I had no idea how much we were asking. I guess we expected them to believe in themselves, and that, as it turned out, was too much. Just one month later, the family sold off the pieces of two humble palm thatch dwellings that stood on the property and walked away from the land.

fourteen

No Go Up, Me Stay Down

*"Strength does not come from physical capacity.
It comes from indomitable will."*

Mahatma Gandhi

Welcome to Stapleton International Airport," the flight attendant announced as the plane touched the tarmac in September 1982, two years after the Prom family had run barefoot through the jungle over dead bodies and under random gunfire to find refuge in Thailand. They had reached the promised land, but everybody stayed glued to their seats with panic-stricken faces, wondering what was Stapleton? After the plane had emptied of passengers, Dani groped for the English he knew, to ask the flight attendant, "We want to go Denver?" The exquisitely manicured woman assured the rag-tag group of Asians not to worry; they were, indeed, in Denver.

Relieved and excited, the six children clamored off the stuffy, sterile-smelling airplane, leaving their motion sickness bags on the seat. No need to access the overhead bins; they had nothing but the clothes on their backs. Immigration officers in Los Angeles had confiscated their only belongings, mostly Asian foods and spices; rumor had it that lemongrass, madaeng and kaffir lime leaf could not be found in America.

They stepped into the busy fluorescent lights of Stapleton Airport and were greeted by Cambodians, including their old friend, Rasmey, from Battambang, and his remarkably plump and healthy family. "How come they're not skinny like us?" Maly wondered. Her envy quickly waned in the thrill of lights and traffic beaming from the enormous city outside the windows. The family piled into a long, low, 1975 brown Plymouth and passed under a spectacular tunnel. They were heading west in the Batmobile, toward the looming mountains, for their first meal in America.

At Rasmey's house other Cambodian immigrants stood back from the straw mats at the center of the floor, where china bowls laden with hot soup and rice were served to the latest newcomers. Maly devoured her bowl of chicken soup, amazed that the curious children did not fight her for their share. Her mother slapped Dani's hand as he reached for a second helping.

"No, no, eat as much as you want," said Rasmey. The children looked to their mother for guidance. "Finish it," Rasmey said, and they dove through their shyness toward the soup pot. Bowl after bowl of sour chicken soup filled their tummies to contentment. Rasmey's children brought plates of fruit to the mat. The bananas and apples looked absolutely perfect; Maly didn't care if their taste was bland. This was the America of her dreams, a place with plenty of food to eat! She wanted to remain on that straw mat eating chicken soup forever. Then the bad news broke.

Rasmey wasn't their real sponsor. He had sponsored too many Cambodians already, when he received Sokun's letter from Khau I Dang. He introduced a dark-faced Cambodian man and his teenage Laotian wife, friends whom Rasmey had found to sign their sponsorship papers. The Proms would be living with these two on a street called Santa Fe. While still distrustful of other Cambodians they didn't know, the family had no choice. Everyone bowed gracefully to thank the stranger, addressing him as Pu to subtly establish the social hierarchy; he was "Older Uncle," to be honored with great respect. The Cambodian social system would buy him time to exploit their ignorance, before they figured out the American system.

With bellies stretched full of warm soup, the eight family members lay down beside each other on the shag carpet of Pu's living room floor, huddling close for warmth, while their sponsor and his young wife disappeared behind an old, pink sarong that hung from the door jam separating the couple's sleeping quarters from the rest of the one-bedroom apartment. A cold draft blew through the cracks in the windowsill, bringing with it a strange, strong smell. Maly plugged her nose to conserve the taste of sweet, sour soup until she fell asleep, dreaming of a glorious ride in the big, brown Plymouth and *dtuk gaw* falling from the sky. She hadn't seen ice for many years, since her father shaved it from a large block at the roadside in Battambang, selling cold treats on hot, humid afternoons to happy people passing by. Here in America, the greatest of luxuries would fall from the sky.

On the morning the earth turned white, Maly could barely contain herself. The Khmer language had no word for "snow" or any kind of phrase to express the coldness of a Rocky Mountain winter. The word did not translate; the meaning of winter had to be experienced. The children went running out the door half-naked and barefoot, wearing only underwear and T-shirts. Maly spread her arms wide and twirled about, trying to catch as much *dtuk gaw* falling from the sky as she could, delighted by light, little pieces of puffed cold. A bitter glob struck her shoulder, lobbed by her brother, Bon Leoun, igniting their very first snowball fight. Many minutes passed before the children noticed how cold they felt. Freezing and wet, they ran back in the house and gathered around the floor grate where heated air rose from the furnace in the basement below, warming their red cheeks, runny noses, wet feet and smiling faces. How could something so happily abundant make them so painfully cold?

For a few weeks everyone tried to politely eat spicy Laotian food prepared by Pu's wife, without complaint. Mother chided the children to take just a little bit, not too much. She believed it was the sponsor's food, even though he used their food stamps to buy it. When the end of the month came, Pu drove everyone in the big, brown Plymouth to the Department of Social Services to get more food stamps. Yet the refrigerator was always empty.

Maly's parents didn't know that they were supposed to keep their welfare checks. When Pu demanded that they hand over the money, $500 per person, they assumed it was the price of sponsorship, paying Pu for rent and food. Certainly they owed Pu a debt of gratitude they could not otherwise repay. No one knew how to cash a check or where the money came from, and Pu didn't bother to explain. He was careful not to mention where other Cambodian families lived and in the huge city, with no transportation, how could anyone find a job?

"We didn't know the welfare was government money," Amanda says. "They just tell us when we arrive you can get this money for six months, and if you go to school, you can continue to get the money. It was hard for my mom and dad to study, especially my mom, she want to work, because if they go to school they still can't get the money, because it's under our sponsor's name."

Sokun and his wife were anxious to get jobs and enroll their children in school. At 55 years old, Sokun's Khmer Lycee education, royal government training, private business experience and command of French were useless; he had to learn English to support his family. Every day he walked five blocks to the adult literacy class, wondering where other Cambodians lived. He hadn't seen anyone since the night of their arrival, and Pu evaded his questions by driving off in the brown Plymouth to play cards and gamble away the welfare money. He even refused to give them a key to the house.

One afternoon Sokun came home and found his wife and children sitting outside in the cold. No one knew where Pu had gone or when he would return. They were shivering in the crisp air of a waning fall day, when a neighbor peeked her head out the door and asked in perfect Khmer if they would like to come in. For many years they'd learned to be cynical about strangers, but they were struggling day by day under the noose of their sponsor's greed. They needed the neighbor's help.

San Da and her daughter had been living in America since before the war and had retained the customary generosity and open hearts of Khmers from before the Khmer Rouge regime. She told them the truth: The welfare money came from the United States government and they were supposed to keep it, not the sponsor. It would only last six months, unless they stayed in school. San Da knew an American who could find them a job where English was not much required. She explained how to cash the checks and pay for food with the funny yellow stamps, and told the children that discarded aluminum cans brought five cents each when returned to a grocery store. They'd made their first friend in America.

A little before sunset the brown Plymouth pulled into the driveway. Sokun's anger exploded as he came out the door.

"We rent that house with the government's money," he shouted at Pu. "Give us the key!" He was no longer afraid of the sponsor's power.

"What do you think, now you are a bad ass because you are in America?" Pu yelled back. "You have to remember that I'm the one who get your ass over here!"

Her father's face was turning red as he yelled from his newfound knowledge and wounded pride. Tears fell from Maly's eyes as she thought, "Maybe he will send us back to Cambodia." She was afraid and angry and started to yell, "My mom is old. We just want the house key because we don't know when you will come home!" Malis pinched her arm to make her shut up. Sokun appreciated the United States accepting them as refugees; he did not want his family to be on government welfare forever. Pu's ignorance was holding them down at the bottom of the well, and he wanted to climb the mountain.

"After living through all that Pol Pot time, our sponsor took advantage of us, too," Amanda says, with a chuckle. The squishy mess of cold, ground pork moving through our fingers absorbs

laughter and the tears of memory. From a distance, Amanda's
first days in America seem pleasantly absurd: the glory of a
church rummage sale; the satisfaction of fake fur on a free coat;
the revolting smell of pine trees; the fascination of dashboards
and upholstery; the fear of a flasher exposing his hairy pink penis
in the street. We add chopped green onion, chilies and parsley
to the mixing bowl, and then spice it with fish sauce and sugar,
packing the meat mixture into sausage casing. "When we first
come here, we are so poor, not one dime to our name," she says,
still laughing. "We don't know how to do anything at all."

Mastering English was the first order of business. Maly's older
siblings were accepted into a special class called ESL, at the local
high school, but she had to wait for additional papers to arrive
before she could enroll. Each morning before school, her brothers rummaged through trash bins in the alleyways between city
streets, collecting aluminum cans. After they left for school, she
separated the precious cans and carefully hid them under the
steps, dreaming of the end of the month when they would return
them to a store in exchange for real money. Maly's job was to
make sure Pu didn't steal them first.

San Da found Maly's mom a cleaning job at a nursing home.
The $3.50 an hour felt like a lot of money to an Asian woman
who considered caring for old people an unpaid filial obligation.
Private thoughts of growing old in America, to be looked after by
strangers, made Neang uneasy. Where are their children? Are
they old orphans? The hallways stunk of disinfected urine and
the elevator scared her, but her meticulous care and eagerness
to please resulted in the occasional tip from a resident that she
quickly squirreled away in her bosom. Accepting money from
the old, white people worried her; what if her boss got angry?
She couldn't afford to give it back. Between the cans, her salary,
and the food stamps, she had enough to feed the children healthy
food. She no longer needed to be stingy; they could eat a whole

chicken everyday if they wanted to. Even so, chiding the children to save some for tomorrow remained an unbreakable habit.

It was nearly Thanksgiving the first time Maly went with her mom to the grocery store, with the strange feeling of green money in their hands. She had found a twenty dollar bill in a parking lot and wanted desperately to hold onto it, but reluctantly she gave it to her mom, just as her brothers handed over their can money. Only a mother can be trusted to buy what is best for the family. The mounds of fresh vegetables and glorious fruits were unbelievable; the carrots looked strange and exotic; how do you eat it? The colorful packaging on endless rows of alien canned goods fascinated her, but it was hard to believe there was food inside, prepared and preserved – how strange. Even the rice looked weird, packaged in little boxes with spice packets. Maly pushed the cart carefully, just as her English picture book showed, until she ran into the giant chickens, frozen solid in a tight plastic sheath. She abandoned the cart to peer into the bin of Thanksgiving turkeys. The giants were on sale! Carefully they hoisted a bird into their cart, thoroughly impressed with the size to which even a chicken can grow in America.

"Cash or check?" the cashier asked.

"Real money," Dani answered, with a wide smile, pouring a handful of crumpled bills and rattling coins into her hands, gathering up the bags and heading for the door. Their hearts began to race when the woman came shouting after them.

"You forgot your change," she said, placing several bills back into his hand. For a minute, they stood dumbstruck by her honesty.

If there was a holiday for giving thanks in their new homeland, the Proms were going to celebrate. The giant chicken sat on the counter naked, staring at the girls and their mother. Without knowing how to turn on an oven, they could think of only one thing to do: Chop it up and throw it in a soup pot with triangular pieces of pumpkin. They chopped a little lemongrass and turmeric root that San Da brought them from an Asian market. Improvising with unproven vegetables and a little garlic, the girls fashioned Somlaw Kako, Neang's favorite soup. The family gathered on the floor around the heater grate to sup on the magnificent bird. No one felt compelled to speak about thankfulness, when every mouthful was silently worshipped.

Private victories at home bore no relation to life in public school, when Maly entered the fifth grade at age twelve to start learning her ABCs. She longed to fit in with the other kids, but how could her classmates relate to a child of war? They were real children; she was only pretending the role. It was December and the kids where cutting green and red paper to make a chain of garland for the Christmas tree. It seemed like a stupid waste of time to Maly. "I don't want to cut paper," she thought. "I need to learn something useful!" Her father paced the floor every night, demanding rigorous study of English. The school principal wanted her to move up to the seventh grade so she could join an ESL class, but Maly refused.

"No go up, me stay down," she insisted. "Me wan learn English."

When she came to school with purple-red bruises all over her body, the principal hauled her into his office and demanded an explanation. Maly didn't have the words to explain that she had the stomach flu, and her mother had used a quarter to rub hard in patches all over her back, torso and arms until her blood vessels surfaced. In Asian medicine, coining is a common practice for moving the congested life force believed to cause nausea. Khmers use the technique regularly on viral ailments. The principal, however, was sure that Maly's parents had beaten her. It took half the day to find a Khmer translator, and when he finally sat down in the principal's office, he repeated the principal's question: "Did your parents beat you up?"

"Ot-tay," Maly cried, "My parents did not beat me up. My parents love me!" Why is he asking this question?, she thought. He should know our culture. We always rub the coin when someone is sick. Then he called her parents. Speaking in that shameful, authoritative tone, he asked them if they beat their daughter. How can he say something like that? Maly felt panic and anger. What if they take me away from my parents, like the translator threatened? She cried, and kept saying, "No, sick, sick, make better." The principal finally believed her and allowed her to go home, but from then on Maly would keep silent about all things Cambodian. She changed her name to Amanda, and set her mind to becoming an American.

Amanda wasn't sure if she should tell her teacher, Mr. Allory, about the girls who picked on her, shoving her into the locker and pulling at the sides of their eyes to make an Asian face, calling her "Chink." "Why do they think I am Chinese?" she wondered. "Cambodians don't have that kind of eye." She liked Mr. Allory. He was nice and let her stand quietly next to him on the playground, while they watched the other kids run around having fun. No one wanted to play with her. She smiled when she saw the mean, brown-haired girl stumble in a game of tag. "Should I tell him that girl always pushes me against the wall in the bathroom?" she wondered. "What if Mr. Allory thinks I am the bad one? Maybe she'll tell him I don't flush the toilet. It's different than the one at home and I don't know how to do it." She was ashamed of that.

Mr. Allory knew Amanda hardly ever ate lunch. Standing in the cafeteria line with her plastic tray, she stared with a furrowed brow at the piles of cheesy noodles and pizza she didn't know how to eat. The smell of milk in a carton made her gag. Sometimes Mr. Allory allowed her to stay behind and eat a package of dry Ramen noodles in his classroom, where the other kids didn't look at her strangely. She scrambled to her knees and tried to pick up her crumbs before Mr. Allory noticed. "No, no," his voice stammered. She looked up with big teary eyes, praying that he wouldn't get mad and kick her out of school. "It's okay. " He hugged her and more tears fell on his shoulder. He must think I'm bad, she thought. He let me copy cursive writing off another paper and I still don't get it right. Mr. Allory smoothed her hair and told her not to worry. "Everything will come in time," he said. She sobbed because she felt unworthy of his kindness.

When the end of the school year finally came, Amanda was eager to make herself proud at the fifth grade field day compe- tition. These kids don't know how good I am at running and jumping, she thought, while the competitors took their turns. She had honed her leg muscles in Khau I Dang, playing endless hours of *lo ning tay ot,* a game like jump rope with a long row of rubber bands stretched between two girls. They started at the ankle and moved the rubber rope up the body all the way to the neck, eliminating the jumpers one by one. Maly was often the last one standing. The girls and boys who pushed her into walls and pulled her hair to tease every chance they got were indeed quite shocked by the shy Asian girl's athleticism. Amanda won first place in both the long jump and high jump, running home as fast as she could to show her parents her blue ribbon. No one was there. She took the city bus to the office building where her mother worked a second cleaning job in the evening. Mom took the ribbon and smiled, saying the magic words she so wanted to hear: "You make me very proud." Then she handed Amanda a mop and told her to clean the bathroom floor.

By the end of the summer, the family had saved $1,000 and Sokun told his wife it was time. Together they paid a visit to the Catholic Charities office and handed over their savings, paying back the donation for their airfare to America. Her father spoke three languages and had once handled import-export trade for a King. Now he was a janitor at a nursing home, alongside his wife, and his children rummaged through trash bins for tin cans. But they were regaining control of their lives.

That evening, sitting on the floor around the heater grate eating *num ba chok*, the same curried rice noodle dish they had eaten on the eve of the Khmer Rouge revolution, Father announced to the children that he didn't want to depend upon the government any longer. "We don't want to live on the government checks; we don't need to be on food stamp," he said. "We can make more on our own." Her parents had learned enough English to get new jobs cutting glass at a window factory. Her brothers worked as janitors at the high school, cleaning up before and after class. Malis and Amanda babysat their little brother and helped the others whenever they could. By the time Sokun was promoted to supervisor at the window plant, his family was off welfare.

After two years of ESL in junior high, Amanda entered high school with newfound confidence, though she was still an oddball – too foreign to be popular, and too far behind to be a scholar. During her junior year she began to dream of becoming a lawyer, when she played the role of defense attorney at a mock trial in civics class, and unleashed the quick, contentious tongue she had inherited from her father. The 'A' she earned in the class bolstered her dreams. Her fresh American convictions began to eclipse the shy, genteel dependence expected from a young Cambodian woman. The family joked that no one would ever want to marry her, but Amanda didn't much care about marriage; she wanted money. Consequently, the interest of a suitor came as a surprise at the Khmer New Year celebration that spring.

Gracefully the women rotated their wrists, with fingers curving upward in the shape of lotus blossoms, dancing beside their husbands in a large circle that oozed to the beat of Romvong music. Amanda loved watching Romvong dances, and so did Punthea Rith; only he was watching her, not the dancing. He was nine years older, an orphan, a refugee and a good friend of her brothers, who'd been waiting patiently for her to turn eighteen. She was surprised when he asked her to dance in the Romvong, and shocked when he asked her father if they could marry. With no living parent to negotiate a bride purse, Sokun gave tradition

some latitude and consulted their birthdates and finger lines; it
all looked auspicious enough. He approved.

Punthea Rith's only living older relative, however, did not
approve. His sponsor, Pali, was a distant relative and she was
quite sure that the daughter of a window factory worker was well
below his esteemed station in life. She expressed her disapproval
by telling him that he'd be better off with a prostitute. Punthea
Rith's family had been quite wealthy in the old Phnom Penh.
His father was a high-ranking officer in the Lon Nol military,
murdered early by the Khmer Rouge after a jealous relative
informed on him. His mother had given him and his sister away
to separate families, before dying of starvation. Although their
circumstances had changed drastically, Pali, who escaped early
and sponsored them from Khau I Dang, expected Cambodians
to recognize their status from the old country.

The engagement ceremony took place during the Festival of
the Dead in the fall of Amanda's senior year, and Pali did not
attend. Amanda decided that she wanted a husband with an easy-
to-remember, distinctively American name. Her fiance accepted
"Andy," at her request. In return, Amanda tried to be an obedient
niece, bowing generously in deference to Andy's older relative,
who called her cheap because she worked.

"Work for pay not cheap," Amanda's mother assured her. "It's
those people who are cheap."

Paying the proper respect was of no consequence. Pali was
not going to attend the wedding ceremony, either, and they
would have to find a replacement for the ancestor-honoring
ritual. Neang asked her friend, Om Bo, to stand in as Andy's
foster mother for the two-day event. A month later, in June 1990,
Amanda graduated from high school with only her new husband
and sister in attendance. She wished her parents and brothers
could see her receiving the diploma, but they were working and
saving, dreaming of a Chinese restaurant to buy.

The dream took them to South Dakota, where her brother,
Bon Louch, now called Tom, washed dishes in a Chinese restau-

rant to learn the business. He reasoned that people have to eat every day, so a restaurant puts a little money in your pocket every day, and he carefully observed the popularity of Chinese-style cuisine among Americans. His wife may be a fine Cambodian cook, but no one knew about Cambodian food, and he couldn't afford to educate people; he wanted ready customers. With the help of a Chinese moneylender, they got into their first restaurant in Mitchell, South Dakota, at the bargain price of $80,000 and a 20 percent interest loan – 15 years after they had been driven out of the family restaurant in Pailin.

With marginal income and no credit, they couldn't get a bank even to consider a loan, so the Asian system prevailed. Mr. Thong was the owner of Indochina Limited, an Asian grocer and oriental restaurant supplier, and he kept tabs on the Asian establishments that came available in small western towns. He procured investments from venture-minded Asians who preferred to profit from new immigrants rather than trust a bank. They split the profits – 10 percent to him, 10 percent to the investor. The borrower, meanwhile, worked his ass off to repay the debt as fast as possible. Thong Heng was happy to loan money to the Proms; they had a built-in labor force that worked seven days a week, sustained by communal food and shelter. As each child graduated from high school, he or she joined the others in South Dakota to help pay off the debt while learning the Chinese restaurant business. Their father, meanwhile, tallied the miles between small western towns in his used silver Buick, to check out the establishments that Thong Heng hinted were good deals. One by one each son acquired a rundown Chinese restaurant in a ranch town of the American West.

Amanda had been waiting tables while Andy learned to cook for two years, to help her oldest brother Dani's restaurant become solvent in Mitchell, South Dakota – home of the "Corn Palace." Finally it was their turn to venture out on their own when her father announced that he found a little fixer-upper called China Garden, in a place called Lander, Wyoming. Oddly enough,

Thong Heng had also found a noteworthy investor: Pali. The conceited in-law still looked down on Amanda but was willing to make the most of her.

Between cleaning tables and making friendly conversation with customers, Amanda made a careful study of American people, becoming increasingly impressed with their unpretentious attitude. She wanted to be just like them someday. Once a man left his checkbook on the table, and she snuck a look inside. She gasped at the thought of having $20,000 in the bank; it seemed like a million to her. That man was a regular customer and didn't act snobby at all. She began to dream of making big money by working for an American.

"My father will disown us if we leave the family business," Amanda said to her husband, while they were playing with their new baby daughter. They were both nervous about raising her far away from family, but Amanda's father was convinced they should open a fourth family restaurant. When they drove to Lander for the first time, and the car finally topped Beaver Rim, a rocky outcrop above the dry, high desert sagelands of the Wind River Valley, Amanda's jaw dropped.

"I thought, oh my god, what have we done, we are going into hell," she says, with a wide-eyed grin. Ten years later, she turned down an offer from a Chinese moneylender to buy her place at 20 percent interest. Now that China Garden is a success, she's a highly respected member of our community and she gives to every cause that walks in the door. When tragedy struck America on September 11, 2001, she wrote a $1,000 check for the relief fund. On yearly trips to Cambodia she visits random villages, drilling water wells. She's the American Dream personified. Even Pali looks up to her now.

fifteen

Beyond Blood

"With all beings and things we shall be as relatives."

Sioux Indian proverb

Spend Thanksgiving dinner in a Chinese restaurant in Wyoming eating free food donated by a Cambodian refugee, and "home" enjoys a whole new meaning. Amanda assigns me the job of greeter. She says she offers the feast because she has known hunger, but I know she also finds joy with all her American friends in the kitchen, carving their home-roasted turkeys, mashing potatoes, and cutting up pumpkin pies for 350 people in our community whom we may not know on a normal day. Many senior citizens come in, or take a turkey dinner in a Styrofoam box for a friend at the Showboat Retirement Home who can't make it out on a cold autumn day. There are oil field workers from the motel next door, a single mom and her kids, Indian families from the reservation, a furniture store owner who assures me she can afford to pay, so I direct her to the donation jar. As a one-woman welcome wagon, I need some skill to set everyone's mind at ease. Whether you're well off or needy is irrelevant; no one will look down on you for accepting generosity here.

A man called "Big Joe" walks into China Garden, eyes downcast as he inquires if this is the place with the free dinner. "It's the place," I say, shaking his hand to welcome him in from the chilly November afternoon. "We're happy you've come to share Thanksgiving with us. Do you want to sit alone or with someone else?" He'd prefer to sit alone; my cheery effort has not eased his embarrassment. I serve up lemonade and coffee and encourage him toward the buffet line. "Make as many trips as you want. We don't want anyone leaving here hungry." Big Joe finally lifts his head and smiles a bit, and I notice that he has no shirt underneath his worn coat. I've never met him before today, but by the time he has eaten three plates of turkey and all the fixin's, we've had a few good laughs about the weather and our dogs. I send him out the door with another meal in a Styrofoam box and give silent thanks for the healing that serving him bestows upon me.

Amanda's busy restacking plates on the buffet, accepting hugs and handshakes from her guests that fill the empty spaces of childhood and reconnect her heart to humanity. She has never spent a dime on therapy, but seems to have found forgiveness for her life's troubles in giving to others.

Maybe that's also the real reason George and I sponsor the Grady Grossman School: We're seeking forgiveness for America for lighting the fuse that would lead to Cambodia's self destruction, and to forgive Cambodia's corruption for robbing the adoption journey of its sacred meaning.

We didn't create Grady or the circumstances that made him an orphan, but we hope one day he'll be proud of the way his life began. His adoption changed the lives of hundreds of Cambodian children who attend our school, and of hundreds of Americans who donate to our school regularly, having learned Cambodia's story. For us, the ties that bind are beyond blood.

What will his legacy be? What will the District Chief of Education do with the thought that jealousy is no good and love is number one? What will a Cambodian-born boy do in America with his interest in outer space? What will a Souy hill tribe boy do with his ability to read? What will a Cambodian taxi driver do with his American Dream? All of these connections happened because Eric Ratanak Grady Grossman was born, and abandoned, and adopted.

Sovann now has a growing business in searching for the birth families of adopted Cambodian children. The scandalous accusations of child trafficking have led many adoptive families to search for the truth. Unfortunately, for many the trail is cold and there is no hope of ever obtaining accurate birth family information. Sadly, many of these adoptive families also live with a painful stigma created by irresponsible journalism. Not one report on the subject of international adoption has bothered to illuminate the causes of Cambodia's child welfare crisis. Convergent forces of poverty, corruption and societal dysfunction have left Cambodia, a nation of 14 million civil war-weary people, with more than 600,000 orphans. According to UNICEF's 2003 estimate, 10 percent of those orphans lost their parents to AIDS; the rest were orphaned by other diseases, land mines, deadbeat dads, domestic and sexual abuse, and no food. A 2005 USAID report documented less than 8,000 of those orphaned children living in child-care facilities. Between 1993 and 2003, only 1,653 were adopted to homes in the United States. Adoption by U.S. citizens remains closed.

Sovann has located more than a dozen birth families, and in each case a birthparent or relative willingly relinquished the children because they had too few resources to raise them. Placing the child with an orphanage, either personally or through a profiteering third party, was the Cambodian equivalent to what our social workers call "making an adoption plan." Adoption system corruption, bribes paid to government officials, lies told to adoptive parents and identities improperly recorded for ease of paperwork processing have been misconstrued into statements that all the children residing in overcrowded institutions in Cambodia are part of a vast baby-buying racket. Would the story be less entertaining if newspapers and television decided to present the myriad positive ways that international adoption is changing the paradigm of poverty and race in our world?

Sovann has turned into somewhat of a paid Cambodian Robin Hood: American parents hire him to do various development projects such as delivering life-changing medicines, school supplies, food, water and shelter to their children's birth relatives and their communities. Even so, he doesn't seem to like his work much. He's trying to support his family without having to go back to the brothel scene, yet performing social work with no training in the psychology of the issues is stressful. In his role as go-between, he has frustrated Americans and Cambodians alike. The language barrier pales in comparison to the gulf of the cultural divide. Once, he hinted a fatalistic view of the path his ambitions have taken, working with people at the bottom of the well out of which he has struggled so hard to climb.

"I think in my past life I must have owned many slaves and been a tyrant," he told me. "That is why in this life I have to bring the healthy food to help all the poor people." He cringes. "But you know, I don't like to talk to them, because they are ugly." The birth families he finds are always poor, usually illiterate, often dysfunctional, and always begging for money. Having mastered e-mail at the Internet café, he dreams of a job in Information Technology. But since there are no jobs, he cannot afford to spend time or money on more computer training. Having forged relationships from the small number of foreigners who come to Phnom Penh, primarily altruistic adoptive parents and humanitarian aid workers, he feels stuck working with the destitute to get paid by the prosperous. Perhaps his attitude will have to change before his bones will float.

Sovann's dream of coming to America remains just that – a dream. Someday I hope our economic development program at the school will give him a documentable source of income. Then, maybe, the U.S. embassy will grant him a visa to visit me for a taste of American-style business training. He has already given Grady a life-sustaining gift, true information about his birth family. I only wish that in return, I could make Sovann's dream come true. He found the needle in Cambodia's chaotic haystack; I will continue to search for a hole in the American dream wall.

As we pass through the seasons and snow blankets the earth, my son's skin lightens considerably, which draws compliments from my Asian friends, who admire his fairness. That offsets the tactless remarks from strangers I hear in the summer, when my little chameleon roasts like a coffee bean into a beautiful, deep mocha color. The range of his tonality is simply astounding. In Cambodia, the deep south of Asia, skin tone is largely a function of how much time is spent under the equatorial sun. Peasants are dark from laboring in rice fields, while light skin is a benefit of a cushy indoor job. Historically, royalty spent their days in the cool stone temples while peasants worked like animals to support them. The skin tone bias speaks to an economic caste system the Buddha sought to dismantle through nonjudgment and loving-kindness. It strikes me as unfortunate that a 98 percent Buddhist population remains blind to enlightenment by an engrained favoritism for fair skin.

Around our house we have endless holidays to celebrate. Christmas is spent skiing in the mountains, followed by International New Year, the feast of Chinese New Year, then Valentine's Day, and finally Adoption Day rounds out March. In any given spring, Easter and Passover might fall the weekends before, after, or on either side of Khmer New Year.

The Colorado Cambodian Buddhist temple is an appropriately ornate interior of a two-car garage attached to a single-story ranch house on the front range north of Denver, where the Great Plains and the Rocky Mountains meet. During Khmer New Year, the temple grounds host a festive, picnic-style party for hundreds of revelers who bring offerings to the monks in residence and welcome the New Year with music, games, comedy and dancing. Grady fits right in, and his parents are the ones whose faces stick out above the crowd like glowing light bulbs. I can't tell if wearing my traditional pamoung sarong, white lace blouse and white scarf thrown properly over the left shoulder helps me blend in a little or stick out more. A lot of people check me out, curious where I would have procured traditional Cambodian temple wear, not realizing how I am related to the little boy holding my hand.

Five sand mounds are piled on the temple grounds with incense sticks and prayer flags stuck in them. It's a miniature representation of Mt. Meru, the place of divine origin bestowing god-like power on kings, conceptually similar to the revered Angkor Wat. Grady plays with other children on the leftover sand pile, and a gray-haired woman quietly pushes a ten-dollar bill into one of the scared mounds, blessing herself to receive good fortune. The sand is said to represent the dirt people take away from the temple on their shoes that must be brought back at the end of the year. Life's journey always comes home to culture. I'm glad Grady will go home with sacred sand on his shoes.

A colorful parade begins, with teenage girls dressed in shiny silk kbens and tiaras, followed by silly old ladies dressed like out-of-shape Apsara goddesses, with white masks for comic relief. The crowd follows the entourage, escorting a statue of the New Year angel around the temple three times, to the rhythmic hop of long drums. Umbrella-shaped trot dancing instruments jingle on a long pole with prayer flags, providing shade for the New Year angel while jangling a call to the spirits of invisible realms. Once the official blessing is bestowed, it spreads quickly around the crowd as people begin running around slapping baby powder and water on each other, wishing, "Sok Sabbai Chnam T'mei! Happy New Year!" Music and dancing carries on all afternoon.

We make a donation and receive a tinny blessing from the clergyman, then remove our shoes and enter the garage temple, bowing three times to the Buddha before the monk blesses our offerings. Pleased that we've come, more Khmer friends escort us to the adjacent house, where we sit on straw mats on the living room floor in big circles, sharing small portions of the blessed food with the Khmer community: homemade coconut curries; sour fish soup; beef satay; fried rice noodles; and green papaya salads. Grady rarely eats Cambodian food with gusto, but on this day he impresses all the ladies with his appreciation of their cooking.

"How can he know about the culture?" one old woman asks, not realizing that I understand her question. Like many older generations, her concern is directed at all the Cambodian-American young people, not just the adopted kids.

"Don't worry, he will know," Amanda tells the woman. "She puts me to shame!" When she hears gossip from her compatriots about how spoiled adopted kids are, Amanda's quick to admonish them by saying, "That's not spoiled, it's love!" She tells me that they're jealous, and I tell her that we choose to love what we can about Cambodian culture, and leave what is pointless behind; that's the Middle Way. Of course, Amanda doesn't have the advantage of reverting to "dumb American" mode when judgment rears its ugly head toward her. For example, she fears the rumors that will stem from her husband's absence today. Amanda's a little too outspoken and not quite ornamental enough, a little too sociable and not quite haughty enough. In other words, she's a little too American.

In the evening, the crowd gathers at a Holiday Inn ballroom in brightly colored silk cocktail dresses and dark, mandarin-style silk suits for the more formal Romvong dancing. When Amanda arrives, she greets me with a big American hug. "Sok Sabbai Chnam T'mei!" In a lower voice she whispers, "When I see you, I'm relieved. Thank god my people are here!" In a room full of Cambodians, George and I are her people.

The spring calendar of holidays finally comes to rest on my favorite celebration of the year – Mother's Day. I give thanks for the spiritual union of my family in the way it began, in a Native American sweat lodge ceremony, sitting side by side with my husband, whose beautiful infertility put us on this road. The power of this sacred medicine guided us to our son and all that I have come to know because of him. On Mother's Day, especially, in the damp heat of Earth Mother's womb, I pray for my son's birthmother. I ask the Creator to expand my heart's capacity to hold the reality that my joy came from her suffering. The image on that blue card settles into my heart where it will live forever, like an invisible emblem on my chest – two women revolving around each other in an energy dance, yin and yang. I understand my joy because I understand her suffering; one defines the other.

The sweat lodge did not fail me. A year later, when typhoid almost killed her second daughter, the birthmother returned to Sovann's home, begging for money for medicine. He took her to an NGO-run children's hospital where the medicine is free and once the girl's health stabilized, he asked why she had walked away from the land we bought for her. She could not work for him for free, she said. They would starve. Sovann explained again that the produce was theirs to keep, all of it, and the land itself would be hers once a farm was established. Still, the landless migrant sharecropper did not comprehend. But this time her uncle was present and he understood, admonishing his niece to apologize and move back onto the land. Sovann purchased a pile of wood, some bags of cement and corrugated steel for a roof, and left her to her own devices. Miraculously her husband rejoined the family, and together they began to build a house and cultivate the farm. At last report the fruit trees are producing well, the daughter is in school and, finally, the birthmother has asked about Grady. Until now, she did not have the luxury of caring. What she needed to happen, what he needed to happen, and what we needed to happen – happened.

I used to really dislike the term *"adoption triad."* It sounded so clinical and slightly dysfunctional, like a kind of weird power struggle. Now it just feels inadequate to define what this evolutionary family experience is, in essence a sacred trinity – birthparents, child, adoptive parents – uniting disparate people through love. In the Earth Mother's lodge on Mother's Day, I thank the Creator for sending me on this journey, to bring back what the people needed to know: Family is beyond blood.

At four years old, Grady sometimes makes sweat lodges at home out of the couch pillows and then goes under it to pray. He knows how to bow three times in front of the Buddha. He knows how to make the sign of the cross in a Catholic church. He knows how to ask the four questions at the Seder on Passover. He'll tell you that his skin is brown like a roasted coffee bean because God made him that way. There are many spokes in the wheel, my son, but they all lead to the same place, and in that center point we all are one.

Drumbeats and chanted song broadcast over the airwaves on the reservation radio station, and I'd better not turn it off or Grady will be upset. He wants it louder. As we drive through the Wind River Reservation on our way north to Dubois for a baby shower, he asks me the name of a town we pass through.

"Fort Washakie," I say.

"Fort Washakie?" he asks. "I used to live here."

I smile and pull over at the convenience store to get a Pow Wow schedule for this summer. The space between Lander, a predominantly white town, and Fort Washakie, a predominantly Native American Shoshone town, often seems more distant than between here and Phnom Penh. Maybe Grady has come home for a reason. After all, old souls are being born right now.

A gold necklace resides in a wooden box carved in the shape of an elephant on top of the bookshelf in our house. Sometimes I take it out and assay the weight of the two gold leaves rolled around either side of the clasp, a heavy contrast to the weightlessness of the chain. I'm drawn to their hidden inscription and I wish I could unroll the golden leaves to satisfy my curiosity. But even if I could read Sanskrit, I'm afraid of violating its prophecy.

A few days before we left Cambodia with Ratanak, we received this blessed token from Men Chan Punleu, a high-ranking Buddhist monk of the Theravada tradition. The pungent smell of sandalwood incense hangs heavy in my memory of Men Chan Punleu sitting cross-legged on a golden cushion, while we offered rice to the Buddha statue, and Ratanak crawled into the monk's lap to check out his saffron robe. Without a care for the informality, Men Chan Punleu scratched Sanskrit characters onto two small rectangles of gold leaf. He rolled the gold leaf inscription around the necklace we had furnished for the purpose and blew on it. Our baby would thus be taking his ancestors' wishes with him to the new world.

After clasping the necklace around the baby's tiny neck, the monk handed George a small Buddha carved in teak wood. I was given a closed lotus flower carved out of ivory. In just a few short minutes Men Chan Punleu had sized us up accurately, George's gift representing enlightenment and mine the potential to blossom. Turning over the ivory carving of a closed lotus flower, bestowed by a high monk when the Buddha blessed us, my mind works endlessly to unlock its meaning.

Thirty years ago, when the decision was made to bomb Cambodia in hopes of "making the world a safer place for our children," was President Nixon thinking about me? I am one of the children for whom this action was taken, and I sink under the burden of responsibility for the inheritance that is sitting in my lap.

Every day now, the TV news gives details of carnage in Iraq. A sense of patriotic duty compels me to watch it, until Grady starts pointing at the blank screen, saying, "Let's watch the war." I don't want him to learn to associate the word "Iraq" with war, the way I learned to associate the word "Viet Nam" with war as a child. Take out communist, insert terrorist; take out Viet Nam, insert Afghanistan and Al Qaeda; take out Cambodia, insert Iraq; and the story is frighteningly similar – same bus, different driver. We brought a war to a country where one didn't exist, overthrew its regime, and inspired a guerrilla force to fight our puppet government, while losing our own resolve for the battle in a foreign land we didn't understand. What have we ignited and where will the escalating violence between Sunni and Shiite Muslims lead? Will Grady be holding an Iraqi child in his lap thirty years from now, wondering how this came to pass?

In the mornings, when Grady sits on my lap in the rocking chair watching the sun rise over the Wind River Mountains, we don't say anything. We just hold each other for a few minutes before our day begins, heavy with preschool and business projects. I listen to him breathe and smell his hair, and remember that what I'm holding here is not just a boy. It's much larger than the two of us. Cambodia's entire story lives in our embrace.

Epilogue

Can one book make a difference? I think so. Or at least, that is what I hope to prove.

What began in 2000, as a one-time fundraising event to constructively pass the months of waiting for our son's adoption to become final, has grown into a life mission. Beyond supporting the education of 485 children who now attend the Grady Grossman School in Cambodia, I have a vision of facilitating a cross-cultural, e-learning relationship between Cambodian schoolchildren and students in the United States and other developed countries. The past six years of lending support to the teachers and community leaders in Chrauk Tiek village has taught me that the relationship matters as much as the money. Friendship empowers good people to stand firm in their resolve to improve their way of living, even in the face of dismal poverty, government corruption, and environmental destruction. Information exchange is the key; thankfully, we now have the Internet to achieve just that.

To learn more visit www.GradyGrossmanSchool.org

My work is all I have to support my mission and that is why I chose to publish this book independently, even though I had a nice offer from a prominent publisher. Within the traditional book publishing and distribution system, there was no way for our education project in Cambodia to benefit; that gave me the fortitude to reject my personal dream and embrace a greater goal.

I believe this book will inspire its readers to take action and make a difference in Cambodia's future. In your hands, right now, is the power to do just that. Please help us spread the word.

What can you do? Recommend this book to others.

Pass out the 10 postcards provided with your book. Twenty-five percent of every book sold benefits education projects at the Grady Grossman School and, in the future, other Cambodian schools as well.

Purchase the book directly from www.BonesThatFloat.com for $24.95. Every copy is signed by the author.

Is there more you can do? Yes; host a Book Discussion.

We are distributing this book through book discussions to raise awareness about Cambodia and money for our education projects. Discussions can be one-time events. You don't have to be a member of a regular book club but if you are, please suggest this book!

A book discussion is a fun way to spend an evening with friends and ignite stimulating conversation, learning about a fascinating culture with a heartwrenching history. To help you prepare, we will send you a Bones That Float Book Discussion Kit featuring a 10-minute DVD of the Grady Grossman School and artwork from the students in Chrauk Tiek village. We'll also provide recipes for great Cambodian appetizers from Amanda Maly Prom's restaurant. During your Book Discussion, the author, Kari Grady Grossman, will call to personally answer your guests' questions.

For more details go to www.BonesThatFloat.com.

Together we can change the world, or at least our little piece of it. Thank you for purchasing this book and helping to spread its message to others.

Organizations to Support

All are operated or supported by adoptive parents of Cambodian children.

Friends of the Grady Grossman School

www.GradyGrossmanSchool.org   Supports the Grady Grossman School, educating the children of five remote villages in Kampong Speu province.

American Assistance for Cambodia

www.cambodiaschools.com   Dedicated to improving opportunities for youth and rural poor in Cambodia in the areas of education, health, rural development, and technology.

The Angkor Dance Troupe

www.angkordance.org   Preserves, develops and teaches the traditions of Cambodian performance arts.

Angkor Hospital for Children/Friends Without A Border

www.fwab.org   A pediatric teaching hospital dedicated to improving the health and future of Cambodia's children by providing medical, nursing, and para-medical education, coupled with the highest quality pediatric care possible.

Cambodia Tomorrow

www.cambodiatomorrow.org   Provides disadvantaged children in Cambodia's orphanages with opportunities to reach their full potential through education and providing for their basic needs.

The Cambodia Trust

www.CambodiaTrust.org   Working for equal rights for disabled people in an inclusive barrier-free society.

The Cambodian Arts and Scholarship Foundation

www.cambodianscholarship.org   Improves the lives of poor, at-risk girls in Cambodia by sponsoring their education beginning in grade school and continuing through college.

Cambodian Living Arts

www.cambodianlivingarts.org   Works to support the revival of traditional Khmer performing arts and to inspire contemporary artistic expression.

Cambodia's Hope / Palm Tree Orphanage

www.cambodiashope.org   Provides survival support for orphans in Cambodia as well as opportunities for education and occupational training.

Khmer Arts Academy

www.khmerartsacademy.org   Dedicated to fostering the vitality of Cambodian Arts and Culture.

A New Day Cambodia

www.anewdaycambodia.org   Helping Cambodia's garbage dump scavenger children by providing shelter, food and education for the impoverished children of Stung Mean Chey.

No Child Left Out

www.nclo.org   Provides supplies and services to ensure that the basic survival needs of orphaned and impoverished children are met.

The Sharing Foundation

www.sharingfoundation.org   Helps meet the physical, emotional, educational, and medical needs of orphaned and seriously disadvantaged children in Cambodia, including the support of Roteang Orpahange where our son received much love and care.

Tabitha Foundation

www.tabitha-usa.org   Works to develop the poorest communities of Cambodia in a self-sustainable manner.

3 Khmer Flowers

www.3khmerflowers.com   Organizes small-scale relief projects in the rural villages of Cambodia: building bridges, schools and houses; addressing water supply problems; helping farmers buy livestock and tools.

Riverkids Project

www.riverkidsproject.org   Works with families to stop child trafficking in Cambodia.

Give the Gift of

Bones That Float, A Story of Adopting Cambodia

to your family, friends and colleagues.

_____ **YES, I want** _____ **copies of** *Bones That Float, A Story of Adopting Cambodia* **for $24.95.**

Please include $5.00 shipping and handling for one book and $1.50 for each additional book. Wyoming and Colorado residents please add applicable sales tax.

My check or money order for $ _____ is enclosed. *Payment must accompany orders. Please allow two weeks for delivery.*

Name: _____

Organization: _____

Address: _____

City: _____ State: _____

Zip Code: _____

Phone: _____

Email: _____

Please make check payable to:
    Wild Heaven Press
    PO Box 707
    Fort Collins, CO. 80522

Even better and faster or to use a credit card, order securely online at:

www.BonesThatFloat.com